BLACK OFFICER, WHITE NAVY

BLACK OFFICER, WHITE NAVY

a memoir

REUBEN KEITH GREEN

FOREWORD BY JOHN P. CORDLE

A note to the reader: Some of the quotations printed in this volume contain racial slurs. The author has reproduced the original, unaltered language to accurately document instances of racist terminology. Discretion is advised.

Scholarly publisher for the Commonwealth, serving Bellarmine University, Berea College, Centre College of Kentucky, Eastern Kentucky University, The Filson Historical Society, Georgetown College, Kentucky Historical Society, Kentucky State University, Morehead State University, Murray State University, Northern Kentucky University, Spalding University, Transylvania University, University of Kentucky, University of Louisville, University of Pikeville, and Western Kentucky University.

Editorial and Sales Offices: The University Press of Kentucky
663 South Limestone Street, Lexington, Kentucky 40508-4008
www.kentuckypress.com

All photos are from the author's collection.

Library of Congress Cataloging-in-Publication Data

Names: Green, Reuben Keith, author. | Cordle, John P., writer of foreword.
Title: Black officer, White Navy : a memoir / Reuben Keith Green ; foreword by John P. Cordle.
Description: Lexington : The University Press of Kentucky, [2024]
Identifiers: LCCN 2024010521 | ISBN 9781985900288 (hardcover) | ISBN 9781985900295 (paperback) | ISBN 9781985900318 (pdf) | ISBN 9781985900325 (epub)
Subjects: LCSH: Green, Reuben Keith. | United States. Navy—African Americans—Biography. | United States. Navy—Officers—Biography. | United States. Navy—Military life. | African American sailors—Social conditions—20th century. | Racism—United States—History—20th century. | Race discrimination—United States—History—20th century.
Classification: LCC V63 .G738 2024 | DDC 359.0092 [B]—dc23/eng/20240305
LC record available at https://lccn.loc.gov/2024010521

This book is printed on acid-free paper meeting the requirements of the American National Standard for Permanence in Paper for Printed Library Materials.

Manufactured in the United States of America.

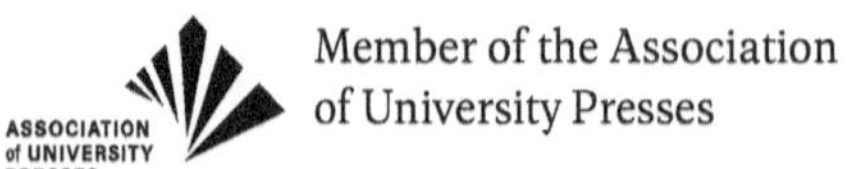

Member of the Association
of University Presses

This book is dedicated to my parents, Parker W. L. Green and Betty Ray Sotherland Green, who told me from an early age that I was just as good as anyone else and made sure that I believed it. With five children and a dog to feed, they bought books that I asked for when the money could have been used for more pressing matters. They both carried secrets that I didn't know or understand until well into my forties. I understand both better now, but particularly my father, in whose footsteps I followed, including making some of his same mistakes. I regret that neither lived to see their son become a naval officer, but I am confident that they would be both proud and amazed to learn that one of their children did so.

I further dedicate this book to all the proud service members who die with their stories untold, and I challenge those who know or have access to them to bring them to life. I encourage minority service members and veterans to write their own stories. History needs these stories.

Contents

Acknowledgments

I would like to acknowledge my sister, Dorothea “Tina” Simmons, for her unwavering support, encouragement, and assistance as well as for being there during the tough times. I would like to thank Natalie O’Neal for bearing with me while I struggled to prepare this revised edition and delayed committing to do so out of fear.

There are many people I would like to publicly thank for their encouragement and assistance but hesitate to do so, as I know all too well the backlash that can result. One who I cannot leave unacknowledged is Dr. John P. Cordle, retired navy captain and “Prolific Disruptive Thinker.” But for his coming to my defense when I was being attacked on LinkedIn and his willingness to take a chance on a self-published memoir, filled with ill-advised acronyms and written without adult supervision by someone clearly self-medicating with alcohol, this version would not exist. His published review set in motion a chain of events that led to this edition. I consider him a friend, an ally, a mentor, a writing partner, and the conscience of today’s navy. I find his own journey quite fascinating, and I hope to read it someday.

Abbreviations

ADJ	aviation jet engine mechanic
BOOST	Broadened Opportunity for Officer Selection program
CBDR	constant bearing, decreasing range
CCS	central control station
CHENG	chief engineer
CLAW-1	Commander Light Attack Wing 1
CLEP	College-Level Examination Program
CMAA	chief master at arms
CMS	Communications Security Material System
CNH	certified navy hero
CNO	chief of naval operations
CO	commanding officer
COMMO	communications officer
DC1	damage controlman first class
DEOMI	Defense Equal Opportunity Management Institute
DOD	Department of Defense
EO	equal opportunity
EOOW	engineering officer of the watch
EOPS	Equal Opportunity Program Specialist
EOQI	equal opportunity quality indicator
FFG	guided missile frigate
FOIA	Freedom of Information Act
GCM	general court-martial
GTMO	Guantanamo Bay, Cuba
HMS	Her Majesty's ship or station
HT1	hull technician first class
JAGMAN	Judge Advocate General Manual
LDO	limited duty officer
LPH	landing platform, helicopter
MN	mineman
MOMAG DET	Mobile Mine Assembly Group Detachment
NAS	naval air station

NATO	North Atlantic Treaty Organization
NROTC	Naval Reserve Officers Training Corps
OCS	Officer Candidate School
OOD	officer of the deck
OP	ordnance publication
OPPE	operational propulsion plant exam
PHM	patrol hydrofoil, missile
PREP	Predischarge Educational Program
SIMA	Shore Intermediate Maintenance Activity
SMCS	signalman senior chief
SSDG	ship's service diesel generator
SWO	surface warfare officer
TAD	temporary additional duty
TAFFY 3	Task Force 3
TAO	tactical action officer
TQL	Total Quality Leadership
TRICARE	Healthcare Program for DOD Military Health Benefits
UNSAT	unsatisfactory
USS	United States ship
VHF	very high frequency
WAVES	Women Accepted for Volunteer Emergency Service
WRNS	Women's Royal Navy Service
XO	executive officer
YN	yeoman
3M System	Maintenance and Material Management System

Foreword

I grew up in a small Georgia town and spent a long career in the navy, much like the author, but this book was a punch in the gut that made me revisit my entire life through a different lens. It literally changed the trajectory of my life and my leadership style. If you lead people, this book will open your eyes to the pernicious and deleterious impact of racial bias, intentional or not, in the form of policy and culture, and open your mind to an entirely new lexicon.

As a white male, I had a paradigm of what leadership is, as it pertains to sponsorship and mentorship, and allyship and advocacy. This enlightening book opened my eyes and showed me how simple symbols such as a Confederate flag (like the one I had on my car in high school) can undermine conversations about diversity and inclusion. I learned a new term—*microaggressions*—and how they can creep into our daily interactions and produce long-term negative impacts on those around us.

I learned how decisions such as naming a ship after a segregationist like Mississippi senator John C. Stennis or a personal appearance grooming standard on shaving and medical exceptions to that standard can disadvantage and disenfranchise an entire population of Black sailors. But I also relearned—or at least had validated—certain leadership traits such as active listening, active learning, and advocating for those with few allies; Keith challenged me to do research and read about things that were new to me, causing me to view my own actions and words from another perspective, resulting in changes to my thinking and behavior. I learned what moral injury looks like and how racist behavior can harm both individuals and national security.

I learned about how, in the course of integrating the armed forces, Black leaders were sponsored by white leaders and vice versa to make incremental progress against discrimination. I learned things about naval history that I had never heard before, explored deeper, and learned about the things that divide—and unite—us as humans.

This book is unique; it should be on the chief of naval operations' required reading list and on the shelf of every leader who desires to create a more diverse and inclusive team.

Dr. John Cordle

Dr. John Cordle is a retired navy captain who commanded two warships, USS San Jacinto *and USS* Oscar Austin, *and was the 2010 recipient of the Navy League John Paul Jones Award for Inspirational Leadership.*

1

Zumwalt's Legacy

Old sailors tell sea stories. The funny ones are told loudly and often; the dark ones are seldom told at all and usually only to other old sailors. Captain Quint, a character in the movie *Jaws*, told one of the darkest ever, about his surviving the sinking of the USS *Indianapolis* in 1945. Unlike most sea stories, the one that follows is largely verifiable, has a mostly happy ending, and as most old sailors would say (but not quite this way), every word of it is true. *Most* of it is, anyway. *It is a sea story*, after all.

The sea sometimes demands a certain ruthlessness; it doesn't care if you are injured, exhausted, scared, or navigating by computer or seaman's eye, or whether you are being treated unfairly. It is as it is; nothing more. So it is with the captain: whether he is William Bligh or John Paul Jones, inevitable ruthlessness will exist and surface, sometimes out of necessity, sometimes just for fun, stress relief, or due to inherent instability. Such is life on the sea.

Those unprepared for rough seas, ruthlessness, or nitwits may be on their final voyage, whether they survive it or not. Some have been in the news lately, and some of them are dead, their final voyage completed. Rough seas can come in many forms and arise quickly, as you will see. Becalmed does not imply safety; you can still have something bearing down on you. Constant bearing, decreasing range—CBDR—every sailor knows this means danger, potential for collision. Recognizing that it exists is the first step; to survive it is the next. A good captain understands that danger is everywhere.

This is why a well-rested, laid-back captain on a ship at sea is rare indeed. Sometimes the biggest danger, often hidden, comes from inside the lifelines, from the sailors themselves. So it was during the racial unrest of the seventies, and so it was with me.

My sea story begins on land and once upon a time, when times were very hard. I was living in a tough time to be turning into a man. Everywhere I went, it seemed like it was uphill, both ways. People were learning that the government had been spying on its own citizens and violating some of their rights. The president, Richard Nixon, was not very popular, and the

Vietnam War was not far from anyone's mind, especially if you were in it or had a loved one who was.

There was fighting at home as well. Things were expensive and sometimes in short supply, or the money to buy them was. People were worried about jobs, climate change, and the environment. The economy was bad, and unemployment was high, especially for Black youth. With political intrigue and misdeeds, simmering racial issues, and economic uncertainty, the country was clearly in a foul and angry mood. From bumblebees to billionaires, times were hard. The year 1974 was a tough one. Everyone was hoping for better times.

Living in the small coastal Florida town of Tarpon Springs, which was largely segregated, I had an especially tough future ahead, it seemed. Even though I owned a car, a rarity for a young Black man in my particular circumstances, I couldn't afford much gas. I couldn't even afford to leave town. High school dropouts didn't bring home very big paychecks. I had quit one job, washing dishes at a mental hospital, when I started my senior year, and shortly after that, I dropped out of school. Weeks later, I got fired from my other job, bagging groceries. My boss resented that I disapproved of him calling some young Black boys, about my age, standing outside his store "fucking niggers" without realizing that I was walking up behind him.

When he saw me, he explained that they had just stolen something out of his car shortly before. My comment that he called them not thieves but a racial slur didn't sit too well with him. The police never showed up, but I was soon gone. Florida's best grocery bagger was now out of a job. My future was dimming.

I thought harder about the navy, which was my dream. Almost every young man dreams of war. Since my sixth-grade teacher in San Diego, California, told us about serving in Vietnam, being shot at and shooting at people, I had wanted to go fight for my country. After boxing champion Muhammad Ali refused to be drafted on religious grounds and famously argued, "I got no quarrel with them Viet Cong. . . . No Viet Cong ever call me nigger," I sometimes wondered whether or not I should.

The nearest town, Palm Harbor, had recently been a sundown town. No Blacks were allowed after sundown: "Welcome to Palm Harbor, Niggers Straight Through." I never saw it, but I'm told that's what the sign used to say as you approached. No ambiguity there. I needed to go farther. Like many young men, I thought the military might be the answer to my problems. Like many young men, especially Black ones, I was warned about going into the military, particularly the navy, which had a reputation, well earned, for being the most racist of the armed services. As did my father,

I read a lot, even then, and so had received this warning from multiple outlets; however, my most strident and surprising warning came from an unexpected source.

I was sure that my father would be happy and proud when I told him that I was going to join the navy. He was neither. His reaction surprised me, and I think it surprised him too. My father had served in the military longer than I had then been alive. He was in Korea in a tank battalion in 1953, and he served on at least eight ships and made four trips to Vietnam as a boatswain's mate in the navy. He was only five foot seven, but he stood taller than that. He lived dangerously, his anchor often dragged, and he sometimes acted like a nitwit. Like father, like son.

His last tour of duty was at the Naval Air Station Jacksonville, Florida, courtesy of the US Navy Brig. I would be in this brig myself someday, but only to visit one of my own wayward sailors.

Rather than make his fifth trip to Vietnam, my father decided to fly to Florida from Hawaii with his second wife (not my mother, who was his first) and her two young sons. He sometimes told the story that he informed his commanding officer that he would not be on the ship when it sailed for Vietnam, and knowing my father, I'm sure he did. In any event, two guys in civilian suits, who looked like they meant business, or so he said, eventually picked him up and escorted him to the brig. He was less than two years away from a lifetime navy pension, but he walked away with nothing. He would go to his grave without explaining why.

I learned early to take my father's advice with a huge block of salt. He had once told me, his five-year-old son, to pour some rubbing alcohol into my butt crack, which I had told him was itching. He said it without looking up from his newspaper, using what I now recognize as his command voice. I would use that same voice in years to come, on the bridge of a ship, saying things like "right standard rudder" or "all ahead two thirds" or, on a hydrofoil, "land the ship." I went back upstairs and did as I was told, despite my mother's more sensible advice to use Vaseline. If a real man like my sailor daddy would use rubbing alcohol, I would too, I reasoned.

Besides, she had called me "baby." Hell, I wasn't a baby; I could count to ten without missing a single letter. He drank alcohol, which seemed to make him happy or sleepy, so it couldn't be bad, or so I reasoned. I poured a little on my finger; it felt cool and soothing and smelled like mint! It was a pretty green color, too, like a throat lozenge. Perfect! If I spilled any, I could see it on the white floor. It would be easy to clean up. Soon, I would be happily sound asleep. I leaned forward and poured just a little bit in my butt crack, like my daddy had said. I felt the effect almost immediately.

Green alcohol went everywhere, and I mean everywhere, including the ceiling. The walls looked like someone had slaughtered a bunch of aliens with a chain saw. It was then I learned how amazingly high I could jump, how incredibly loud I could scream, and how unbelievably fast I could run, buck naked, down the stairs, without touching a single one. I also previously had no idea that I could climb all the way to the top of my mother's head. My mother tried to comfort me while my father tried to apologize, but it was way too late. My father learned the power of a father's ability to influence his son's behavior. I learned that "there be dragons" in bottles labeled "alcohol," to be extremely skeptical of my father's advice, and how to live through a good sea story. None are things a five-year-old should be learning from his father.

The future is full of big surprises, many of which seem obvious when you can finally look back. John F. Kennedy said that his biggest surprise after he became president was that things were actually as bad as he had been saying they were. I think about my father when I hear that Kennedy story. I wonder if he would have been surprised at how right, and how wrong, he was about the navy. In this book, you can now compare and contrast the backgrounds and experiences of two different sailors, both of whom have written about their military experiences, and I describe some of the experiences of Bill Goss, who is the other sailor. Unlike Bill, I have experienced numerous encounters with discrimination and racism. I survived them all, sometimes just barely. Some important ones are detailed in these pages. Bill spent his last navy tour working for an admiral in Jacksonville, Florida, and fighting a deadly skin cancer. At about the same time, I spent my last tour working indirectly for the same admiral in Jacksonville.

There were only about four thousand Black sailors in the navy back in 1941, and most of them were stewards—that is, cooks and servants—for the officers, none of whom were Black. During World War II, the navy would commission 268,000 officers (dozens of them Black) and enlist more than 100,000 Black sailors. By 1974, the number of Black sailors was still low, and less than 2 percent of officers were Black.

Dennis Nelson II, son of a navy steward, and his son, Dennis D. Nelson III, may be the first Black father-son duo to retire as US naval officers, both as lieutenant commanders. Dennis D. Nelson II was likely the first Black officer to write about minority service policies; Lieutenant Commander William S. Norman, Zumwalt's minority affairs adviser, helped make those policies into a navy-wide reality. Virtually any Black officer who sticks around long enough will be the first Black something-or-other, even now. On November 13, 2020, it was announced that Rear Admiral Alvin Holsey would become the next commander of the navy Personnel Command and deputy chief of naval personnel, thereby becoming the first Black one.

The generally accepted definition of *mustang* in the navy is an officer who has served at least four years of enlisted service prior to earning his or her commission, usually without a break in service. The typical mustang is a hotshot young petty officer or chief who gets commissioned through the limited duty officer or chief warrant officer programs. I did not. They are technical and managerial experts in a particular field. The navy benefits from their expertise and leadership. I was different. I served in both administrative and technical ratings and also served two years outside of both of those ratings as an Equal Opportunity Program Specialist, definitely a non-career-enhancing assignment. In a herd of mustangs, I was a unicorn.

Zumwalt's three major personnel concerns as chief of naval operations (CNO) (1970–74) were addressing regulations and practices dealing with personnel behavior, improving operational schedules, and increasing the ability of bright and talented young men and women to obtain more responsibility and greater opportunity for advancement. I am a direct beneficiary of the initiatives of Admiral Zumwalt; a living part of his enormous legacy. His headstone in the Naval Academy cemetery simply says what he truly was: "REFORMER."

Before I could begin my own resistance-filled naval journey, I would have to focus my mind on my own present and future, which weren't looking so good. At one point, it was a real question of whether I would have any future at all, other than as a tragic statistic.

An angry young man pointing a sawed-off shotgun at my chest took my future in his hands. "Who you callin' a bitch?" he said. I then saw my future in mere seconds and not much more. I was barely seventeen years old. The way I had gotten myself here was by making three mistakes, any one of which could have gotten me killed. First, I, an outsider, had inserted myself into a dispute between people who all knew each other well. Second, I had spoken brazenly before I understood what was happening. (I had seen this done before, and I should have known better.) Third and potentially most fatal was that I had brought a knife to a gunfight. The knife I carried in my pocket for self-protection was about as useful now as a copy of *Robert's Rules of Order*.

Suddenly no longer feeling so cocky, I decided to try reason. I remembered some advice I had heard years earlier, attributed to a cop: "Never dare a man holding a gun in your face to shoot you. That is a quick way to wind up dead." Like most angry young men, the one pointing the shotgun at my chest wanted one thing more than he wanted to kill me. He wanted respect. I had just said some derogatory things about his sister, who had been stabbed by my girlfriend, and he took it personally. This stabbing, with a small kitchen knife, was as big a surprise to me as the shotgun, although it shouldn't have been. All of this madness had originated because my girlfriend had laughed at the girl during an argument earlier in the evening. It was all very stupid. It's an old story that poor, stressed people will take out their frustrations on the most convenient targets, who are often each other.

While I was reasoning with the angry young man, I saw my eighteen-year-old brother, Ray, easing away from the small crowd. I knew that he was heading for my father's house to get the .38-caliber pistol that was there. If he came back with either my father or the pistol, I knew things would get much worse. I kept talking, and I came to realize that this guy really didn't want to shoot me. If he had, I would have already been dead. I don't remember exactly what I said to him, but he lowered the shotgun. And that's when the trouble really started.

One of his sisters quietly stepped forward with yet another gun, a pistol, and announced that she was going to "kill the bitch" who had just stabbed her sister. (Was I the only fool here with a knife? No, my girlfriend was the other one.) It's much easier to get away with calling someone a bitch if you have a pistol in your hand and your brother has a sawed-off shotgun. The sister was clearly the more dangerous one; she was calm and determined. My girlfriend, who was a decade older than I was, had quietly tried to engage her cloaking device and disappear behind me as other people frantically tended to the girl she had just stabbed. I wondered why the hell these people kept pointing guns at *me*. I had not hurt anybody!

I started talking again, keeping my girlfriend behind me as the woman with the pistol tried to circle around me and get off a clear shot at her—an effort my girlfriend was really helpful with, making sure I was between her and that angry woman with the gun all the time. At one point, the woman with the gun aimed it at my knee, and I just knew she was going to drop me with a shot in the leg and then kill my girlfriend. I was pretty sure if that happened, I wouldn't be playing any more basketball. By now, I was wondering whether my brother, if he made it back in time, would shoot someone or get shot along with me. I was the bookworm of the family; my brother, Ray, was the dangerous one. If I got shot, my brother wasn't going to waste any time talking.

Thinking back on it, I was more afraid of Ray than either of the two angry people who had pointed guns at me. My brother had more than once sent me running for my life, and I knew even then that he was capable of really hurting someone, including me. In the end, that night no one died or got shot, and I later had a long, harsh talk with my suddenly much-less-attractive and soon-to-be ex-girlfriend.

Shortly after this stressful night, I told my father that I wanted to join the navy and that he'd need to sign the papers for me to do so, and he said: "Hell, no, the navy is too racist, and I'm not going to sign any damn papers for you to join." I had just almost gotten shot, and it was not a racist white guy who did it. Nonetheless, in some ways, this was an understandable response from an uninformed Black father in 1974.

The navy had a long-standing reputation for being hostile to Blacks and, as a result, having very few, by design. Did my father think that the navy was more dangerous than my current environment?

I had lived in military housing and grown up around sailors, on navy bases at San Diego; Norfolk, Virginia; and Newport, Rhode Island. We had US Navy blankets at home. They just showed up somehow. My father was a sailor, "Old School." He was not uninformed; he was experienced. He could curse, drink, fight, lie, and tell sea stories with the best of them. Boatswain's Mate First Class Parker W. L. Green earned letters of commendation for his outstanding leadership and performance and also received nonjudicial punishment at captain's mast for inciting a riot while Zumwalt was CNO. Captain's mast is the administrative procedure used by commanding officers to address minor disciplinary charges stemming from violations of the Uniform Code of Military Justice. I hope to pull that string someday.

What racism had to do with my father's decisions, I'll never know for sure, but what I do know has taken me years to understand. When my father refused to sign for me to enlist and warned me against it, he wasn't really angry or unreasonably difficult. He was, I now recognize, traumatized and simply afraid. How could someone who had grown up in the military, both army and navy, be afraid for his own son to serve? Not afraid of the enemy, but of his fellow sailors?

Lieutenant Commander Bill Norman, Zumwalt's minority affairs assistant, gave an interview to author Wallace Terry about the Black experience in the '60s–'70s navy for his national bestseller *Bloods*, published in 1985. This book is an oral history of the Vietnam War by Black veterans, in their own words. My father's story about his Vietnam experiences would have been a great addition to this volume, based on the sea stories I heard him tell.

Almost two decades later, I would have some of the same enraging experiences as an officer that Bill Norman had. A self-admitted "discrimination" hell-raiser, he resigned his commission before Zumwalt retired because too many admirals were gunning for him and weren't bashful about telling him so. Can't say I blame him. He had a giant bull's eye on his back, and he knew it. The book *Zumwalt: The Life and Times of Admiral Elmo Russell "Bud" Zumwalt, Jr.* by Larry Berman adds a bit more to his story and legend. You should read it.

The opposition to the changes Zumwalt made was formidable: President Richard Nixon, himself a former naval officer; Secretary of State Henry Kissinger; Admiral Thomas Moorer; powerful southern senators and congressmen, such as Mississippi senator John C. Stennis, chairman of the Armed Services Committee; many senior officers; retired and active-duty military members (officer and enlisted); and much of the general public. That he was able to withstand the pressure and prevail against such opposition is remarkable.

My father was too late to warn me away from the navy. At almost eighteen, I was too strong, smart, and careful to get discriminated against. I knew that the navy was now an equal opportunity employer; the CNO had said so himself. My favorite pair of pants when I was seventeen was an old pair of navy dungarees (bell-bottoms) that my father had given me. Eventually, they were so dry-rotted that I had to patch them up with many denim patches across the front of both legs and on the seat. I wore those pants until they disintegrated like an old dishrag.

Zumwalt said that there was no Black navy, no white navy; there was only one navy, and nothing mattered more than performance. What I didn't know, and perhaps my father did, was that just because the CNO gave an order did not mean that it would be carried out.

After mulling over my father's warnings and considering my options, I returned to the navy recruiter's office to negotiate terms, having initially gone a few weeks earlier to feel them out. He wasn't particularly excited to see me again (I would later learn why), but he did give me some more brochures, let me watch some films, and gave me some papers to fill out. I would have to take a test to see if I qualified to join the navy and at what job. All the documents stated that the navy was "an Equal Opportunity Employer." An equal opportunity was all I wanted. I took the entrance exam and waited. In the meantime, I tried to avoid my stepmother and scrape together enough money to keep my car from being repossessed. I picked oranges. It was way too hard. I soon quit.

After my test results came back, the excited recruiter called me. I didn't know that the navy was then restricting the number of Blacks (and whites) who scored poorly in their entrance exams. Statistically, I was likely to be one of them. He had probably seen plenty of young Black kids like me and turned most of them away. No point in getting my hopes up. The *Washington Post* wrote about this in 1976.

Zumwalt had earlier talked to the National Association for the Advancement of Colored People (NAACP), among other organizations, about his recruiting efforts and his logical rationale, and they gave their tacit approval. Sometimes, if you are logical, you can talk and achieve understanding with your perceived enemies, even if they're pointing a gun at you.

The recruiter, and a backup, drove twenty miles to my house to talk to me. Unknown to me until more than thirty years later, I had scored in the top 7 percent of Black men taking the entrance exam and in the top 30 percent of all young men taking the exam that year. In the recruiter's eyes, I was a prize catch. All he had to do now was to tell me enough lies to get me to sign up. Black, white, or lime green, I was now a much more attractive prospect.

I didn't understand the significance of my test results, but I had already learned that the year before I quit high school, I was reading at a two-year college level. In the dead-end Florida school system, with no prospect for any scholarship or family support for college, I could have been a genius, and it wouldn't have made much difference, at least not to me. I had been in three different high schools, two in Florida and one in Tennessee, and I was having trouble adjusting to both the new schools and the curriculum. I needed just a little help, but the teachers weren't exactly helpful. I simply gave up trying. As the recruiters talked to me, they also tried to convince my father to return to the navy and serve for a little more time so that he could earn his navy pension. He informed them, with abundant profanity for emphasis, that he wasn't going to sign any papers for me to join the navy and he sure as hell wasn't going to go back in himself. They laughed uneasily, but he wasn't smiling or kidding. They probably knew why he felt this way, even if I did not.

After the recruiters left, I talked to my father again. He would not budge. He had always told me that I could do anything I put my mind to; he didn't believe it but felt obligated to say it anyway. I didn't dare share my officer aspirations with my father. He could no more have envisioned his son becoming a naval officer than he could envision a Black president. If I had told him that I intended to become an officer, he would have likely said something to hurt my feelings. Like many fathers can do to their children, he could hurt me without intending to and not know how to fix it if he did.

My mother was another story. She was a churchgoing woman all her life. When my father spoke of God, there was almost always blasphemy involved. I'm sure she regretted letting me go live with my father after I turned sixteen. He thought church was for funerals, and he didn't like funerals. His first funeral, when he was twelve, was that of his own father, who had been an army stevedore during World War II.

My father's father developed emphysema and ultimately died in a Veterans Administration hospital in Nashville, Tennessee, in 1948. I don't ever recall my father, who grew up as an only child, talking about his own father, other than to say when he died.

A proud man often doesn't want to bring up the fact that he grew up without a father. To compensate for this, I think my father joined the military at an early age, earned his jump wings in the army, and served in the infantry in Korea. I imagine that a navy boatswain's mate with a set of army parachute wings was a rare sight in the Vietnam era, but he had them. He never talked about his Korean War service. I have pictures of him sitting in a tank, but that doesn't mean that he saw combat. My mother's daddy was murdered before I was born. Both my mother and stepmother signed the necessary papers, which satisfied the recruiters, and I was soon off to boot camp in Orlando, Florida. I was going to miss my long hair.

2

Bootcamp and Almost Becoming a Mineman

I attended boot camp in sunny Orlando, Florida. It was March 1975. By then, the navy had undergone some positive changes, but if I was going to become an officer, there was a lot of tradition to overcome.

By 1975, 7.2 percent of the enlisted population was Black, but only 1.4 percent of the officer corps was. In 1940, the approximately four thousand Black sailors, overwhelmingly stewards, were a miniscule percentage of the total force.

On the first day of boot camp, there was a lot of running, sweating, swearing, marching around, and screaming, and there were bewildered guys of every size and description trying not to pee their pants, attract attention, or show the anxiety that was in their hearts. The collective thought bubble over most of our heads was "What the hell did I get myself into?" Once they shaved our heads, took all our clothes, and dressed us alike in dark blue uniforms (the color of toilet bowl cleaner—they also made sure we knew that toilet bowl cleaner had more potential for success than we did), it was almost impossible to remember who was who from the day before.

In boot camp, we learned pretty quickly that if, by some miracle, any of us stupid, crawling maggots actually survived and made it to the fleet, only one out of a thousand of us would ever make it to master chief petty officer, the pinnacle of the enlisted ranks. How many, I wondered, would ever get a commission and become an officer? This information was so depressing that I flushed it from my short-term memory. I had to face the reality of statistics. I had not yet learned the irrefutable fact that 98.6 percent of all sailors' statistics are made up on the spot, so I was pretty bummed.

Within the first few days of entering boot camp I came face to face, literally, with a problem that would follow me throughout the rest of my career and my life. After they shaved our heads, took our clothes, put us in our uniforms and yelled, marched, and ran us into submission, I began to think clearly enough to notice the problem. We were required to shave every day, and we didn't have much time to do it. When I looked in the mirror, I saw a face full of small bumps and pus-filled scabs, and my face burned like it was on fire—the parts that had hair on them, anyway.

I, like many men of African descent, have this problem. When you take a sharp razor and run it across your face, you've just put a sharp point on hairs that are probably going to curl into your skin. This is very painful, causes a localized infection, and looks bad. The only way to get this hair out once it grows into your skin is to lift it out with a needle, tweezers, toothpick, or some other instrument. If you don't get it early, it may continue to burrow into your skin, deeper than an inch. Trust me, this is true. If you shave over this bumpy mess, it only makes things worse. The condition is pseudofolliculitis barbae (PFB).

When you see a Black man with a two-tone face, the darker area shows what a lifetime of scarring has done to his skin. When I used to watch my father pick at the hairs on his face, I had no idea that I would someday do the same thing. Three of the four Black guys in my company had this problem to some degree.

Luckily, the navy was aware of this problem, and allowances were made, provided you were medically diagnosed and had the proper chit to allow you to not shave daily. I carried one for many years. For a few years, I wore a full beard. Thanks to Admiral Zumwalt, this was one of the many new privileges allowed for enlisted and officer personnel alike.

Despite this official understanding about my hair and skin problems, they were still a big problem for me in boot camp. We were marching with rifles when the company commander called for us to halt. Before I knew it, he was in my face, screaming and calling me every kind of dumbass you could imagine. Between the spit, hot breath, and profanity, one or all of which smelled like an ashtray, and the shock of receiving the brunt of his wrath, I heard something about my exhibiting poor military bearing by reaching up and scratching my worthless-ass chin, which was supporting my equally worthless mouth, which I did not dare open to speak. He grabbed my cap and pulled it down so far on my head, my ears stuck out like wings. I could feel all the eyes grinning behind me.

I was expecting more discipline when we returned to the barracks, but none came. More than forty years later, I still wonder, was he not harder on me because I was Black or because he understood how difficult the condition was?

At boot camp, I was surrounded by white guys from all over the United States, and Texas. I was the first Black guy that many of them had ever really talked to or closely associated with. Some of us got to be really friendly, and we had many interesting conversations once things calmed down. I think some of them were surprised that we Black guys were pretty much just like they were, once we started talking. Every night, we would say good night to each other just like they did on the television show *The Waltons*. There were four of us Black guys, the only visible minorities: Dwight Stewart, Carl Gardner, Rickey Taylor, and me. Carlos Rivera was Hispanic; he didn't fit in, complexion wise, and he had big Dumbo-sized ears. We accepted him anyway. The fact that I still remember the names of these guys after more than forty years makes me smile. After graduation, I never saw any of them again. All debts and all friendships usually terminate upon transfer, it is said. I can tell you that I was the most handsome of the bunch. I know this to be true because I was voted "Most Handsome Nigger" by my fellow recruits during our impromptu "awards ceremony" as we were preparing for graduation the next day. There was no plaque, no prize, just bragging rights. I did not actively seek the title. After flipping them the bird and telling them what to kiss, I could not help but smile. We were now like a family; they didn't know any better, and there were much worse awards being handed out.

I never let words bother me much because I was pretty good with them myself and was happy to exchange insults with any of my peers. I have been playing the dozens since elementary school. Where I grew up, if you couldn't stand hearing your friends say the most terrible things about your momma anybody ever heard, you weren't going to make it. It toughened you up. You developed a thick skin for verbal insults, and you also learned how to dish them out.

I'm embarrassed right now for some of the things I said about some nice ladies who went to church regularly and asked Jesus to watch over us wayward children. In the 1970s, many men felt that the worst thing you could call someone in boot camp, or anywhere else, was a homophobic slur. The more macho you acted, the more likely you were to be called one. We all dished out regionally specific, profanity-laced, culturally distinct versions of such perceived insults, usually followed by vivid descriptions of what Jody was doing to the opponent's girlfriend at that exact moment, usually with solemn affirmations from the peanut gallery.

In boot camp I narrowly avoided one fistfight, which most likely would have resulted in severe disciplinary action or possibly administrative discharge. One of the white recruits tightly grabbed me by the arm to prevent me from walking on a part of the recently buffed deck, but the deck was an excuse. He was the squad leader I had replaced, and I think there was some resentment lingering. He was an aggressive New Yorker, and had we met in his neighborhood, we might not have been buddies. We got past it without violence, but we could have both ended our navy careers right there.

Up until then in my life, when a white guy grabbed me, it was usually because he had first pretended to befriend me and then I had ignored him after he called me a "nigger" in front of his real friends. This sometimes emboldened him, and he would sometimes grab or attack me (usually from behind). This didn't happen until I started high school in Tennessee after I had lived for eight years in San Diego, California. Three "friends," three sneak attacks, three real quick ass whippings, and then the word was out: "Leave that quiet, four-eyed skinny new California kid alone; he doesn't know the rules or follow the script and will call you a motherfucker in front of the eighty-year-old female English teacher while whipping your ass in the cafeteria, but only after you spit in his face while he is eating." That specific scenario happened twice.

I would not allow myself to be paddled by the vice principal/football coach for fighting back and simply defending myself. I told him so. He never tried. I must have looked like I would resist.

My first real exposure to religious conflict also occurred in boot camp. Someone's mother was sick, and the company master at arms asked us to say a Hail Mary for her. At the time, I didn't know a Hail Mary from "Proud Mary," and I thought singing "Proud Mary" was inappropriate just then. But someone else did have a problem, not just due to not knowing the prayer. Plitman, whose first name I can't recall, was Jewish, which didn't mean anything to me then. It was easier to divide the white guys by whether they did or did not pay attention in English class or whether they did or did not talk funny. Plitman had been getting lightheartedly teased for being Jewish, and sometimes the teasing had an edge. He was apparently a little touchy about his religion. He exploded in a profane tirade and pent-up expressions of resentment, as though he had been personally attacked or something. An argument followed, but then things settled down.

In boot camp, we kicked ass under our good leadership, especially during Sports Week, the competition between companies for bragging rights and sports pennants that improved your standing. Having three fast Black guys, and one sort of fast white one, on your relay team in boot camp was a definite advantage, even with the one white guy running the last leg. We thought about fielding an all-Black relay team, but that would have been overkill and would have discriminated against the white guys. We were unknowingly practicing affirmative action. Nobody complained.

When we finally got to go on liberty, despite all the other friends I'd made, we four Black guys all hung out together, along with Rivera. Truth is we were comfortable with it being that way. Among ourselves, we could talk like we were used to talking. Even though we laughed and joked and drank with the rest of the guys, we also realized that we were viewed differently, and we saw ourselves differently, too.

On the first day of liberty, near graduation, we were allowed to go to the on-base club. I got so drunk that I was soon under a table, and an equally drunk first class petty officer was trying to get me up before I got into trouble. My shipmates got me back to the barracks and then tucked me into my rack, with my head hanging over a big metal bucket ready to catch the remaining contents of my stomach.

I don't remember much about that first drunken night as a sailor. I wouldn't have many more. Long before I had entered boot camp, I had already begun the slippery slope of trying to drown my sorrows and stress with alcohol. Thankfully, I refused to do drugs, and I caught myself before too much alcohol damage was done. I do remember that many of those who helped me were white, talked funny, and had not paid much attention in English class. It didn't matter. I was their shipmate, and they were mine. After graduation, I got to spend a couple of days back home, received some effusive displays of affection for my spiffy new uniform from my soon-to-be ex-girlfriend (who was already stalking her next soulmate), and then flew to Charleston, South Carolina.

Mineman Class A School provided introductory training to the mineman rating specialty. At the time, the entire mine force worldwide consisted of around five hundred personnel, all men, fewer than ten of whom were Black. Very few minemen would ever serve on ships; they served overseas and at select locations in the United States. I reported for duty at the Fleet Mine Warfare Training Center with about twenty-five other guys. I was initially the only Black student in my class, but eventually, I was joined by my friend David D. Mack, an air force veteran, who came from a previous class. We are still friends.

Only seven of us survived to graduation. We alternated between bored and scared, watching people slowly fall away and thinking about how a wrong move could ruin your day.

When the instructors spoke about mining the Ho Chi Minh Trail, which Zumwalt planned, and the difficulty the enemy had in trying to disarm or avoid them, it really gave us pause. The absolute worst class I remember in this school was what I like to fondly remember as "Slow Death by Schematics." We had to learn the electrical and mechanical schematics of various mines, line by line, mine by mine. The senior chief mineman instructor taught this exciting class in a dull, dry, deep monotone as he dragged his pointer across each schematic, pointing out the really interesting parts. Think Ben Stein in uniform, only bald, fat, and not rich. With the class right after lunch, we quickly got sleepy and bored.

To compensate for this, he would sometimes, just as we were all about to fall out of our chairs, rouse us to wakefulness by shoving his cigar deeply into each nostril, twirling it around dramatically, lovingly inspect the results, and then sticking it into his mouth with a satisfied look on his face. It always did the trick; as disgusted as it made us, and knowing what was coming, I could never look away. I was going to watch this damn train wreck happen.

We would thereafter try very hard to concentrate on what he was saying rather than thinking about the disgusting spectacle we had just witnessed. Despite his best efforts, this class was where we lost the most people. After this segment of the course was taught, we were finally down from twenty-five to only seven people.

As school progressed, I was treated differently, and it was not subtle. I had bought the navy's equal opportunity propaganda hook, line, and sinker. "You can be Black, and Navy too" was one of the recruiting slogans at the time, but it was not quite true, from my perspective. I was trying to be navy first, but being Black kept getting in the way. Several disturbing trends emerged as I went through the fleet mine training school.

First, my uniform was always immaculate. My boondockers (boots) were spit-shined so well that I would see the staff looking at them as I walked down the passageways. None looked better. One of the chief instructors on the staff once casually asked me where I had gotten my Corfam (shiny synthetic) boondockers; he did a double take when I told him they were standard issue. I spent almost as much time shining my boots as I did studying. I scored well on all written tests, seldom getting anything less than an A.

I was never singled out for praise or recognition for my appearance at the weekly inspections, or my grades. One of my classmates, Ralph McClusker, was consistently praised at inspection for his appearance. He was tall, good-looking, blond, and white. I looked at least as good as he did, and my boots looked better. So did my grades. We stood right next to each other; I was tall too. He'd get the recognition; I'd get the silent treatment. Ralph reflected light; I absorbed it, like a black hole.

This blatantly discriminatory staff behavior was noticed by my classmates. They would sometimes ask me why I never got any good comments. I would usually say that I didn't know, and when I asked them why they thought I wasn't praised, they would lower their eyes or look away. I never got an answer. I didn't need one. Subtle messages were being sent. Were the instructors trying to show my classmates how Black sailors should be treated? Was I being pressured not to do so well or perhaps to quit? I also noticed that although on written exams I would score As, when we had to demonstrate proficiency (we called them *practicals*) in a specific task or explain the workings of a piece of electrical or mechanical equipment, I would score a B or C, never an A. This was my first encounter with what is called "rater bias." I'd have many more similar experiences.

My classmates, some of whom were struggling academically, would almost always score higher than I did during these practicals, and I helped them practice. How could this be? I was suddenly getting dumber when someone had to evaluate my performance subjectively. While doing one of these demonstrations, my instructor evaluator interrupted me and quietly asked how I kept my fingernails from breaking. At first it confused me. What the hell? Fingernails?

Then it dawned on me that he might be implying that I was gay. I pulled up my other hand and showed him all the broken, dirty nails on that one, from working on my car, and said I just haven't broken the others yet. I kept my nails well-trimmed after that and a little dirty if I could. Things looked like they were going to change, starting in 1980, but it would take a while longer. AIDS, homophobia, and Ronald Reagan had a lot to do with that.

The most blatant unfairness I dealt with involved a navy correspondence course, Tools and Their Uses, which we had to complete on our own time. I finished the course right away; I even enjoyed it. It helped me, as I had a 1965 Ford Fairlane 500 that required a lot of tools and prayers to keep running. Some of my classmates, having seen that I'd finished my course first, asked if they could look at my completed course before I turned it in. I happily obliged. It apparently got "looked at" a lot. I didn't care; some of them were struggling to keep up. Later, we had a surprise quiz on the contents of the course. The class genius, David Badger, and I were the only ones who passed the test. I waited for the staff to congratulate me for passing the test, but it didn't happen. We promptly were chewed out and told that all of us would have to take the test again.

This was the first time I challenged the way I was being treated. There was no ambiguity here; this was not fair. I asked for an explanation of why I was being required to retake a test that I had already passed. This was unjust, and I told them so. Ultimately, I didn't have to retake the test, but I was under resentful suspicion. I helped my shipmates, and I was punished. I outshone my shipmates, and I was punished. Unwisely, I had shown some assertiveness. It would cost me, a lot.

These instructors couldn't have had much experience with Black sailors. They were simply acting according to their own prejudices. My high grades were not anomalous by now. They still couldn't imagine how a Black guy could pass a test that none of the white guys did. It was obvious that I hadn't looked at anyone else's paper, wasn't it? I couldn't understand why they seemed to resent me for doing well. Was I doing too well? I didn't know that the country was in the infancy of a more conservative turn, and there was a growing resistance and backlash to the civil rights gains, like school busing and affirmative action, as well as resistance to the "intrusion" of Blacks into areas where they were not wanted. I was essentially an unwanted intruder.

One day David Mack (my only Black classmate) and I were walking near the school at lunchtime, and one of the senior officers—I believe it was the commanding officer—pulled up alongside us in his pickup truck and told us to get in; he'd give us a ride. We told him we weren't going far, less than a block, but he firmly insisted. As we entered the truck, I couldn't help but notice that the metal dashboard was plastered with Confederate flag stickers, "The South Will Rise Again, Forget Hell" slogans, and the like. It was like a shrine to the Confederacy.

In this man's mind, I thought, I should still be enslaved. I instantly sensed danger. What did he want? Did he want us to cut the grass, shine his shoes, or something sinister? I looked in the mirror to see if there was a car tailing us. Here I was on a US naval base, in broad daylight, and I was confused, worried, and scared.

As he drove, very slowly, he quietly asked us questions about school, and although the talk was ostensibly pleasant, his tone was slightly ominous. He asked us if we were having any problems in school but was really, in a roundabout manner, ensuring we weren't by pretty much telling us how good things were there. After he dropped us off, Mack and I just looked at each other in disbelief. What the hell had just happened? Neither of us knew what to say. He had never spoken to us before and would not again.

I'm pretty sure that when we did speak, the words "Racist Redneck Cracker" were worked into the conversation, with all due respect, of course. (I knew Black sailors talked like this because my daddy did, and he was one.) The officer may have been a traditionalist, someone who opposed Zumwalt's changes, but I didn't recognize them yet; I was too young and green. Mack and I both felt like we had just been warned, without understanding why. This was my first experience with navy "discrimination damage control." It would not be my last.

And as it turned out, Mack and I soon found out just why we had been "taken for a little ride." A Black student in another class within the school command had formally complained of discriminatory treatment. Unlike the rest of us, he had the stones to actually speak up about it and even put it in writing. Ultimately, this made it more tolerable for the rest of us, at least for a while. Every Black student (the few there were) in the school's command was interviewed. I was asked a few questions about how I was being treated and whether I believed I was being discriminated against. I could tell what the desired answers were.

I could have said quite a lot by then, but all I was comfortable saying was that no matter how good my uniform and shoes and personal grooming were, I never received any positive or encouraging comments during the weekly personnel inspections. This was the only thing I could prove, and I had witnesses. Behold, a miracle cometh! The very next uniform inspection, I was told by my class leader, Mineman First Class Lord, that my shoes looked good; however, the way he said it, sarcastically, made it seem like he thought I had been begging for a compliment or something. I wanted to spit, and I knew exactly where. I didn't say anything, but I did blink a message in made-up Morse code: F-U-C-K Y-O-U! By then, my shoes really didn't look much better than anyone else's or, at least, not as good as they had looked. I had quit trying to impress the school staff and instructors. In subtle and not-so-subtle ways, they made me know that I wasn't really welcome, and my efforts to shine, literally, were wasted on them. I never knew if any of my white classmates were interviewed about this discrimination complaint and investigation. They could no more truthfully articulate to me the instructor's racism than they could their own.

Our class leader was named Tony. Being the class leader made him smarter than the rest of us, especially me. I once won five dollars from him because he insisted that the command master chief had a gold band on his combination cover. I knew better. He insisted we bet, and I, the son of a sailor, easily won.

Tony also once tried to convince me, during study hall (we didn't always study, sometimes we digressed), that someone being called "a nigger" had nothing to do with skin color. "Anybody could be a nigger," he said. I said, "Nigger is only used to refer to Black people." We argued about this for quite a few minutes. Finally, exasperated, I asked him, "Would you call Ralph a nigger?" Ralph McClusker, sitting nearby, was tall, good-looking, and white. Surprised at my question, he said no. I asked why not? Tony said, I swear, "Because he's not Blaaaaaa—"

He almost choked as the tentacles of enlightenment circled his windpipe and squeezed it shut. I didn't have to say anything else. The rest of the class was pretty much silent after this last exchange. Some of the good ol' boys in the classroom knew that this was a losing argument on Tony's part, but I guess they figured I could handle this one myself. I had firmly established myself as the racial slur expert, both by how I was being treated and by being the only one there who was "Blaaaack." I'd made my point. The black sheep is always black; he knows it, and so do you and the rest of the sheep.

Admiral William J. Crowe, chairman of the Joint Chiefs of Staff from 1985 to 1989, said that when he and his wife were stationed in Charleston, he never met anyone who thought the South had lost the war. South Carolina was the only southern state that had a Black majority population after the end of the Civil War, which was a source of contention during Reconstruction. But of course, after that came Redemption. I wondered a lot about what life must have been like in those days. I knew I easily had it better. I regret that I didn't speak up more forcefully or complain about the disparate treatment I was subjected to during this period—but at the same time, there was no clear authority that was safe to raise these complaints to. And even though I said very little about my treatment, I would pay a big price nonetheless.

Finally, it was time to graduate. I was the number-two student academically, behind Dave Badger. I was a shoo-in for the school's honor roll, which we had been told about on the first day of class. I would have my name engraved on the brass plaque at the school for all to see how smart I was. My classmates had started to happily kid me about it. When they carved your name in brass somewhere, you were hot shit, dead, or both. I had repeatedly calculated my GPA, and I knew I was above a 3.6, the cutoff for the honor roll. Alas, this was not to be.

I had survived the technical rigor, booger-eating instructor, culturally biased (redneck-oriented) instruction, and differential evaluation. What was left? What I could not overcome was the racism. When grades were released, I found that, somehow, I had just barely missed honor roll by the tiniest of margins, fractions of a percentage point, a fingernail away. My "official" (by their calculations) GPA upon finishing the course was 3.57. Immediately, I wondered if I had miscalculated. Or, I thought, might I have lost a fraction of a point somehow by whining about no one noticing my shiny shoes? Should I challenge them? Request an audit? Quit? File a discrimination complaint?

The truth was there was no way these guys were going to allow a Black guy's name to be added to that honor roll. This was not a new phenomenon. It would take systematic reviews of World War II awards to minority service members, ordered by President Bill Clinton, many decades later, to reveal the extent of the denial (attributed to racism) of the appropriate earned recognition (the Medal of Honor) to these men. Their lesser awards were upgraded to the Medal of Honor to correct this injustice.

I didn't get my name immortalized on the school brass plaque. I did, however, qualify, based on my grades, for accelerated advancement to mineman third class. This meant an immediate promotion, more money in my pocket, and a jump start to my career, if I chose to make the navy my career. I submitted my special request chit and waited for my required promotion board.

The promotion board was easy enough. The toughest question I got was "What would you do if you gave an order to a white guy and he didn't follow it?" My answer was "The same thing I would do if it were a Black guy," and then I explained a little about my philosophy of leadership, which I had learned, mostly in boot camp, from reading comic books and the *Encyclopedia Britannica*, following the civil rights movement, and watching John Wayne movies and Mighty Mouse cartoons. To me, even then, it was an asinine question.

I was really surprised at who asked this promotion board question. It was one of my favorite instructors, a senior chief. Was he trying to help me? Trip me up? I was well enough read on the Black experience that I understood where the question was coming from.

I passed my board, went to the uniform shop and happily bought some nice new mineman petty officer insignia for my uniforms. I eagerly waited for my promotion ceremony. David Badger, the smartest guy in our class, applied and passed his board but was denied, I later learned. He was a Yankee. In my case, there was a big, insurmountable problem. I had enlisted as a reservist, in a special slot. This meant that I went to boot camp, A school, and then to my reserve unit for inactive duty for the next five or so years. If my father was right, I could put up with racism one weekend a month, so long as they were going to pay me to do it.

"Sorry," Mineman First Class Lord, my class adviser, told me, "but you can't be advanced." There was nothing that could be done. Why wasn't I given this important information until after my board? I wanted to stay, but they said I couldn't. There is nothing for you here. Muhammad Ali fought to stay out of the military; I had to fight to stay in.

My father was right. There was racism, but I had dealt with stuff like this before, and I could handle it. I sadly packed my bags and left for home. I looked at that shiny brass plaque on the way out. No job, no girlfriend, no future that I could see. I did have very shiny shoes. As I checked into the reserve unit in Tampa, Florida, the personnelman first class petty officer looked through my service record while I stood at the counter. I was wondering what I was going to do for the next five years. As I pondered my romantic relationship and career options, the future changed again. The clerk jerked his head up in surprise and looked at me, asking if I knew I had qualified for accelerated advancement. I said, yes, I did. He asked why I had not accepted it. I explained what I had been told about it.

He got this quizzical look on his face and asked me sharply who exactly told me that. I told him that my class adviser, Mineman First Class Lord, had. From the disgusted look on his face, I knew I'd been lied to. Why would they get rid of a smart, motivated guy like me, with my shiny shoes and all? This decision had likely been made at the command level. I learned from him that I could have reenlisted on the spot. Father 1, me 0.

The post-Zumwalt navy was trying to do better toward minorities, but where the rubber met the road, resistance was sometimes strong. This was racism in its most raw, blatant, and economically driven form. I would have been taking a position and money that some white guy was entitled to, as they saw it, and no smart-ass, sissy-looking young Black kid was going to do that if they could help it.

The navy's Affirmative Action Plan was issued slightly after I was turned down for promotion. I wasn't asking for, getting, or expecting affirmative action; I was expecting equal treatment and opportunity. I ultimately got neither one. I was already suffering the discrimination my father was worried about and had experienced himself. I simply had no idea that it would be so open, so normal, and so seemingly casual. It was institutionalized. The personnelman, a white guy, asked me if I wanted to be advanced to third class and return to active duty. By this time, I was embarrassed, and I was angry. I had not known enough to ask questions, read the directives, ask for a waiver, something! I wouldn't make this mistake again. I had no mentor or person to ask for help. I would have been a lot better off if my father had actually had a conversation with me about the future. I said yes to active duty, no to accelerated promotion.

The senior chief who had asked me the white guy question was always polite and professional toward me, and I had sometimes thought about asking him for advice. I'm glad I didn't. You'll understand why in the next chapter. His question was the only time the subject of race was mentioned by the staff.

3

Yeoman in the Mine Force

While I was cooling my heels, waiting for the required paperwork to be processed to permit my return to active duty, which took three months, I had a lot of time to kill. One day, I went to a matinee to see this new *Jaws* movie. I was OK until one particular scene. Usually, they would warn you when the shark was coming. *Duuuuhhh duuuumm*. You can't forget that music. I laughed every time someone would scream when he or she saw the shark. Didn't those people hear the music? What suckers! Anyway, this one scene caught me by surprise. Chief Brody (Roy Scheider) was throwing chum off the back of the boat and bitching like a real sailor, when suddenly this huge shark head broke the surface and tried to eat him. The idiots forgot to play the damn music!

All hell broke loose in that theater. Several little old white ladies in front of me screamed like the shark had just grabbed them. I jerked my legs off the floor so fast and so high that they knocked the bucket of popcorn out of my hands, or maybe the popcorn went flying because the hands that had been calmly holding it were now clawing for the ceiling with all their might.

In the middle of all this, I heard someone scream, "*Godddddammmmmit!!!!*," and they sounded like a terrified little girl. When I finally calmed down, I realized that it had been me. By now, I was busy trying to calm the acrobats who were steadily doing all kinds of fancy tumbling tricks in the pit of my stomach and listening really hard for that damn stupid music. Would they forget to play it again? I was so glad to see that rubber shark die.

I hurried out, shaken. It was a long, long time before I was comfortable going into the water again. I would think about *Jaws* many times, being a sailor and all. The shark is never mad at you; it's just doing what sharks do. With people, though, it's personal.

But the waiting period did not last forever. Soon enough I was back in Charleston, assigned to Commander Mobile Mine Assembly Group. I returned as a seaman, now behind my classmates in experience. I was now one of the 5 percent of Black sailors then serving in a technical rating. Only one in twenty sailors in any technical rating in those days were Black and usually very junior. I was one of them. Eight percent of the new recruits in the navy in 1976 were Black.

Personnelman First Class Forrester "John" Barker Jr., the personnel office supervisor, cheerfully checked me in, happily welcoming me aboard. While he was looking through my records, he all of a sudden jumped up from his desk and asked me to walk down the passageway with him. I immediately got worried. Was I in trouble?

Barker had seen from my service record that I could type well and that I had done very well in "A" school. He asked me if I would be willing to work in a nice warm office, typing stuff for him, instead of out in the hot or cold equipment bay doing maintenance on dirty old dangerous mines.

This was an easy decision. He didn't care whether I was pink, purple, or pumpkin. He was shorthanded and needed help, and I was just the man for the job. After I started working for him, I would learn that he had been the Atlantic Fleet Sailor of the Year the year before. Because of him, I became a yeoman.

He was the first person in whom I confided that I was interested in obtaining a commission. In my very first performance evaluation, he highly recommended me for consideration as a future officer. Largely because of this early encouragement, I believed it was possible. He was the brightest spot in my years in the mine force. He went on to become a chief warrant officer himself. Neither of us could envision that when we talked on the phone years later, I would outrank him.

Shortly after settling in, I was standing duty one night, and between compound watches, I was playing pool with one of the guys in the break room. His name was Jimmy. From North Carolina, he had an easy southern drawl and was really laid-back and friendly. We started talking a little about the music we liked, and eventually I must have been looking at him rather funny. He looked at me and calmly said, "What, you didn't know I'm Black?"

Looking at him in disbelief, I said, "Are you?" He had been in this movie before. Jimmy pulled out his wallet and showed me pictures of his parents and his siblings, including a family portrait. Jimmy had curly blond hair, light eyes, maybe blue, and was as pale as a biscuit. His family portrait, however, looked like one of those Benetton ads, or an Obama rally; people of every hue and hair color.

Jimmy became my main man. We went to see the Commodores in concert together, and he drove. He had an old Ford too, like me, only his was nicer and all painted the same color. As a guy who could pass for white, he had a lot more exposure to white people's true feelings than I did. Jimmy told me about his first day in Mineman A School, in the class right after mine.

The instructor walked into the class, looked around, and said, "At least we don't have any niggers in this class."

This was the same senior chief instructor who had asked me the white guy question and whom I had thought about confiding in about the treatment I was receiving from some of the other instructors. He had been so nice to me face to face. How do you respond to something like that? I was shocked to learn that the person I had considered confiding in and asking for advice and help resented that I was even there. I had to learn to read people better—and fast. Jimmy approached the instructor after class and informed him that he was in fact Black, not white. The instructor informed him that he was not prejudiced, but he could not deny what he had said. Jimmy wisely didn't file a complaint.

No wonder, as the *Guide to Command of Negro Naval Personnel* had said, in 1945, "Negro sailors are wary of white people in authority over them." It hurts to know that while I was working hard, trying to be all that I could be, craving acceptance and appreciation from the people for whom I worked, they were actively trying to undermine me, limit me, and actually looked down on me. My performance showed that I was entitled to be there. Jimmy's did too.

After working briefly in the personnel office and the administrative office, I was deployed to Mobile Mine Assembly Group Detachment 5 in Sigonella, Sicily, for six months. Although I was still a mineman seaman, I was going to fill a yeoman second class (YN2) billet. A yeoman is an administrative job. Blacks were largely clustered in clerical and nontechnical service ratings in those days.

There were no YN2s on the staff, so they sent me. The twenty-five-man detachment included a lieutenant, a chief or senior chief, a leading petty officer, various petty officers and seamen, and a storekeeper, if we were lucky. I quickly learned my job and started looking for more things to do.

I soon learned that the ordnance publications (OPs), technical manuals used to perform maintenance, were badly out of date, *all* of them. These manuals were critical to the proper maintenance on these mines. The frequent changes and updates to these publications for immediate action were left undone and had been piling up for years. Some had as many as ten such changes. Without being told to, I spent many hours updating them. I didn't want to get blamed for out-of-date publications if we had an inspection. I had proximity.

I also learned a lot about what my leading petty officer was doing. He spent a lot of time on the watch bill, making room assignments, filling out routine paperwork, coordinating pack outs, and such. I offered to help.

Once I gave him something I had written, and he asked me who helped me write it. He didn't believe that I had written it myself at first, but he came around.

Soon I was doing the watch bill, room assignments, and lots of other stuff. I built a mailbox with slots in it so the guys would quit coming in to my office bugging me. I stenciled on it "good news, bad news, and no news." We got some of each. My senior chief and the lieutenant were not especially good writers. I had been reading lots of correspondence, instructions, and messages, and I was picking up the military lingo and style.

In my job, I would make corrections and suggest rewrites, which my superiors quietly accepted. Gratitude was hard to spot. I think it made them uncomfortable that this young Black kid was showing them how to be better writers—but not uncomfortable enough to stop accepting my suggestions and recommendations.

Three enlightening things happened during this deployment. First, my leading petty officer wanted to put me in for sailor of the quarter. I had been a big help to him, and he knew how outdated the publications had been. He wrote up my nomination, had me type it, and presented it to the senior chief, who was sitting a few feet away in the next office.

The senior chief read it, and announced in a loud and annoyed voice, "Why are you putting him in for this? This won't do him any good; he's just a fucking seaman! I want to put MN1 [mineman first class] Lemieux in for sailor of the quarter; he's trying to make chief!" He sounded angry. He marked up the recommendation, inserting Lemieux's name and position where necessary, and gave it to me to type. The lieutenant, my officer in charge, was aware of this. I dutifully typed the paperwork, giving full credit to someone else for all the hard work I had been doing.

They never spoke to me of this, and I never mentioned it. I lost a lot of respect for these men after this. They showed no shame at any of this. A few days later, at morning quarters (muster), in addition to speaking of what a good job MN1 Lemieux was doing, the senior chief announced that MN1 Lemieux had both been selected as detachment sailor of the quarter and been nominated to the headquarters command for sailor of the quarter. My leading petty officer later apologized, but I told him not to worry about it. Imagine how difficult it would have been at this point for me to tell my father, "Dad, you were wrong about the navy."

A few months into the deployment, we received orders for new people, which included a young fellow I did not especially get along with. He was a young Black man from Chicago or somewhere "up North." I'll call him Kenny, because that was his name.

I assigned Kenny to room with one of the other guys who had a vacancy (we were assigned two per room), and I assigned a white guy whom I knew and liked to my room, as I also had a new vacancy. My buddy Mack, the other Black guy in my class, was rotating back to Charleston. I thought it had been a happy coincidence that Mack and I had roomed together.

Imagine my naive surprise when Kenny arrived and started moving his stuff into my room. I informed him that he was supposed to room elsewhere, and he said this was the room to which he had been assigned. I knew better. The room assignments had been changed by my leading petty officer because nobody wanted to room with a Black guy if he didn't have to, as was gently explained to me. This intervention had saved not one white guy this indignity, but two. I relinquished the room assignments responsibility after that. "Fuck 'em," I thought. My previous roommate, Mack, was my friend. Kenny and I were not friends—Black not friends. In fact, we barely got along with each other. We both learned at the same time that no one wanted to room with us. Didn't make us friends, but it gave us something in common. We liked each other's music, if nothing else.

Lastly, I soon learned that the long shadow of racism extended to the local Sicilian civilian community. I was sitting in the enlisted club with my friend, our Black detachment storekeeper, and my recently acquired girlfriend. Her name was Ventris C. Giles, and she was from southeast Washington, DC. She was an air traffic controller, and she would go on to have a stellar career in government as Ventris C. Gibson. She chose me because I was one of the only men there that wasn't pestering her. Our storekeeper liked to joke that every month, his wife sent him some money and told him to go buy himself the best piece of tail he could find, and every month he would go buy two just OK pieces. I don't know if his wife sent him any money, but if he ever bought anything with it, it was a girly magazine or a box of donuts. Anyway, I went to go get us all drinks from the bar.

After standing there for a while, I got impatient. The bartender was ignoring me. A guy walked in and sat down right next to where I was standing, and the bartender walked over and took his order and served him right away. He continued to ignore me. I tried to get his attention, and he kept ignoring me. I finally angrily slammed my hand down on the bar as he was walking by and asked him what I had to do to get service. He started flailing his arms around and yelling at me, "You no service! You no service!" and telling me to get out. He was a local Sicilian.

I left the bar area and found the club manager and angrily explained to him what had happened. He politely explained to me that the bartender had the right to refuse service to anyone. I persisted. So he went to the bar, and I followed him. As I was explaining what had happened, the bartender was yelling that he had not seen me and that I was causing trouble. The guy who had been served beside me spoke up and said that what I had described was exactly what had happened and that I had not been causing any trouble at all. I walked away, vindicated yet disgusted, and explained to my friends what had happened. A waitress came over to take our order, and I angrily waved her away. We seemed to have been invisible up to that point; that was the first time she or any other staff had approached us. That's why I had gone to the bar in the first place.

I wondered whether in fact the bartender had not seen me. Logic ruled this out. I was six foot one, bald as a cue ball, wearing an orange-and-white football jersey and big, shiny glasses, and standing at the only patron station for some minutes. Oh, yes, I was also the only Black person in the bar. Funny that. He would have seen me instantly if I had reached my hand into the tip jar, I bet. I resisted the urge to wait for him after he got off work. I wanted to make sure he would remember me if I walked into that bar again and that he would think twice about abusing me or treating me unfairly.

I was beginning to understand the power of documentation. I went to work the next day and typed a letter to the base exchange officer, who was in charge of the club. I explained what had happened, sticking to the facts as I saw them, what the base regulations said about discrimination, and how this had negatively impacted me. I requested that he correct this situation. I dropped it off at his office with his secretary.

I never discussed the situation with my immediate superiors. I didn't think it would help. The most amazing thing happened after that. I received a phone call, asking me if I could come to the exchange officer's office the following day. When I got there, he apologized and explained that I would not have any more problems at the club and to come to his office and tell him if I did. I thanked him.

When I entered that club a few days later, you would have thought Zumwalt himself had just walked in. They swarmed me like I was a celebrity. At first I thought it was some kind of joke, until I saw fear in their eyes, including the manager's, actual fear of a Black seaman. Strangely, this only pissed me off more. I was polite, but I was fuming inside.

This was the first time I truly learned the power of the pen. I had carefully composed my letter, forcing myself to take all the emotion out of it and just state the facts. Whether or not I was purposefully discriminated against was not the issue. The issue was that I was treated poorly, I had responded appropriately, and the issue was resolved. Everyone involved learned valuable lessons, and I might have saved someone from getting into trouble, one way or another.

Once, I went to Catania, the nearest city, and walked around with Mack. He warned me to be prepared for a lot of gawking. I watched an old lady who was staring at us so hard from across the street that she walked right into a telephone pole. I suppressed a laugh. No one was rude or mean to me, but I felt like a zoo animal.

Bill Goss flew to Munich one weekend and came back with a great story. He had asked several of us to go with him. No one did. He had a wonderful time, having met a bunch of southern belles on college vacation and gotten invited to travel for free on their tour bus. He said we had really missed out on a great trip. I don't think he understood that *he* might not have had such a great time if I had been with him. There is a really good chance that he would not have been invited to join them had I been with him.

Before I left Sigonella, I was officially nominated for sailor of the quarter. I had a new chief and officer in charge. I still didn't make it. Perhaps my nomination looked suspiciously like the one that had been submitted a few months before with MN1 Lemieux's name on it.

Back in Charleston, I returned to working in administration again. After work, I would sometimes go to the library. One day, to my everlasting gratitude, I found a book that would help shape my future and moderate my growing resentment at my treatment. Surprised to see it, I pulled it off the shelf and looked at the cover.

The name of this book was *On Watch*. It hit me like a bolt of lightning—this was by Admiral Elmo Zumwalt! With his bushy eyebrows, sharp features, pointy ears, dress khaki uniform with gold-encrusted shoulders, chest full of ribbons, and piercing look, he seemed like a cross between Mr. Spock from *Star Trek* and a wise old Klingon, with a low tolerance for stupidity and bullshit.

Intelligence, fearlessness, and impatience radiated from his face on the cover. I knew immediately that I would read it. Little did I know the impact this book would have on my thinking and my future. Flipping through it, one picture caught my eye. There was an artist's conception of a high-speed hydrofoil patrol ship, a PHM. The *Pegasus*, the prototype of the class, was being launched at Renton, Washington, in November 1974.

This was probably the coolest-looking little ship I had ever seen, skimming *above* the water, on some sort of skis. I later learned that they were called foils, hence the name. I imagined myself on one of these ships, holding on for dear life. Another artist's conception was of a new class of patrol frigate, with gas turbine engines, with a helicopter flying above it. Both would also play a role in my professional future.

Being only nineteen years old at the time, much of what I would read in this volume was above my head or of little immediate interest—strategy, Henry Kissinger, the Russians, military budgets, boring crap like that. Who cared about that drivel? What was *not* above my head was the section of this book that dealt with people: "Chapter 7: Programs for People," "Chapter 8: Mickey Mouse, Elimination Of," and, most especially, "Chapter 9: Sailing Second Class." When I read chapter 9, with its detailing of the daily indignities those minority sailors, officers, and their families had to endure, written by the admiral who has just recently been the chief of naval operations, I began to understand why my father had been afraid for me to join the navy. I also got a better idea of the road ahead of me.

Those three chapters should have been required reading for all naval leaders, and they still should be. To get a taste of the treatment Black sailors endured, read *SUBIC: A Sailor's Memoir*. It's written by Dr. Barbara Perkins-Brown, EdD, about her father, Bobby Earl Perkins, who lived and suffered through these demeaning days in the Philippines. It might break your heart. It has a happy ending.

All these years later, I wish I had paid more attention to the chapter he titled "The Rickover Complication." Political intrigue, psychological intimidation, targeted officers, inspector general investigations, careers sabotaged—all of that stuff was way too heady for a nineteen-year-old Black seaman.

Reading about the report on race relations at the two major installations in the Philippines, conducted by the Naval Investigative Service in 1970, at the behest of the base commander, was sobering. I learned that examples of types of prejudice and discrimination centered on some eight general categories. *Eight?* Hell, I didn't even know there were *that* many ways to be discriminated against in the navy in 1970. Of everything in this report, one sentence stood out: "More than one Black man referred to his desire to be treated like a '*human*.'" When I wrote my letter in Sigonella, Sicily, I was expressing the same desire.

I was quickly redeployed to the North Atlantic Treaty Organization (NATO) Ammunition Depot, Glen Douglas, United Kingdom, assigned to MOMAG Detachment Four, still a seaman. We lived on HMS *Neptune*, a submarine base, known locally as Faslane, near the town of Helensburgh, Scotland. Every day, we would take a long bus ride through the beautiful countryside and then enter a NATO ammunition depot to work with Scottish nationals, many of whom had wives who worked in the cafeteria where we ate lunch every day. We were well fed, and it was always delicious. To this day, I don't know what most of it was, and I never cared.

The minemen performed maintenance on mines for US and NATO ships. Our living quarters were connected to the building that housed the WRNS (Women's Royal Navy Service) barracks. We could hear and sometimes see them happily chirping every evening, sometimes on their way to or from the showers. Some of them would sometimes come visit us and chat incessantly. This was not something that we ever, ever complained about. I worked for the senior (as far as I knew) Black mineman in the fleet, Mineman Chief Roosevelt Wyatt. It was the first time I had worked for a Black man in the navy. It was also the first time many of the other guys in the detachment had also. I took it a lot better than some of them did.

My officer in charge was Lieutenant Kenneth R. Martin, a mustang, as were many mine force officers. He was a very good officer. Bill Goss and I flew over on the same flight. In the airport terminal gift shop I bought a book called *The Save Your Life Diet* by Dr. David Reuben, because I couldn't find anything else to read. After both of us read it, we decided to add more fiber to our diets.

We bought some wheat bran in town, and within a week, we were both farting up the place so badly that my leading petty officer threatened to make us walk home from work rather than ride in the vans. We tried to outfart each other. Bill always won. He was bigger. I went to Scotland because they needed me. Bill received orders to Scotland, which he desperately wanted, because the admiral he worked for as a driver pulled some strings and made it happen. Bill's story of his great deployment to Scotland took nine sentences in his book, *The Luckiest Unlucky Man Alive: A Wild Ride*. My story is a little more complicated.

The OPs were as neglected as the ones in Sicily, so I went to work. This indicated a leadership problem. I also had furniture made for our office by the local workshop on the base, and I again helped the leading petty officer with his duties. When the grassy hills covering our weapons magazines caught fire, I helped put it out with high-tech equipment like pieces of fire hose nailed to strips of wood, beating the flames down while trying not to catch on fire or get blown up. I fell on a tall blade of grass and thought I had punctured my eardrum as it jammed into my ear. The pain and the ringing eventually went away.

Lieutenant Martin was a much better writer than my last detachment officer, and Chief Roosevelt Wyatt was no slouch either. They were a good team. Chief Wyatt looked out for me. I looked out for him also, because I picked up bad vibes from some of the guys toward him, and I soon found out why.

Late one night, I was lying in my bed, reading. One of the few Black minemen lived across the hall from me, MN2 Homeboy (wink). Three Blacks on the same detachment had to be some kind of adverse record, because there were only a dozen or so in the entire five-hundred-man mine force. My detachment leading petty officer, several other petty officers in the detachment, and at least one of the British sailors we had befriended were drinking and talking loudly in the room across the hall from mine, next to my buddy Homeboy's.

Our walls were thin, and sounds carried down the hall and through the walls easily. Sometimes this could be interesting, or frustrating, if you listened closely (and sometimes even if you didn't). The talk this night quickly turned to Black people, but they used the more derogatory racial slur. Two were bad; three were nearly intolerable. They were complaining about having to work *with* Black people. They were complaining about having to work *for* Black people. They were complaining about having to sleep *near* Black people. Apparently, *with*, *for*, and *near* made up some kind of racist trifecta!

I had not seen any Black sailors in the Royal Navy, but there might have been some there. I lay there, contemplating my next move. This loud conversation was clearly for the benefit of Homeboy and me. I worked with these guys every single day. I drank and ate with some of them on liberty. I took care of their records and professional affairs. I had tried to help some of them get laid. Was this how they really felt about *me*? Did I really know these white guys at all?

Was it the alcohol? How did the rest of the detachment feel about us and about what they were saying? I wanted to get up, get dressed, put on my boots, my foul weather jacket, and my gloves and give them a chance to run *from* a Black person. This night really got to me. I lay there, fuming and sick at heart. I shouldn't have been surprised. Many years before, I had read the autobiography of comedian Dick Gregory, titled *Nigger*.

I usually didn't let words bother me, but I was now being told in no uncertain terms how my coworkers and friends really felt about me. All I had done was try to take advantage of the same opportunities they had.

Black people tend to avoid situations with white people where alcohol is involved because of exactly this kind of behavior. I had done nothing but try to support and work with these guys, and they apparently hated me, at least when they were drunk, in a group, and full of liquid courage.

Maybe it was because some of the local girls didn't care if our skin was black, or maybe even worse, they liked that we were Black. The next day, I asked Homeboy if he had heard any of that discussion, and he said he had not. I didn't believe him.

When I informed Chief Wyatt, he said he'd been hearing that crap for years. I believe he'd been to our facility in Subic Bay and faced the crushing discrimination permitted there. I can only imagine what he put up with for almost twenty years. He said that some of these guys were not happy that some Scottish women were attracted to Black guys. This attitude had persisted since Black servicemen began serving overseas. Was this really the problem? I had a lot to learn about microaggressions, which I had never heard of back then. All the rage and hurt I was beginning to feel building up in me were going to need an outlet, and it wasn't long in coming.

I'm not sure if the navy's Affirmative Action Plan exactly covered any of this. I doubt any of my shipmates had read it. I don't think it said "Thou shalt not call thy shipmates racial slurs, whether or not thou hast consumed mirth-making spirits." I don't think it would have made any difference. I now better understood my father. At work the next day, I was clear-eyed and full of understanding. I started planning my exit. I didn't think I could tolerate much more of this treatment.

Some of the local girls told me that my shipmates told them that I had a tail. My "friends" were making fun of and ridiculing me behind my back and attempting to curtail any of the local ladies' budding interest in me. Just as was done to Black service members by their fellow white service members in World War I, World War II, and Vietnam. When I asked Chief Wyatt about that little tidbit, he wryly informed me that it was not my "tail" the ladies were curious about. In attempting to reinforce one stereotype, my shipmates were generating speculation about another. It was nice finally to have a mentor who could break things down so I could understand them.

Finally, an older man who had been watching this nonsense took charge of my love life. He owned the pub where we often hung out and where my chief moonlighted as a bartender. He walked up to me one night and asked me, "What the hell is wrong with you, boy?" Momentarily befuddled, I asked him politely what was wrong. He pointed to the pretty girl behind the bar, who was very cute, shy, and friendly toward me. We had been chatting occasionally as I'd order a drink and making eye contact for months but nothing more.

I was well aware that she had been politely ignoring or shutting down any man who flirted too aggressively with her or behaved improperly. She always seemed to have a smile for me. I was such a gentleman. He said in a very loud voice, "Boy, are you stupid or what? When in the hell are you going to stop tiptoeing around and ask that girl out?" She blushed, I laughed, blushing too, and the crowd began to tease me mercilessly. Having been called out so publicly and gotten the explicit stamp of approval from someone we all liked and respected, I had to do something!

I eventually asked her to dinner. She insisted that I come to her house to pick her up and meet her parents. Nice mother, suspicious and rude father. She browbeat him in front of me for being rude, and off we went to dinner. He was right to be worried. I had ideas. She did too. So began my first trip across the International Race Line.

One night soon after, a group of us were walking back from the on-base club having had a few drinks, and the talk turned to the Ugandan dictator, Idi Amin. He was quite the news item during those days. Jim, one of the British sailors who had been loudly complaining about Black people with my detachment leading petty officer that recent drunken night, asked me if I knew what AMIN stood for. Jim had no girlfriend. When I said no, he looked me straight in the eye and loudly proclaimed, "Africa's Most Ignorant Nigger!" A. M. I. N. Clever that was. Jim had been drinking, but he was not drunk.

Before I could stop myself, I laughed, just like I would have if Mack had said it. I looked at Bill Goss, who had a look of sheer horror on his face. I think that this was the first time he'd ever experienced something like that happen, at least in front of the Black guy. I didn't respond. I was too conflicted. It *was* funny. I respected Jim for looking me straight in my eye, and I hated him for thinking he could say something like that to me in total comfort. No one else laughed, probably having heard it before. I didn't hang out with Jim much after that. There were to be much more serious incidents later, in which people and feelings would get hurt, after which nothing would ever be the same.

I had by now taken the mineman third class exam and passed it. This was great news! I was sure, however, that I no longer wanted to be a mineman. I was sure that a yeoman had broader opportunities for success in the navy. I never wanted to hear a bunch of guys complaining about having to work with, for, or near me again.

Lieutenant Martin submitted a message to the Bureau of Naval Personnel requesting that I be advanced to yeoman third class vice mineman third class. I'd completed all the YN3 requirements. To my surprise, the request was approved. A Black mineman was a rarity. A Black yeoman was common. I could blend in. I put on my YN3 crow proudly and prepared to leave the mine force behind.

Lieutenant Martin also nominated me for sailor of the quarter, only he did it by message vice the usual letter, so that the base message center personnel (the ladies), who handled our message traffic, read it and told me and their friends how glowingly he spoke of my accomplishments during that quarter. Captain Cyrus R. Christensen, whom everyone called Combat Chris, our skipper back in Charleston, was sure to see this message.

I wasn't selected, but several of the ladies had read the message and were effusive in their congratulations. I wanted to get out of Charleston and the mine force as soon as possible after I returned from this deployment to Scotland. Several things happened that strengthened my resolve.

The first involved my friend David Mack, who was assigned to our sister detachment, about an hour away, in Machrihanish, Scotland. We had a holiday picnic (July 4, I think), and Mack and others drove up from there. There had been some tension between Mack and a few others during our last deployment, and I had intervened to prevent a fight.

Resentments lingered on both sides, and Mack didn't make it any easier. He was older than some of us, and he would needle you if he found a soft spot. As the alcohol flowed and the words grew from good-natured barbs to words more pointed and serious, all hell broke loose. As you probably know, the words most frequently spoken in English before the shit hits the fan are "What the hell you looking at?" Statistically, that sentence starts 78.379 percent of all fistfights. People were yelling and screaming, and Mack and one of my other friends were swinging wildly. We got them separated, but the white guy picked up a wine bottle, broke it, and started coming after Mack.

The civilian who cleaned our barracks, who was like a surrogate mother to us, stepped between them and tried to stop him. He was too drunk to listen to her, so I pushed her out of the way and tried to reason with him myself. This failed, so I popped him in the mouth, hard. He ceased to be vertical, a threat, or a problem. I had, however, created another one. His Scottish girlfriend jumped on my back and commenced calling me every racial slur she could think of, with a Scottish accent.

I finally got her off my back, but I had to knock her hand loose from my shirt, and she tore it almost half off my body. I stood there a moment, looking at the madness around me and trying to decide whether to shit or go blind, but I did neither. I did what seemed like the smartest thing to do under the circumstances—I started walking home.

I was miles away from the base, and it was getting dark. Someone was liable to get hurt if I left. Tough shit. I just wanted to get the hell out of there. As people piled into the various vehicles and started leaving, some of them pleaded with me to get in a van, but I ignored them. I was disappointed and disgusted with the entire situation. I didn't understand why we couldn't all just get along. I felt like the Rodney King of Scotland.

I must have been quite a sight from the rear: a tall Black guy, all dressed in black, with a big little Afro I had grown to keep my head warm, the remnants of my red sleeveless shirt hanging off my back, marching like I was leading an insurrection. I had a long-sleeved black turtleneck under it, or I might have frozen to death. Fortunately, a kind Scottish family picked me up and dropped me off at the base before it got too dark.

Later the guy I punched, who had a great sense of humor and really was my friend, apologized for being drunk and stupid and thanked me for not letting him hurt anyone. He also told me that his jaw really, really hurt. I apologized, but I didn't mean it. Mack and I didn't see each other again for months. Alcohol and lingering resentment made for a dangerous combination. I was far from being the senior man there. Hell, the guy I punched was senior to me. The next incident in Scotland was much milder and calmer, and no one got hurt, except me. Several of us went on a weekend trip to Edinburgh, Scotland. We visited castles, dungeons, and museum attractions, some got tattoos, and drank beer. The most amusing items we saw were the chastity belts on display, with their unusual shapes in various openings and colorful explanations of their use. It was a great trip, initially.

Then racism reared its ugly head. I began to hear this voice from down a side street. It sounded like the angelic voice of a child singing in the movie *Empire of the Sun*, when this young English boy movingly sings opera as he watches Japanese fighter pilots take off near his internment camp during World War II.

It is beautiful singing. If you remember the tune, picture it, only substitute the words with a beautiful version of "Niiiiiiiggggggerrrrrrrr, goooooo hoooooooome you fuuuuucking Nigggggggggger!" He had his hands cupped to his mouth and would arch his back and sway in the rhythm. At first, my friends pretended not to hear. But it soon became too loud and persistent to ignore. This kid couldn't have been much more than ten years old. How in the hell did he even know what the word meant? Tradition, I guess.

He hated me and wanted me to know it. He probably doesn't remember me, but I have thought of him often, every time I rub my memory across that little scar he left on my soul. I want to tell him that I would have risked my life to save him if he were in trouble, and I wonder what beliefs he passed on to his own children. I pray that he didn't scar them as well. When I think of this incident, I want to laugh and cry at something my great play friend Richard Pryor said. He said, "It's a wonder every nigger in America ain't crazy." I was just about ready to go home.

I was to have one more truly exciting but depressing adventure in Scotland. One evening, I was with one of my buddies, MN3 Donald Plack. We had walked down to the base club, a two-minute walk, to imagine playing chess with all the beautiful women we'd see there.

I usually had no problems at all there, but I had witnessed fights break out without much warning. I didn't want to be caught with slowed reflexes, so I didn't drink much when I went out. A Royal Navy sailor I didn't know decided that I was a problem. I was darkening up the place, all by myself.

He stood beside me and gruffly asked me for a light. I informed him that I didn't smoke. After a while, he started poking me in the side, asking me repeatedly for a light. I again informed him that I didn't smoke. He was standing inches away from people he knew well who each could have given him one, and he wasn't holding a cigarette. He had been drinking. He would relent for a while, and then poke me again, harder. Plack eventually noticed him and asked me if everything was all right, and I said it was.

I finally turned to look the guy in the eye menacingly and asked him if his mother knew he was out this late. He said yes, so I decided to leave his mother out of the rest of this. I then told him not to poke me anymore and provided him with the universal "I'm about to whip your ass" signal, which was moving my jacket from my right arm and draping it over my left arm. I was now locked and loaded, safety off.

When the guy poked me again, this time much harder (now, you knew he would), I caught him in the chest with my right elbow, bouncing him off the wall and emptying his lungs. Then, as he hung momentarily in the air, I released all the pent-up rage and frustration I'd been feeling into his jaw through my right hand. Deprived of both air and equilibrium, he did the smart thing and fell down hard. Only then, when he hit the ground, did I consider my situation.

I, a Black Yank, standing in a club full of well-lubricated British sailors, had just knocked out one of their mates, and I was with a white American guy who had probably never been in a fight in his life and who was probably going to switch sides. British sailors weren't squeamish about blood. I'd seen them beat each other over the head with heavy Ravenhead beer mugs, and it wasn't pretty. I waited to get clocked in the back of the head, and when it didn't happen, I grabbed Plack by the arm and led him out. The music had stopped, and the room was completely silent as everyone stared at me like I was some kind of wild animal. I felt like one. Everything was moving in slow motion, and I was as alert as a zebra at a crocodile-infested waterhole.

As we hurried toward our barracks (I wasn't quite as cool as I was trying to appear), Plack was peppering me with questions, jumping around excitedly, but I wasn't listening to him. I was waiting. Sure enough, this roar came up from behind us, and I turned around to see a charging bunch of people, some in uniform, some not, some sober, some not—all pissed.

I handed Plack my jacket, told him to run, and pushed him toward the barracks. I felt like that baboon in the famous *National Geographic* picture, about to be killed by a leopard. I was going down fighting. The first person who reached me was never, ever going to forget me. I didn't expect to be able to do much after that.

It must have surprised them that I just stood there waiting for them, because they stopped a few feet short of me (out of striking range), yelling at me all at once. I finally held up my hand and, when they quieted, said, "I want to tell you something. I didn't come down here looking for any trouble, and I'm not looking for any now. I am just trying to go home to my room." One of the uniformed members, a shore patrolman, told me that I'd have to go back with them and go to the base police station. I went with them, and Plack came with me.

We got back in time to see them carrying the guy out, eyes closed and very limp. "Oh God," I thought, "he's dead." As far as any of them knew, I had beaten him up for no reason. I was enduring many loud shouts of "You fucking animal!" and such, but no one touched me. I was not yet safely in a cage.

At the police station, I wrote a detailed statement. Fortunately, Plack also wrote out a statement, and we were both sober. Lieutenant Martin counseled me the next day, having gotten a call about his young Black bloke, but I never heard any more about it. When I read the police report, I saw that the guy's pitiful written statement looked like a drunk had written it. Of course, he was totally innocent, the victim of a brutal Black Yank. I never went back to the club. Message received. I was ready to go home. The guy later approached me on base and said I had gotten him into a lot of trouble and that it was, of course, entirely my fault. I politely disagreed with him and eventually walked away before he poked me again.

Lesson learned—it's hard to get into trouble if you're minding your own business and sober, but not impossible. Bigger lesson learned—when you see trouble brewing, walk away. If it follows you, walk faster. If it keeps following you, turn around, look it in the eye, and ball up your fists. Sometimes you can reason with trouble; sometimes you can't. The great white hunter and the African bush mother will both tell you that when you hear an angry lion roaring, the safest thing you can do is run toward the roar. The lion is trying to spook you into running into the jaws of the pride that are waiting for you in the opposite direction. Run toward the roar and the bully. There is less danger there.

I soon also had solid evidence of racism within my command. I had asked to extend my tour in Scotland some time before and was denied after our white detachment storekeeper had requested an extension and been approved. This detachment was a plum job because I received per diem in an amount that gave you the equivalent of first-class pay for being at only a third-class petty officer level. There were differences between us other than race.

He was married to a Scottish national. I was not. I was a mineman. He was not. He turned the extension down after it was approved. They turned mine down flat, just as when I applied for accelerated advancement and to stay on active duty. He could stay; I could not. It would have saved them money, and they were short both yeomen and storekeepers.

When I returned to Charleston, I learned that they wanted me to deploy again really soon to the lovely Souda Bay, Crete. I assumed that the publications there were out of date too. They could respectfully kiss my ass, I thought. I was getting the hell out of there. I negotiated for and received orders to Naval Station Guantanamo Bay, Cuba, by way of Legal Clerk School, and prepared to reenlist. I was done with the mine force.

The admin office chief, Yeoman Chief Petty Officer John Henry Murray, wanted me to reenlist at the annual command ball, which was being held in October, in conjunction with the Navy Ball. I didn't want to. I just wanted to go quietly. Shortly after I got back, I married the woman I met in Sigonella: Ventris Giles (now Ventris Gibson), a former navy air traffic controller, who would go on to bigger things in government, at the Veterans Administration and the Federal Aviation Administration, and the city government in Washington, DC. In 2022, she would be confirmed as the deputy director of the United States Mint, the first African American to lead it.

She had departed Sigonella in order to be discharged from the navy while I was in Scotland, and I stopped in to visit her in Washington, DC. Her mother was determined that I wasn't leaving town without marrying her daughter, as she somehow got the idea that I was a prize catch. It was probably my Scottish accent. I got gently strong-armed into the wedding. Her stepfather was a minister and her mother, very persuasive. We got married in their living room. Ventris wasn't hard to look at, and I wanted a wife and a family. I can't say either of us was madly in love.

The skipper wanted to do a reenlistment at the ball as a retention tool, and I felt pressured to be a team player. I reluctantly agreed to the "request," and I soon regretted it. At the ceremony, after he reenlisted me, the skipper loudly announced, "We gotcha now, boy," and slapped me on the back, giving me a little shove away from him. I was the entertainment. Looking at the faces of my new wife and my Black friends, I could see that they were embarrassed and angry too. I felt stupid and humiliated. No thanks, no recognition, no fair winds and following seas. In the end, leaving this place, I didn't want to be laughingly remembered as somebody's boy. I had done a man's job, and I knew it. The Big Navy and Marine Corps are debating whether to add the word "respect" to their core values. I have some thoughts on that.

I understand why some service members, like my father, have bittersweet memories of their service. I was proud that I had served in the mine force. I detested the way I was treated. I knew I wasn't anybody's boy, and I worked hard to prove it. This was not my father's navy, but it still had work to do. Bill Goss went home to New Jersey, enrolled in Rutgers University, and worked on mines one weekend a month in the reserves. It was ten years before I saw him again.

When I went to the legal clerk course as a petty officer third class, I was granted a one pay grade waiver to attend. I was being ordered in to fill a petty officer first class billet in Cuba, "fleeting up" two pay grades. I did greatly benefit from my time in the mine force, working independently and performing duties that would aid me in managing a heavy workload with little assistance and not much time to learn. I had begun to realize that my skin color was always going to be a factor, and I was studying human behavior and leadership.

At the justice school, I sailed through because I'd been exposed to so much. Up to this time, I hadn't been exposed to drugs in the military, so I was surprised on graduation night when some of my classmates smoked a joint to celebrate as they were packing to leave. Remember, this was 1977. Drug use was still pretty common.

4

Guantanamo Bay and Captain's Mast

When I arrived at Guantanamo Bay, Cuba (GTMO), in December 1977, several things had changed in my life besides duty station. My wife, Ventris, left Charleston and went to live with my mother in Tennessee, and I had completed the requirements for my high school diploma between deployments via the Predischarge Education Program (PREP), created for sailors without one.

As I studied the materials in preparation for the various exams we would have to take, I realized that I already knew all of the material, or I thought I did. I asked the instructors if I could just take the tests. I passed all the sections with flying colors, except the one for math, which I quickly passed after a bit of study. I was not a stupid kid, and I was an avid reader. I was beginning to learn how important education was, and I intended to get a lot more of it.

There had been a 30 percent reduction in force at Guantanamo, and this had a direct impact on me. The navy was shrinking, saving money to build more ships. I worked for a Black yeoman chief petty officer, YNC Robert E. Brown, and a Black yeoman first class, Charlie Baldwin. They would be not only my bosses but also my mentors and friends. I would also meet a guy I could really have used in my previous command, aviation jet engine mechanic (ADJ) First Class Ronald Fulton. He was an Equal Opportunity Program Specialist (EOPS), and he was a busy, beleaguered man. We had many conversations about racial injustice and the insanity of it all, and he would impress me greatly with his spirit and determination to ensure that people were treated fairly.

My job would put us in contact with some of the same people, and he was vocal about the injustices as he saw them. This did not make him universally popular. He loved Admiral Zumwalt. We talked together about the admiral and the bad old days he had lived through. Once, Ron Fulton's office was broken into and trashed, "at the hands of persons unknown," because he was doing his job so well. The intruder(s) left some written racist calling cards. The perpetrators were never found. Ron was rattled, because his family had been threatened. Because of him, even as busy as I already was, I would eventually volunteer to teach sailors Navy Rights and Responsibilities, Cultural Expression, and Women in the Navy workshops.

During one of these workshops, while we were discussing words that were potentially inappropriate, I shared the story of being called a "boy" at my reenlistment ceremony. A chief petty officer, a white country good old boy, spoke up and said that he called people "boy" all the time and that he didn't see anything wrong with it. The class was filled with both Black and white male and female sailors. Rather than challenge him, I simply asked the class whether anyone in the class resented being called a boy. Every male hand in the room went up, and some of the female hands shot up as well. After looking around, the chief looked angry, but I think that boy learned a valuable lesson.

In taking on my role at Guantanamo, I had relieved a female yeoman first class and a male chief, and I didn't feel prepared for this workload. I was responsible for receiving all of the raw report chits for the naval station and typing the charge sheets for the legal office for courts-martial.

Some of the petty officers writing these report chits left something to be desired in their communication skills. I would often have to figure exactly what these sailors had done and what to charge them with. Many of these had been written in anger and were a mangled mess. GTMO was short on dictionaries. The disrespectful language was often very colorful, as sailors are often very explicit in expressing their displeasure. The colorful language, stated word for word in the charges, was often enough to make you belly laugh. Throw in the mix of accents, verbal dexterity, and colorful euphemisms, and it was almost worth paying to attend captain's mast.

Captain's masts could also be very emotional and stressful for all concerned, especially if you were standing on the wrong side of the podium. However, depending on what issues were raised, they could also be extremely amusing. I will never forget a particular young man named Barnhill. I used to know his social security number by heart, having typed it repeatedly on multiple documents because of the frequency with which he was placed on report and administered punishment at captain's mast. He ultimately left the service to pursue other adventures and spend more time with his family.

On one of his last trips to see the captain, John H. Fetterman Jr., Barnhill stood there absentmindedly as the list of charges was read and the captain recapped how many times he had already been there. When Captain Fetterman asked him if he had anything to say, he said, quite cheerfully, "I sure will be glad when that administrative discharge gets here." Barnhill was tired of being held accountable for his misbehavior and just wanted to be discharged and put the navy in the rear view mirror. Without missing a beat, Captain Fetterman said, "So will I!" I never saw so many people try so hard not to laugh in my life.

Mast was usually stressful and often enlightening. Many sailors did not feel they had been treated fairly, or that they got a chance to tell their side of the story. In many cases, they were right.

I was responsible for compiling statistics for the naval station regarding discipline, race, and gender for submission to higher authority. These equal opportunity quality indicator (EOQI) statistics were eye-opening. By the end of my two-year tour, I had become convinced that Black sailors were often treated more harshly than their white counterparts. Not only did I see this with my own eyes, but the EOQIs bore this out. From what I've read, they still do, in every branch of the service; the statistics and my observations closely reflected what the overall Department of Defense statistics indicate to this day.

Per Martin Binkin and Mark J. Eitelberg (1982), in *Blacks and the Military*, "The average black Army recruit had a higher level of education than his or her white counterpart, and minorities, especially blacks, from 'better' backgrounds and with 'better' credentials are disproportionately attracted to the armed forces." This tendency might be explained by high unemployment among young Black men and the lack of funds within the same group to attend college.

Furthermore, white entrants were coming from the least educated sectors of the white community, that is, nonmetropolitan areas. These people were the bookends of the most segregated areas of society. The middle class largely avoided voluntary military service during the 1960s. This had implications regarding military discipline. During the Johnson administration and Vietnam War–era force buildup (called Project 100,000), middle-class white men were avoiding service; so, Black men were being drafted in large numbers, and poor southern and not well-educated white men were making up the rest of the deficit.

The problem was largely cultural. I will try to explain it as I saw it. Most of the petty officer supervisors were southern white men. Not all, but many. They had subordinates of various ethnicities and backgrounds, but they themselves had had little intercultural exposure and therefore had difficulty communicating effectively to their subordinates. All involved, both enlisted and officers, behaved in ways that reinforced the stereotypes they held. In some cases, some involved in conflict situations acted according to established tradition and norms. They misinterpret each other's body language and behavior. They have different sensitivities to language. As usual, the guy with more stripes wins.

Factor into this equation peer pressure, command pressure from higher-ups, and other factors, and you can see potential problems. All, or nearly all, of the accused I saw were technically guilty of the charges against them. Let me also say that many of the supervisors were guilty of the countercharges leveled against them, such as discrimination, racism, and "selective" enforcement and prosecution. But you can guess who was held accountable.

An inner-city kid is not going to respond to verbal criticism and admonition the same way as would someone from the Midwest or a community in the South. At captain's mast, young Black sailors would often challenge the charges against them, attempt to interject facts and perceptions on how they were being mistreated outside the scope of the charges, and appear belligerent. They would often assert that they were being treated differently than some of their peers who may have committed similar offenses. This in turn would piss off the supervisors, who were defensive and unprepared or unwilling to address those issues.

Oftentimes, I would have to translate, elaborate on, or interpret what was being said. The Black young men and the older white men had trouble understanding each other. The commanding officer would chastise the young men and women for attempting to deflect the blame for their behavior. Seldom was credence given to their complaints. Rarely would their allegations be taken seriously. After all, just a few years before, Congress had decreed that there was no institutional racism in the navy, just a climate of "permissiveness," and the 1973 congressional subcommittee had decreed that poor leadership and Black "thugs" were responsible. In 2022, Marv Truhe's book, *Against All Tides: The Untold Story of the USS* Kitty Hawk *Race Riot*, blew a hole in that finding big enough to drive the USS *John C. Stennis* and the *Carl Vinson* through, without scraping any paint. Truhe was a defense counsel for several of the sailors who had been accused of assault or other charges, such as inciting a riot on board a naval vessel, and the truth, from their point of view and backed up by evidence, is a damning indictment of the navy's legal system, and the congressional findings.

I recognized and had lived the frustration these young men expressed. If you have experienced significant discrimination in your life and your exposure to authority figures has been largely adversarial, you are likely to have perceptions of bias in your interactions. Sometimes you're right; sometimes you're not, but you feel it either way. Sometimes, after you experience discrimination, both subtle and blatant, you lose confidence in the system that you've been taught to believe is fair and impartial because that's not what you see.

If in fact discrimination is what you are experiencing, and no one listens or looks into your accusations or complaints, that may embolden the perpetrator or set a precedent. Resentments build and communication suffers. It's hard to communicate when you're hurt, scared, and angry. Many of these young people would come in talking tough to me but wilt immediately upon standing in front of the captain. It was often difficult for me to keep from laughing as I watched the knees shake on these previously bold badasses.

This seldom happened with the young Black guys. They'd speak their piece, stand tall, argue, and look people in the eye. Where they came from, showing weakness was often dangerous. They were often justifiably angry and didn't mind showing it. I'm sure they often appeared arrogant or insolent. Some of them had previously had guns or worse pointed at them. I had. I was not far removed from these guys in age, race, and attitude. Here's what Elijah Anderson, a longtime New York City schoolteacher, said in 1980 on the subject of Black youth:

> The newly emerging picture, be it widely applicable to blacks or not, is that of an assertive, struggling young person who will not "take the shit" his forefathers did. This new black person is especially sensitive to what could be construed as racial prejudice, slight, and discrimination. . . .
>
> Add to this new image of militancy, the growing problem of youth unemployment, and a stereotype of black youths being primarily responsible for urban street crime, street gang activity, and general incivility, and one is faced with the specter of a nearly "unemployable" person.

If I didn't know better, I would think that Elijah Anderson could see into the future. Bill Norman had said something very similar to Wallace Terry in *Bloods*. They had talked to a lot of these angry young men themselves.

In Dennis D. Nelson's landmark 1951 book on the integration of the navy, he titles one chapter "The Negro and Military Law." I wish I could include the entire chapter here. It simply cannot be said any better than it was back then. Thank you, Google Books, for digitizing it and putting it on the internet. Here are a few tidbits:

> The average Negro has learned from long experience that his chances for securing justice in the courts are extremely poor in those sections of the country where discrimination in other things is legal. . . .
>
> And it is generally accepted as a foregone conclusion that no court will render a judgment against a white citizen in favor of a Negro plaintiff

> in areas where relations between the two races are traditionally more or less strained. . . .
>
> The lack of respect or confidence in the law or in those who administer it in civilian life must be taken into consideration in weighing the merits in the acts or violations of regulations of such persons as appear before military courts. This in no wise suggests or condones leniency or any treatment of Negro culprits that differs from the treatments of others. There are, however, many situations involving minority personnel that frequently warrant consideration of the social aspects involved, and of the impact of their experiences with civilian law and courts. Otherwise justice will not be equitably or adequately administered and the punishment meted out will only increase resentment and disrespect for law and authority.

I saw this disparate treatment of whites and Blacks firsthand, twenty-five years later, with Blacks consistently receiving harsher punishments for the same offences. The bulk of Nelson's law chapter dealt with the situation of a young man charged with desertion after leaving his post in Green Cove Springs, Florida, and receiving a court-martial for desertion in 1949. He had been gone for just under six months. The letter submitted by his defense counsel is perhaps the most eloquent summation of a particular individual's presumed thoughts and reasons provided in mitigation and extenuation that I have ever read. The letter stated that Jacksonville, Florida, was one of four places that the Bureau of Naval Personnel considered not suitable for the utilization of Negro personnel. This was because of the prevailing hostility toward Blacks in the area. The other three places were in Georgia and South Carolina. From my perspective, it hadn't gotten much better by 1980, when I arrived in Jacksonville as a young petty officer.

A poignant quote from this letter is as follows: "There have actually developed within this man physiological and psychological fears which are exceptionally deep-rooted in a persecution complex, in feelings of insecurity, bitterness and frustration which have been prevalent through much of his naval career. Following the war years, [he] found difficulty in finding work comparable to his training and experience—so since the Navy offered him a better way of life in spite of the lack of advancement opportunities in his first 'hitch,' [he] reenlisted."

The young man had been an outstanding sailor in all respects, but the psychological effects of rampant, bewildering, persistent discrimination, unfair treatment, and lack of a support network and suitable social outlets (he was from Cleveland, Ohio, and his family and friends remained there) took a devastating toll on him. The crushing discrimination and unfair treatment he received both in Jacksonville and Green Cove Springs ultimately made him leave the area, with the intention of eventually turning himself in to authorities in Washington, DC. He had previously reenlisted with the specific assurance that he not be sent to the South to serve, based on his experiences. The navy did not honor this agreement.

The eloquent letter resulted in the young man being convicted of the lesser-included offense of unauthorized absence instead of the more serious charge of desertion and ordered that he be sent to the Navy Rehabilitation Center at Norfolk, Virginia. After a little more than three months of his five-month sentence in "racism" rehab, his commanding officer commuted his sentence, and he moved on with his life. I would later learn that my father had experienced something similar, causing him to go on unauthorized absence until picked up after six months and returned to military control. He was not court-martialed but instead separated with an honorable discharge, and an RE-4 (not eligible for reenlistment without a waiver) designation. He received no counseling but did receive a glowing final evaluation that said he was the best petty officer the forward deck department had ever had from the commanding officer of his last ship, the USS *Independence*. The *Kitty Hawk* incident had occurred while he was "away" from the navy. I'll likely never know exactly what drove him to throw it all away, months away from retirement eligibility.

The young man clearly had been traumatized. Don't know if he was "cured" or not, or if he served in the South or anywhere else again. I don't even know his real name. I don't know what advice he would have given his own son. I see ghosts of my father in his story. I served almost my entire career in two of the places previously considered unsuitable for Negro personnel.

This Guantanamo job taught me the true value of a wheel book. Many sailors who wound up in trouble could have used a wheel book. A wheel book is (or was) a little green notebook in which the bearer (identified as the wheel or the big wheel) writes down important information that he or she is planning to use to burn your ass or protect his or her own. Among other things, the wheel book contains what you were told to do, when you were told to do it, whether you were late for muster, whether you got the haircut you were supposed to get, and damaging information like that. There may be an app for that now. If not, there should be. Get busy. Make some money.

I saw many sailors get buried under the crushing weight of the wheel book's documentation. Talking trash never stood up to written documentation. I never saw an accused reach in his pocket and pull out a list of reasons why he was in fact not guilty or document his own specific lists of grievances. You don't think like that when you're young, but if you are in the navy, you better learn how. Let me give you an example. You're getting all the crap details or jobs. You're tired of it. You complain. You're told to eat shit or worse. You get mad and go on unauthorized absence or something stupid like that. That is not a good plan. You lose because you have no documentation of the wrongs committed against you.

Here's a better plan, the one I tried to follow. Do the detail as if your life depended on it. Do the next one too. When the third one comes along, ask why you're getting these details and others are not, if that's the case. Whatever the answer is, write it down in your wheel book, with dates, times, and names. (What, you don't have one? Get one.) Make sure your boss sees you whip out your wheel book and write this down. Next, check yourself. Was the answer you got plausible? Have you been doing your job to the best of your ability? Is there new information you didn't know? Is this a problem or an opportunity?

Were you told that you were the most reliable person for this job and that you were chosen because your work ethic and performance were valued? Do not assume anything. Be sure you understand. Do not be afraid to ask questions. Be direct but open to information that does not fit your belief system. You just may be getting screwed. If you are, you have put your boss on notice that you're aware that you're being treated differently. You've put him or her on notice that you're a team player. You're on the team that has the wheel books. This may or may not solve your problem because the problem may be you.

In a scene in the movie *Glory*, a young Black recruit, Corporal Thomas Searles, a childhood friend of the commanding officer of the regiment, Colonel Gould, is being chewed out. Both are educated Northerners: one white, one Black. The soldier is apparently being picked on by the Irish sergeant major training the men. Colonel Gould intervenes, and the sergeant major tells him to let his friend, whom he considers the worst soldier in the regiment, grow up, grow up some more. The colonel understands, but it pains him. In the end, everyone benefits from these actions. Do you need to grow up, grow up some more?

During this tour, I participated in my first and only "race riot." Failure to communicate effectively and poor leadership were factors. I was right in the middle of it. In the subsequent official base police report, I was the only person there who was singled out by name for my actions during the riot. It's not what you think. I was serving as the only Black shore patrolman and the junior one on duty.

Several ships happened to be in port, and as usual, most of the women on the base stayed away from the enlisted men's club when the fleet was in town. It would have been easier for a fleet sailor to dig up a pirate's buried treasure chest in the base commander's front yard than for him to get laid by some woman he met at the club.

A bunch of these sailors—young, Black, bored, angry, horny, and quietly getting drunk, started getting loud and boisterous. At first, it was lighthearted, but I could see the mood changing and what was developing. I spoke to the senior man present and suggested he ask them to tone it down. He refused and looked a little scared. The shore patrol supervisor eventually made rounds to the club, and when he showed up, I approached him and suggested that he talk to the guys before things got out of hand. He looked at them, said he didn't see any problem, got in his truck, and hauled ass.

As these guys got louder and more aggressive, absent any leadership intervention, I saw them watching me. I'm sure they guessed correctly what I was saying, adding to their amusement. I several times considered going to ask these guys to behave but thought better of it. In their eyes, I would have had "Uncle Tom" written all over me. I would have been laughed at, called unflattering names, or, worse, become a target. I wish I had tried.

Being a third class yeoman didn't help either. Male yeomen were sometimes called "Tit-less WAVES," a derogatory term—WAVES then being the common term used to refer to female sailors. In their minds, I was probably the closest thing to an available woman they would likely encounter that night. Things got worse. Just as the club was closing, these guys were standing up chanting, pumping their fists, and all but daring anyone to challenge them.

The shore patrol supervisor had returned and belatedly tried to deal with the situation, but it was too late. I saw a bottle sailing through the air, and then all hell broke loose. Chairs and fists. Almost all the targets of these fists and chairs were white. I saw a small Filipino first class petty officer shore patrolman backing away, terrified and screaming, and waving his nightstick at a young man who was approaching him with a broken beer bottle in his hand and murder in his eyes.

I ran over and stood between him and his potential assailant, and I wasn't waving my nightstick. I had it cocked behind me. After we exchanged some harsh words, using language we both understood, he backed down. I escorted the shore patrolman to safety. How his pants stayed dry I'll never know.

Ultimately, we got all these guys out of the club, but the melee continued outside. The higher-ups on the scene then decided to get everyone else out of the club. These were the scared shitless people who didn't have the good sense to leave sooner. I thought this was crazy.

I pleaded with the supervisor not to do this. I said we needed to go outside and deal with those rowdy sailors, not send them targets of opportunity. When they persisted in clearing the club, I finally lost it and started yelling and beating my nightstick on a chair, telling the shore patrol supervisors that they were going to get these people killed. My head was pounding. I was angry, embarrassed, and frustrated.

They didn't listen to me. I looked just like the guys who were causing the problem, and I was beginning to act like them too. Fortunately, no one was seriously hurt. None of the sailors were arrested, but some were identified after they got back to their ships. In the subsequent police report, I was singled out for my actions as a shore patrolman in helping control the situation—not quite what I expected based on my behavior.

Not long after this, I would nearly derail my career, not for the last time. I was sitting in the barracks, playing cards with some friends, when we heard a young white sailor loudly arguing with his girlfriend. I had seen him at mast before. Suddenly, he turned and threw an empty glass tumbler, as hard as he could, and it hit smack-dab in the middle of the table where I was sitting on the level below him. Shattered glass went everywhere, and I was sure someone had been cut. Had he hit anyone in the head with that glass, it might have killed them.

I was the first one to reach him, having been the only one who actually saw what happened. I asked him what the hell was wrong with him, but before he could answer, I slapped him hard flat-handed on the side of his face. He went down. I turned around. Panic gripped me as if I were suddenly surrounded by sharks.

Running up behind me were the people with whom I had been playing cards, plus some additional volunteers, all carrying chairs, pool cues, and beer bottles. They weren't rearranging the furniture or taking out the trash; they were going to finish what I started. No sense in all of us going to jail, I reasoned. I managed to hold them off him and was relieved when the base police showed up almost right away.

This mean, alcoholic bully got into a lot more trouble and was soon administratively discharged. For my reaction to the situation, I had to eventually stand in front of the executive officer who told me that as the base discipline yeoman, I could not go around punching people, which I knew. He dismissed my case with a warning. As I turned to leave, he said, "Petty Officer Green." I turned around expecting the worst. He looked up from his cluttered desk and said, "Just between you and me, I would have knocked the hell out of that son of a bitch too." Then he laughed. I felt better, but I didn't laugh.

My boss, Captain Fetterman, assumed command of the naval base a few months after I got there, and he hit the deck running. He made many improvements in the quality of life on the base. He was a no-nonsense guy but a people person. You could tell he was going to be an admiral soon, and by 1981, he was.

He had the misfortune of having to preside over dispensing military justice for a large (more than sixty persons) drug bust on the base, involving many communications personnel, some of them senior petty officers with high-level security clearances. This was stressful for me also because I knew some of them from having worked with them in the same building. Some of them came to me for advice, and I said, "Don't do drugs, OK?" (This line later became famous on *South Park*.)

Other than that, I suggested they become acquainted with their new best friends, extenuation and mitigation. Some of these people had promising careers at risk. Several of them requested to speak privately at captain's mast, which was their legal right. I never knew when this would happen, and I never knew what was said. I had no right to know, and neither did anyone else. On one particular day, a senior petty officer asked to speak to Captain Fetterman in private, after initially speaking openly to the assembled group.

Captain Fetterman, fed up, angrily said no, that this was going to be discussed in the open, with everyone present. At that moment, in anger and frustration, he made a big mistake, exposing himself to the possibility of a formal complaint that might possibly have been forwarded to the secretary of the navy.

I always stood directly to the right and a step or two behind him, his right-hand man in case of problems. I knew my job, and I did it. I quietly stepped forward and whispered, "Sir, he does have that right." I had intervened before with quiet information and feedback. On this occasion, I became the target. He turned to me and yelled, "Don't you dare tell me my rights! I know my rights! Don't tell me my rights! I'm sick of all these people wanting to speak to me privately. We are going to deal with this right here!" This was totally and completely unexpected. The first time a pissed-off navy captain yells at you, you remember what he says. I felt like I'd just tried to take a baby bunny rabbit from a hungry saber-tooth tiger.

I quickly said, in my best ghetto voice, "Wait just a damn minute. Don't you yell at me 'cause you're mad at that sumbitch. I'm just doing my damn job. That's why you tell me to stand here, to keep you from stepping on your own dick. I'm going to let this slide right now, but we'll talk about this when you get finished." Of course, no one in the room was stunned, because I said this only to myself, as I stood there, smarting. The truth is he had just given me a giant wedgie without laying a hand on me.

What I did was say, "Yes, sir," and step back into my usual spot. Then a funny thing happened. He calmed down, hesitated for a minute, and then ordered everyone to leave the room except for the accused. He did exactly what I had advised him to do, which was to follow the regulations.

This regulation exists to protect the integrity of the process, the rights of the accused, and ultimately to give an individual the opportunity to inform the captain directly of facts he doesn't know but that are pertinent to the proceedings. This was the first time I was yelled at by a senior officer for doing my job. It would not be the last.

Chief Brown told me afterward that I had done exactly the right thing and that I should continue speaking up when necessary at mast. He told me that the captain wasn't angry with me; he was just blowing off steam. He tried to make light of it, but I saw the look on his face when it happened. I resolved that once I was an officer, no one was going to yell at me again, and I sure wasn't going to yell at anyone like that. Boy, was I really stupid back then.

I continued to do my job, but I would have closed my eyes and winced if I'd seen Captain Fetterman get ready to step on his crank again, I'm sure. I wasn't ready to get yelled at again, even if I was right. A few years later, I was reintroduced to Rear Admiral Fetterman by a future boss, Captain James T. Matheny, as he toured our command. He didn't remember me. But the navy's a big organization, and he had a lot of responsibility.

While all the drug cases at Guantanamo Bay were going on, a barracks that housed some of the Jamaican civilian workers burned down, completely destroying the building. These workers lost everything, and they had worked hard for it. In the charred and smoking rubble, the investigators and firemen found wads of burnt cash so big you could barely hold them in your hand. Many of these men were saving money to return home and build a better life. I was the small claims investigator for the base, and I processed all the small claims under a few thousand dollars.

These incidents, the drug bust and the fire, were in addition to my normal workload, which was enough to keep two people busy. I was swamped. My mentor, friend, and fishing buddy Chief Yeoman Robert Brown was a great help to me during this time. He helped me set up, at his suggestion, a big whiteboard in my office, listing all my outstanding items, recurring items, and other pertinent details and tasks. It was a big to-do list. This was a valuable tool, which I continued to use (although reduced to the size of a legal pad) for the rest of my military life.

Chief Brown tried very hard to discourage me from becoming an EOPS, but I didn't listen to him. We talked about racism in the navy, and he'd been in a lot longer than I had. He regretted not accepting his commission. He also strongly encouraged me to try to get a commission. He told me the best way I could make a difference in the navy was to become an officer and get some gold on my shoulders. Despite my workload, I managed to earn my associate of arts degree through a series of classes on the base, the College-Level Examination Program (CLEP) exams, credit for work experience, and military schooling.

I had purposely decided to avoid some of the quicker avenues available to me to obtain a commission after hearing two senior officers in my chain of command speak disparagingly of a Black junior officer on the base, in front of me, referring to him derogatively as a "BOOST product." I respected these officers, and if they thought being a BOOST product was bad, I'd avoid it. BOOST stood for Broadened Opportunity for Officer Selection and Training and was designed to prepare promising sailors with educational deficiencies to obtain commissions by bringing them up to speed.

This stupid decision probably delayed my commissioning by several years at least, had I been selected, and it was very immature and prideful on my part. I should have taken advantage of this opportunity. Admiral Jeremy Boorda, the first mustang officer to become the chief of naval operations, took advantage of a similar program to earn his commission. He had been a personnelman first class when he got selected. If you're eligible for any military commissioning program, and you're serious about it, apply for it. Pay no attention to those who disparage your choices. Get there any way you can. The pay is better, but you'll earn every dime.

Perhaps my proudest moment while serving in Guantanamo Bay had nothing to do with anything professional but something more important. The Seabees had the biggest, whitest, strongest, cockiest, and hardest-hitting softball team in the league. The players looked like muscle-bound construction workers, which, essentially, they were. Even their mustaches had muscles. Admin, my team, looked a little different. Our team had mostly small, skinny Hispanic and Black guys and sissy white guys. Yeomen, personnelmen, and legalmen; you know, wimps. Somehow, we wound up playing the Seabees for the base championship. They had really kicked our asses before, in the regular season.

The night of the big game, it was apparent that the game was about more than softball, judging from the spectators. The Seabees cheering section looked like a Sarah Palin rally, minus the one Black secret service agent. The admin side looked like an Obama rally, only more culturally integrated. A lot of the Jamaican civilians came down to watch the game. Nothing personal against the Seabees, but they weren't a diverse bunch. They had open contempt for us, lacking in functional gonads as we were, and we returned the disdain. When they weren't looking, we would think mean thoughts about them.

As the game wore on, with them pounding home runs over the fence every inning and us chipping away with singles, doubles, and the occasional home run or triple, you could feel the tension rise. It was David versus Goliath. They tried to pound us into oblivion, and we tried to give them the death of a thousand cuts. The game stayed close, and, in the last inning, in our final at bat, we pulled ahead.

We won! We won! No one had expected us to! My God, the Tit-less WAVES had beaten the Gladiators! While we celebrated, I prayed that they wouldn't send their wives and girlfriends out onto the field to kick the crap out of us while they packed up their gear. Nothing tempers a well-earned victory like unearned public humiliation. When the cheering died down, and we had smoothed out our skirts and fixed our makeup, we met them on the field to shake hands, just like the big boys did. Suddenly, they didn't seem quite so cocky. They had this look in their eyes that said, "Congratulations, you girls beat us fair and square."

Some of us wimps even dared to make brief eye contact with them. All of us walked a little taller for a long time after that. We had live sperm for a whole week! My only child, a son, was born nine months later. Thank you, Seabees. (My only child's given name is Alexander Rashad Green, but he is now known professionally as "Kaimbr.")

When I left Cuba, I was heading to the Defense Equal Opportunity Management Institute (DEOMI) as a student in the EOPS class. I wanted to help further the aims that Zumwalt articulated, the One Navy ideal. I had seen that in some ways, my father was right. There was true racism in the navy. It wasn't always blatant; however, it was there, and it was harmful to everyone. I wasn't rank qualified for this job either. You had to be, at minimum, an E-6. Although I was higher ranked than when I arrived at GTMO, I was still only an E-5. The navy sent me anyway. I was learning that the navy would sometimes waive requirements for people who demonstrated exceptional ability or drive. I received a Navy Achievement Medal for my service at Guantanamo Bay. I hoped that by becoming an EOPS, it would make me a more attractive prospect as a naval officer. I could do both what Chief Brown and Petty Officer First Class Fulton recommended. Would not an officer with equal opportunity training and experience be more valuable to the navy?

Sadly, my wife and I separated shortly before I left Cuba, and we never got back together to make it work. I have had no more children, but I have had three more wives and four stepchildren. My last wife and her two grown children came and went more than ten years after my military retirement. Alex spent several summers and holidays with me or with my sister when I was at sea. I eventually got custody of him during his fraught high school years, but not before a test of wills between his mother, me, and my then wife, who thought that her two children were more important than my own son.

5

Equal Opportunity Program Specialist and Hard Knocks

I reported to the Defense Equal Opportunity Management Institute (DEOMI) at Patrick Air Force Base, near Cocoa Beach, Florida, in January 1980. The institute was established in 1971, originally named Defense Race Relations Institute and then renamed DEOMI in July 1979. Politics. I was the junior student. There were few navy personnel in this class; the navy was still lagging in filling these billets. It was not considered a career-enhancing assignment.

Equal Opportunity Program Specialist (EOPS) students attended a four-month course. We learned about the Department of Defense (DOD) equal opportunity programs, programs specific to individual services, and how to assist commanding officers or supervisors effectively in implementing and maintaining these programs. Before you can do that, you have to come face to face with your own issues. For many of the white students, it was often a theoretical exercise.

If you're a minority or a woman, the school taught that what you've probably believed your entire life is true. Discrimination and prejudice exist, and they adversely affect people just like you and the organizations you serve. What students may learn here for the first time is that institutional racism may have a negative impact on the service or civilian command in which one serves.

There were some politicians who might have benefited from attending the executive-level programs at this school. Senator John C. Stennis, from Mississippi, who was chairman of the Senate Committee on Armed Services from 1969 through 1981, was one. Senator Stennis is known as the "Father of America's Modern Navy" for his work in the Senate. Admiral Zumwalt recounted how, when he was preparing for the congressional hearings in 1972, Senator Stennis told him that Blacks "came down from the trees a lot later than we did." Presumably, the senator was trying to be helpful.

Today, Black and other minority sailors proudly serve on the aircraft carrier USS *John C. Stennis*, and one may someday command it. The ship has had at least one Hispanic executive officer. Eddie Hebert, the Louisiana representative who had aggressively chaired the committee on racial disturbances in 1973, died on December 29, 1979, a few days before I started this school.

Congressman Hebert opposed school desegregation, and both he and Senator Stennis signed the infamous Southern Manifesto, which protested the 1954 *Brown v. Board of Education* decision. In retrospect, how could he possibly have found that there was institutional racism in the navy? He had to get reelected, and being soft on "the Negro question" was problematic. He chaired the House Committee on Armed Services from 1971 through 1975, the year I joined the navy.

According to Stennis's biographer, he called the conference table in his senate office the "Flagship of the Confederacy." When he surrendered his office to newly elected senator Joe Biden in 1988, Stennis told him that the infamous Southern Manifesto was planned and written at that very table. In June 2020, I wrote an article for *USNI Proceedings* magazine titled "The Case for Renaming the USS *John C. Stennis*" and recommended that the ship be renamed the USS *William S. Norman*, in honor of Zumwalt's minority affairs assistant who did so much to bring the navy into the twentieth century, while Stennis tried to keep it in the nineteenth. That article received widespread and international attention, and I await the navy's response. I wish Admiral Zumwalt had lived to read it. He would have understood.

At this school, we learned about intercultural and interpersonal relations, organizational effectiveness, racism, sexism, justice, and injustice—just the most amazing curriculum you could imagine. The instructors tried to teach us how to talk to senior officers without getting yelled at. I never quite got the hang of that. Each of us received twelve undergraduate credit hours for attending this school, and six hours of graduate-level credit. The graduate-level courses were in interpersonal communication and instructional methodology—I want you to remember that; it will be relevant later. This included a practical demonstration of our skills, judged by experienced and outstanding instructors. (Remember that too.)

This school had an amazing library, and we were required to use it. Each student gave presentations on subjects approved by the school sponsor or class leader. I remember a report I did on the death penalty.

We had inspiring guest speakers at this school. One speaker I wish we'd had there was Mr. Clarence H. King Jr., a former navy steward. King also founded the Urban Crisis Center in Atlanta and authored the book *Fire in My*

Bones, published in 1983, which tells the story of how the navy's opportunity to get some of the best race relations training in the world was derailed because he kissed a white woman, who worked with him, during the training. This was designed to provoke a reaction and, boy, did it ever.

The Charleston, South Carolina, base commander at the time, Rear Admiral Graham Tahler, kicked him out, saying, "No Black man is going to kiss a white woman on my base." He apparently didn't know what was going on in Scotland. In his memoir, King named names, pointed fingers, and called a spade a spade.

The guest speaker I best remember is Dr. Ted Paynther (not his real name) from Kent State University. He started lecturing us about how bad Black people were. When a woman spoke up, he spoke about how bad women were and where they belonged. No matter who spoke up, he attacked that person. One of the army officers in my class was really cracking up at this, and I hated him for it. When things were about to get out of hand, the leaders broke up the assembly and sent us back to our classrooms.

Everyone was tense and angry, and to add insult to injury, the staff then rubbed salt in our wounds. We were sternly lectured about losing our composure and how we were expected to behave. We were told that we might have to deal with this type of behavior from one of our bosses and getting upset was not going to be helpful.

I didn't want to talk about the speaker's comments. I wanted to talk about the army officer in my class who had been laughing at us as this was going on. When I called him on it, he straightened up and apologized, stating that he would account for himself after the lecture. I had held him in high esteem before this happened, but now I had a very different opinion. When we got back into the auditorium, the atmosphere was tense. Dr. Paynther started speaking calmly and quietly, and he told a story that included, among other things, his experiences of infiltrating the Ku Klux Klan.

Near the end of the fascinating story, he told us that his mother was Black, his father was Black, and that he was Black. I was sitting near the front of the stage, very close to him, and I could see that the hair on his arm had suddenly stood up. I can't imagine what it was like for him to put us, and himself, through this, provoking and baiting us, and then revealing that he was Black. He was preparing us for some of the pushback we might face while trying to do our jobs. I'll never forget him. Talk about stress. I wanted to go up on the stage and hug him. He was by far the best speaker we had, in my opinion. I wish he'd written a memoir.

When I looked at him, I thought about my friend Jimmy, with his light eyes, curly blond hair, and Black parents. I had begun to think about dropping out of this school. As great as it was, I could see some hypocrisy around me, in the behavior of some of the staff. This lecture, more than anything else, convinced me to stay. Many people who wanted to graduate failed academically; I had to stay, for them.

The problem with this school was that many commands weren't sending the right people, in my opinion. What could an E-5 do? I thought that every commanding officer and executive officer should be attending this school or a version of it. They are the ones who truly have the power to lead substantial cultural changes through top-down leadership.

The junior petty officer or commissioned officer sent from this school to "advise" his or her seniors is often facing an uphill battle. They are armed with information and knowledge that is mostly useless if they don't have the buy-in from and confidence of their bosses. This was to be my biggest problem. Before I left this school, I'd see an example of this for myself. As one of the few navy people, I stood out, and I was the junior student there. Neither of these facts worked to my advantage.

A tall, charismatic, very handsome Black army captain on the staff took a very intense, personal, and unwelcome interest in me. This entire staff had apparently been specially screened for handsomeness, even the women. His name was Captain Wayne Q. Williams, the student control officer. He called me into his dark, private office to chat. He said that he thought my hair was too long and that the comb that protruded from my back pocket, which I had been carrying for years, was too big. To him, I simply didn't fit the picture of what a good soldier was supposed to look like, I guess. The problem was, I wasn't a soldier; I was a sailor, and I wasn't breaking any regulations. He was pretty direct at expressing his displeasure. I don't think he had ever heard of this Zumwalt guy. No matter; I had. Time to practice what I'd learned.

I looked around the office and didn't see any weapons, so I explained a few things to him, trained sea lawyer that I was. I told him that I wasn't in the army, I was in the navy, and that my hair was well within navy regulations, as was my comb. When he didn't instantly kill me with the tip of his index finger, I got bolder. I told him I saw lots of combs just like mine in the back pockets of people all over the base. Unfortunately for him, it was an air force base, not an army one.

I explained that a little skinny comb like the ones the white guys used wouldn't comb anything but my mustache or my beard, which he didn't like either. Weren't we here, I asked, to learn how to support diversity and accept differences between people, as long as we followed the regulations? Didn't he love Martin Luther King Jr.? Jesus? Did he want me to pray with or for him? Right about then, I think he was wishing that I were in the army.

I thought it was ironic that here in this Mecca of tolerance, diversity, enlightenment, and knowledge, I was getting hassled by a Black officer when I wasn't doing anything wrong. When I asked him if the people who were walking around with wallets that protruded from their pockets (aka, white guys) were breaking any regulations, he said that was "different" and that I was setting a bad example. I didn't agree, and I told him so, respectfully.

We were being taught to hold our own when dealing with authorities, and I was learning. I could have gotten a close haircut and switched combs, but I was making a point; I was an asshole! I was not doing anything wrong, despite the fact that it made "some" people uncomfortable. Being different was making me a problem, even here.

From this supportive, intellectually stimulating, and welcoming environment, I went to what was, for me, a snake pit. That's too strong. It was more like a spider hole. I was going to Jacksonville, Florida, which a few decades before was considered unsuitable for assignment for Black navy personnel because of pervasive racism. Had times changed? I was going to find out.

I reported to Commander Naval Surface Force Readiness Support Group, in Mayport, Florida, in April 1980. The decade of the so-called naval renaissance was just beginning. I didn't know the extent of the bias and subtle discrimination that were prevalent in the overall navy at that time, as was eight years later readily acknowledged by the secretary of the navy and the chief of naval operations, but I was about to find out. The parking lot was filled with Confederate flags and similar sentiments on the car bumpers and windows, and the near lily-white staff consisted mostly of crusty chiefs and above. Many of the officers were mustangs in the engineering fields. For me this was a lot like being back in the mine force, only with a different, less important, and unappreciated job. I would have to figuratively dodge mines rather than work on them.

The navy and the country were soon entering the Ronald Reagan presidency. Reagan would never have a good relationship with the so-called Black representatives and organizations of the era. The navy would have some inner changes and turmoil of its own. The first female midshipmen from the Naval Academy graduated in 1980, and women would continue to fill billets on certain types of navy ships in ever growing numbers. Janie Mines would write about her experience as the first Black female midshipman to graduate from the Naval Academy. It wasn't pretty. Meanwhile, Secretary of the Navy John Lehman announced plans for a six-hundred-ship navy, which meant that many more personnel would need to be recruited to man them, and support them. Janie Mines would be one of the first female officers ever assigned to a navy ship.

Secretary of Defense Caspar Weinberger spoke during 1982 at a gathering in Washington, DC, honoring sixty-four Black flag officers from various services. That same year, the Brookings Institution published its previously mentioned study, "Blacks and the Military: Studies in Defense Policy." The publication highlighted successes as well as problems, concerns, and strategic recommendations.

I was the second EOPS to serve at my new command, and I was the first Black one. The first, a white chief petty officer, from South Carolina, was coasting to retirement. I kept a wary eye on him. He kept bragging about what an easy billet it was at his retirement ceremony before heading home to South Carolina. We would have different perspectives on that. If Charleston, South Carolina, was the South, then Jacksonville, Florida, was the Old South. In some ways, it still is. I've lived there for more than forty years. Battles over Confederate monuments on public property are still raging years after the killing of George Floyd, and that's a blemish on the city. My new skipper sternly and promptly told me when I checked in that he didn't have any race-related problems, which he made very clear, and it was going to stay that way. I got that message loud and clear too. I was an E-5; he was a navy captain. What the hell did I know? I would find that almost all the leadership on the ships in the Mayport basin had the same opinion. I sensed no hostility to equal opportunity or affirmative action when meeting with them, but I did sense a reluctance to probe too deeply or to acknowledge what problems existed. There was danger in turning some of these rocks over; it was easier to tamp them back into place. Promoting equal opportunity would be the least of my responsibilities.

Following a couple of unpleasant incidents out on the town, I decided to stick close to the base. One bartender would not serve me at a local club, a large one, where I was one of the few minorities there. The manager said she could refuse service to anyone, at her discretion, when I complained. Couldn't I buy one drink? I had money and a military ID. Nope. My letters to the Jacksonville Chamber of Commerce and the owner of the club went unanswered. I got the message. Not welcome.

Civilian communities around military bases were not always welcoming to minorities, but you learned to adjust and where to go. Jacksonville's reputation from the 1940s was changing, but slowly. When I attended another club, the DJ played his apparent favorite song when there were too many Black people in the establishment. The lyrics stated that Black people can't play rock and roll but in graphic, racist language. I guess they never heard of Jimi Hendrix.

It was hard to dance to, anyway. I was experiencing firsthand some of the resentment to "social intrusion" expressed by whites who did not want Black people trespassing into areas they traditionally claimed as their own, including their neighborhoods, as would be written about in the Brookings study.

I had no clue where to go for entertainment. I once followed a car full of attractive, smart-looking girls who were obviously going out for the night. Once they got to a club, I walked in the entrance behind them. Things looked promising. Surely some nice, beautiful woman would be in there who had also likely read the latest issue of *National Geographic*, and I was very anxious to talk to her about it. Outside the door, where you paid to get in, was a sign that said, "The French Quarter is a gay bar, and we intend to keep it that way!" Uh-oh. What do I do now? What was a straight young Black sailor to do? I had never been in a gay club before, but I had seen what happened to gay people in the military. I went in. No man—or woman, for that matter—approached me. There must have been too much white showing around my eyes. The music was good, I could get a drink without a hassle, and nobody bothered me. Being Black was not a problem here. I had served with sailors I thought or knew were gay, including officers, and I would do so again. Some of the people having a good time in that club were sailors. They apparently knew where they were welcome. Had I known then about the prevailing tactics of the Naval Investigative Service toward suspected gay service members, I never would have gone in. It was a rough time to be gay or to be suspected of it.

I primarily worked for Master Chief Career Counselor Davy, whose first name I don't remember and never used. I taught certain segments in the retention classes for the fleet sailors on the base. He allowed his students to smoke during class, and he did so himself. I, a lifelong nonsmoker, had a problem with this. There was a long-standing DOD directive, signed by the secretary of defense, that stated smoking was not allowed in classrooms, among other places.

After a while, I asked Master Chief Davy if we could eliminate the smoking because it was causing me problems. I showed him the DOD instruction. He looked at me directly in my red, watery eyes and said, "Hell, no." I had spent my entire life not smoking; I had just left a DOD school, and nobody smoked in classrooms there. Tired of my complaining, he agreed to put out the smoking lamp, but only when I was teaching. This made me very, very unpopular with the students, at least 90 percent of whom were white.

I wasted a lot of time explaining to them why they couldn't smoke in my class but could elsewhere. They had no problem telling me what I could go do to myself, as if I could. Sailors.

They quickly decided that I was a poor instructor, despite my expertise. In their end-of-course critiques, I was usually identified as "that Black second class petty officer," and they said the entire class was very good, except that I sucked—not that I was incompetent, ignorant, or ineffective; I just sucked, big time. They weren't all bad, but plenty were. I'd never gotten critiques like this before. I was failing and had no defense. I had my suspicions but no proof. I had to act.

I put in a chit requesting captain's mast, stating in a letter I attached to the chit that smoking in classrooms should end, as required by DOD mandate, because it was causing turmoil and resentment toward me from the students. I also attached the DOD instruction. The next day, Master Chief Davy told me that he'd "intercepted" my chit, "disapproved" it, and passed it up the chain. He also told me, "In my fucking classrooms smoking is permitted and if you don't like it, you can go find yourself another fucking job." I thanked him kindly for the information.

The commanding officer received my request chit, signed it "Disapproved" as had everyone else. He never saw or spoke to me, but put out a memo prohibiting smoking in classrooms and everywhere else in the instruction.

Maybe he wanted to do this all along, but needed a catalyst. Hello, catalyst. This filled me with dread. As on the set of *Cheers*, everybody knew my name. People I didn't know began to eyeball me. The staff included a Black storekeeper and a Black engineering chief. They smoked too. I had almost single-handedly provided sailors and visitors a smoke-free environment, with an assist by the secretary of defense.

The skipper transferred soon after. Master Chief Davy took it surprisingly well, even cheerfully. He still called me "Buddy." There were several master chiefs on the staff. I was not yet familiar with master chiefs. I wish my father had told me about them. I was about to receive a master class in retaliation. I took college classes on weekends and after work. I worked at the Mayport enlisted men's club as the night manager, often forty hours per week. I had previously passed CLEP exams as a seaman. I took a couple more. Once Master Chief Davy and the other EOPS chief (the retiring one) heard from me how easy they were, they took the CLEP English Composition examination. Both failed it. They said the test was very hard and that "someone" must have changed it since I'd taken it. I was glad that the rules of English composition changed only after I took the test. Neither of them took any more exams. I scored in the ninety-seventh percentile on the African American history exam.

I received a questionnaire from DEOMI after six months, asking how useful the training was. I said that of the nine general tasks they asked about,

I spent 0 percent of my time on six of them and 1–10 percent of my time on the other three. Of the thirty-seven specific job tasks they asked about, I never performed thirty-five of them and performed the other two less than once monthly. Damn. For the section titled Importance of EO Knowledge and Skill Areas (of which there were sixty-four), I considered them mostly critical or very important. I had good skills; I just wasn't able to use them. I wanted to.

Part 6 requested that I list the five most important skills I learned that were required of me in my billet. I said: (1) intercultural communication, (2) white working class, (3) instructor techniques, (4) concepts of personal, institutional/cultural sexism, and (5) values and attitudes. In the free-form comments section, I also said, "Dealing with sexism (individual) and racism, covert and overt, from higher ranking individuals: no E.O. command support involved was a problem."

Asked for my advice, I said, "Seek training for COs and XOs—senior personnel." I also said, "The instructors and instruction were for the most part outstanding. Certain areas could be condensed with a little effort, which would allow more time to process the enormous amount of information presented. I personally feel that educating the TOP people is the most effective way to bring about changes—and also the most difficult to accomplish. Thanks for everything!" I was unknowingly echoing the beliefs and intentions of Admiral Zumwalt when he spoke about the core leadership problems of the navy.

I soon got hit between the eyes by the reality of retaliation. Because I was a "poor instructor," Master Chief Davy convinced the new skipper that I needed remedial training. He had documentation in the form of signed negative critiques. How could I argue with that? I tried. The critiques often referred to my race and generally said that I sucked. Not one mentioned smoking. Despite no one auditing my classes to see how I performed, Master Chief Davy arranged for me to attend Instructor Basic School in Little Creek, Virginia. Anyone could see he was trying to "help" me—he was a career counselor, after all, and had a binder full of negative critiques that indicated I was not performing up to standards and expectations. I would soon learn how that binder came to be.

Master Chief Davy likely told the new skipper that I was an imbecile, too junior to be filling this billet I was in. I doubt he mentioned the "Smoking Fiasco." This was what affirmative action (think *woke*) gets you. The incoming president, Ronald Reagan, with his strong opposition to affirmative action and quotas was setting the tone. I worried that my next performance evaluation would say that I was not performing sufficiently to warrant promotion or retention, despite the fact that I had just received a Navy Achievement Medal for my performance at my last challenging assignment. Moreover, there were no specific objective complaints about my lack of knowledge, presentation, or performance. I just sucked.

At Instructor Training A (Basic) School, students gave five presentations. The staff graded everything from appearance to voice, along with techniques and rigid adherence to an evaluation sheet, with a satisfactory or unsatisfactory grade. I received more than two hundred "satisfactory" grades and two "weak satisfactory" scores. One was for oral questioning; the other, for "labeling" on the presentation I gave on growing an avocado tree. My props were an avocado pit, a glass, and some toothpicks: two tough to label. Hey, it was subjective. I received zero unsatisfactory grades. I was still Black, but magically, I no longer sucked, as Master Chief Davy's binder clearly indicated. I gave two presentations that were close to my heart. One was on the *Bureau of Naval Personnel Manual*, which I taught for Davy weekly, and the other was on the French and Raven's five bases of power, which he was showing me daily, and I would later teach to sailors and junior officers on the waterfront.

For the latter, the staff evaluators said I was a subject matter expert. The most common question I got was "Why are you here?" Because I was a "subject matter expert" on the uses and misuses of power, I knew, but didn't say. I was again "almost" an early graduate, but I had a cold for my next-to-last presentation, and I didn't quite make the cut, even though I was satisfactory in everything. Many of my fellow classmates said I should have, and they were surprised when I did not. By now, I knew the drill. I was still as Black as I was in Mineman A School, remember?

Not long after I got back and resumed sucking, I finished one of my presentations and turned the class over to Davy. The lounge was right next door, and although I normally went right back to our office, this time I stopped in the lounge for something. Through the wall, I could hear Master Chief Davy really bad-mouthing me, explaining to the all-white class that I was the reason they couldn't smoke in the classes anymore. Not the secretary of defense, not the commanding officer, but me. My supervisor and shipmate told them to remember that when they completed their course critiques.

Finally, with a clap of thunder and lightning, and some of that dramatic horror movie trailer music, everything became crystal clear to me. My worst fears were confirmed. Had he been doing this with each class? Almost from the beginning, he had been engineering my failure. He had been pounding my ass real good, wearing a star-studded condom. I was almost beginning to believe the critiques myself.

I fought the urge to walk back and confront him. Instead, I went to my division officer, a lieutenant, and said I needed to talk right away. He could tell I was upset. He was on a call and said we'd talk later. My stomach was churning from the betrayal, desire for revenge, and fear for my future. What else was this low-down bastard doing to harm me? He was going to write my upcoming performance evaluation!

I seethed, pondering my options. I wanted to call my father for advice, but I was ashamed. I should have; he would be dead in less than a year. He and Chief Brown would have said, "See, Slick, I tried to tell you." This wasn't supposed to happen to anyone. I felt helpless and trapped. Davy had all the cards: bad course critiques, my remedial training, the confidence and admiration of the commanding officer, and Lord only knows what else. He was expertly setting me up for the kill, while smiling at me and calling me "Buddy." I decided to run toward the roar, as children are taught in the African bush.

After about an hour, Master Chief Davy walked cheerfully into the room, happy that he'd soon have a bigger pile of critiques to show that, despite his best efforts to help me, I was hopeless. I had clearly been promoted to the level of incompetence. He would eventually recommend a transfer to a job I could handle, like making publication changes or something. No point in continuing to try to polish a turd. No matter how much you polished it, it was still a turd.

With as much nonchalance as I could muster, I said that I had heard the stuff he was saying about me to the class, I had suspected all along that he was bad-mouthing me, and I finally understood why I was getting bad student evaluations. Never breaking eye contact, I said that I would no longer teach classes for him and that he could explain why to the division officer. I had a yellow legal pad on my desk, with some scribbling on it, beside the binder that held the DOD and navy equal opportunity and discrimination directives. He knew I knew those cold.

I looked like I'd been seriously busy and highly motivated. I left the impression that I had something else up my sleeve. I did. Street smarts and jungle smarts. "Until the lion learns to write, the hunter will always be the hero of the story" is an African proverb. This lion was now prepared to pencil whip the hunter. He had been sneaking around behind my back. I came at him face to face, man to man. It was time to look him in the eye, hard, with open contempt. I finally, truly understood some of the Black guys I had watched at captain's mast a few months before. The wheel book tells only part of the story.

At first he denied it, and when I repeated exactly what I'd heard him say, he then fell to pieces. He canceled the rest of the classes for the day and went home. This surprised me; I had expected continued denial or a counterattack. He now saw me as dangerous, and he was afraid and unsure what to do. So he ran.

When my division officer found me and said he had time to talk, I said I had already fixed the problem. He looked concerned, because I was angry, but he didn't ask any questions. When asked where Davy was, I said that he'd canceled classes and gone home. With a raised eyebrow, he left my office. The right question would have opened the floodgates, but he didn't ask any. By now, I trusted no one in the building. Had he been in on this? Had the skipper? Davy had been performing an administrative "buck breaking," and some people surely knew what he was doing, laughing behind my back.

My father was starting to look smarter all the time. Had anything like this ever happened to him? Would he have told me if it had? I doubt it.

Smoking conflicts were one thing. The combination of racism and discrimination retaliation and gaslighting were quite another. When the wagons were circled, they weren't going to be circled around me but around the popular master chief. I didn't know what might have happened, statistically speaking, if I had filed a formal complaint. The statistics on this were frightening.

The next day, Davy and I had a little talk, which he initiated, and things got better. The negative critiques magically stopped. I think he was grateful that I didn't drop a dime on him. I never told anyone on that staff what he had done, except later my new boss and savior, Daniel Ziparo.

Shortly after this exchange between Davy and me, Signalman Senior Chief (SMCS) Petty Officer Daniel Ziparo arrived. Thank God, he had just graduated from EOPS school himself. He had been assigned in Mayport before, and he was very sharp. He soon pulled me aside to talk privately. He told me he was hearing lots of negative talk about me, and he said that what he was hearing did not match what he was seeing with his own eyes. He told me that I had better be careful and to watch my ass. He told me, point-blank, that there were people there who were out to get me. Was this buck breaking conspiracy bigger than I thought? He said he would look out for me but I needed to keep my eyes open too. I struggled to say "thank you" because something was wrong with my throat.

My eyes were now completely wide open, but I could feel them filling up with tears. This man had just met me, but he could see that I was trying to do a good job. He looked me in the eye, talked to me like I was a man and a human being, and with respect. Having just received some very good training, he understood what was happening. He knew about the uses and misuses of power too.

I struggled to remain composed. I could feel my heart pounding in my chest, and it felt like everything was moving in slow motion. I'd had more composure when a shotgun was pointed at my chest. At least then I knew what I was up against. What, exactly, had I done to deserve this treatment? Had I really done anything so terrible? It took all I had not to break down in tears. When I went home that evening, I think I did.

I was learning how a guy could be a star in one unit and a shithead in the next one. I wasn't doing anything wrong, unless expecting the people for whom I worked to comply with the written orders of the secretary of defense, as I was expected to, was wrong.

I realized that Chief Yeoman Robert E. Brown had been trying to protect me when he advised me not to volunteer for an equal opportunity billet. I finally understood how Ron Fulton, the EOPS in Guantanamo, felt after his office was trashed and his family threatened. While he stood there talking to me, looking at the racist graffiti on his office walls, with tears on his face, he had asked the same question of me then that I was asking myself now. Why?

Senior Chief Ziparo, who soon made master chief, probably saved my career. I got a little nervous when he got promoted, but I needn't have worried. He had just completed some of the most intense training on race relations you can get anywhere in the world. This can be difficult for white people, and I saw many appear to be overwhelmed at some of the issues and realities they were forced to confront. For Black people, and other minorities, including women, this was stuff we had learned all our lives, but it was hard for us to confront these realities also. For Ziparo, this was eye opening. He told me so.

I am truly thankful to have had him as a boss, a confidant, and a friend and protector. We went on to become a great team. We were trained in and conducted substance-abuse prevention courses. After Davy left and Ziparo became my boss, my standing slowly improved. In 1981, the chief of naval operations placed increased emphasis on leadership and management training. To support that effort, Vice Admiral John D. Johnson Jr. (Commander, Naval Surface Force Atlantic) established three leadership mobile training teams to teach leadership on the waterfront. Mayport, Norfolk, and Charleston were the locations. Ziparo and I were on the Mayport team. The May 1982 issue of *Surface Warfare* magazine contained an article with pictures of what we were doing. It was great training, and many benefited from it. My new skipper said in the article that "this is a quick way to provide that climate [leadership techniques] to the ship, and boy it's great, it's really great." I was to learn that his enthusiasm about the training I was helping provide to the sailors on the waterfront did not extend to me.

We supplemented the two-week leadership management and education training with a three-day course for people who had not yet made it into that pipeline. I loved this job, thrived in it, and we were a team in the true sense of the word. This three-day course would do until people could attend the backlogged and mandated two-week leadership course. I learned a thing or two teaching these classes. I loved it.

Also in 1981, I applied for commissioning under the Enlisted Commissioning Program. I had good evaluations, lots of college credits, and had been consistently recommended for officer programs since 1978. I thought my required three-officer interview board went well. Unlike during my mineman special promotion board, the subject of race never came up. When I read these write ups, I was devastated. A supply officer to whom I had never spoken trashed me regarding my leadership potential. He didn't see any.

He said "demonstrated educational achievements did not necessarily" mean I would be a good officer. I was teaching leadership to the fleet weekly, but he didn't think I had the potential to lead. Demonstrated educational achievement and advancement potential were primary selection criteria. By what standard was he judging me? It was subjective.

My executive officer, Commander J. M. Stuck, personally apologized to me about the write-up, but there was nothing he could do about it. I didn't yet understand how these things worked. If the commanding officer disagreed, he could have asked the supply officer to reconsider his assessment. He did not. There was not one flaw in my record or my application. The flaw was in the race of the applicant, based on the treatment I received from him. I was not selected. When I watched President Ronald Reagan rail against affirmative action and talk about "Morning in America," I felt that I knew what midnight in America looked like. It looked like me.

I passed the first-class exam as an early candidate and was promoted early to E-6, which wasn't easy. You had to have "demonstrated higher knowledge of such topics as your rate and leadership skills." No one could say that I didn't earn it or qualify. The computers controlled this. No subjectivity. I had typed out the entire YN3 and YN2 rate training questions and answers, put them in a notebook, and studied them daily. I had put them all on a cassette tape and listened to them constantly. When sent to instructor school for remedial training, I took them with me.

My roommates knew the potential questions and answers for the YN1 exam. We would recite them when we got dressed in the mornings and at night while I studied or prepared my presentations. Both roommates were engineers. Both were Black.

In 1981, the percentage of Black sailors serving in pay grade E-6 was 6.7 percent. For the three chief ranks, the average was 5.6 percent. I put on my first-class rank insignia, commonly referred to as a "crow," and became one of the most senior Black sailors in the navy, and I'd been in for only a little more than six years. Few sailors had ever had any training in race relations. Black role models were hard to find, and I certainly didn't feel like one.

I like to think my father would have been cautiously proud. He died in 1981, in Sacramento, California, of heart failure. I was devastated when I got the call. He was forty-six, and I had not seen him for at least a year, but we had exchanged letters. I flew out and sat by his bedside while he lay there comatose. I hope he heard the things I told him. I said I was proud of him. I didn't talk navy. I didn't want him to have painful memories or new worries as he transitioned.

Somehow, the word got out in the command that I was pretty good with a pencil. No one ever mentioned my writing skills to me, but they apparently talked among themselves. Maybe it was all the evaluations I typed for the command, which wasn't my job. I'd fix them as I went along, without asking. Maybe someone read my application for commissioning. One of the staff master chiefs, T. J. Thomas, asked me to look at his chief warrant officer commissioning program application. I was happy to. He was a serial applicant, and I could see why he wasn't accepted. He was an engineman, not an English major. I rewrote both his application and the endorsement by the commanding officer as if they were my own.

Thomas was the only applicant selected from our command and the only one who had asked me for help. I was proud to attend the commissioning ceremony for Chief Warrant Officer Thomas, conducted on board the USS *Yosemite*, where he publicly thanked me for my help. He didn't have any problem asking a junior Black yeoman for help. He was Black too. No one else had ever asked for my help before him, but that changed after his selection. I helped all who asked. We were all shipmates.

Master Chief Ziparo and I were also required to review the equal opportunity programs of ships under our purview. This included the human relations council instructions and records, the ones that Admiral McCain was worried about usurping his authority. Ziparo took his responsibility seriously in this area, but we never really had much support. When we critiqued the various commands' affirmative-action plans or their equal opportunity programs and instructions, we often got pushback. They often took our comments personally. Mostly, we were viewed as a necessary evil.

As I prepared to transfer, I realized that I had overcome a lot. I had gone there to try to help people better understand the navy's regulations on equal opportunity and equitable treatment and had nearly left in disgrace. My skippers had treated me like I had "I'm a problem" tattooed across my forehead. I had taught sailors and officers leadership skills. I had advised commanding officers on their equal opportunity programs. I had counseled sailors on their careers and professional problems and taught drug and alcohol abuse prevention classes. I made sure that all of my professional and personal growth accomplishments were well documented, including my educational accomplishments and my desire to obtain a commission.

What my recent evaluations did not say, and I could not control, was that I was recommended for commissioning. This silence spoke volumes. My skipper could not technically control what an interviewer put on an appraisal form for my application for commission, but he could control what he said in my evaluations. He did. This is called "damning with faint praise." In this case, there was virtually no praise at all. There were, however, specifics of my accomplishments, which I provided. More than that I could not do.

For thirty-three months' service, and my monthly cash contributions, I earned a plaque, which is more than I got after two years of stellar performance in the mine force. I'd paid for that plaque about three times over. When the chief yeoman in the admin office asked me if I wanted the skipper to present it to me, I firmly told him that "I would rather you slid it under my door." He grinned as he turned to leave. I'm sure the chief told the skipper exactly what I said. I hoped he would. I wasn't trying to be disrespectful. I was trying to be honest. It might not have been the smartest thing I've ever said, but that's how I felt about my situation. I had been humiliated by one commanding officer at a ceremony I did not ask for, trying to be a team player, and I wasn't about to let it happen to me again. That commanding officer was simply insensitive or a traditionalist, but I had thought he liked me. Truth is, I also by now had a chip on my shoulder, and I knew it. When I came back from lunch, the plaque was sitting in my chair. I still have it, somewhere, and I'm proud of it. It is brass, and it has my name on it. But as with my Charleston departure, I never received a letter of appreciation.

Master Chief Ziparo told me years later that he had submitted a Navy Achievement Medal award recommendation for me on three separate occasions, and each time, it was lost, misplaced, and finally "forwarded" up the chain of command. One day after hours, he checked the award files and found his recommendation had never left the command; it wasn't even in award files. Round file (aka trash can), most likely. Ziparo was awarded a Navy Commendation Medal right away. I earned one too, easily. I was as good as he was, maybe better. I had simply been on the wrong half of the team—the dark half.

As if to reward me, the navy transferred me to Commander Light Attack Wing 1 (CLAW-1) at Naval Air Station Cecil Field, Florida. I had hit the jackpot and worked with some of the finest people ever. I am forever grateful for this psychological get-well tour and the fine people who helped make it possible. It happened just in time.

At CLAW-1, my supervisor, Chief Yeoman Robert Amberson, was a nice guy. My division officer, Lieutenant Jo Ann Peterson, was very professional and supportive. She pulled me aside on several occasions and told me she was impressed with my performance and my potential. The chief of staff and the commodore were great. No one seemed to care that I was Black. I felt appreciated, and I worked hard. Captain J. T. Matheny, the commodore, would often give me stuff to type, and I would sometimes make editorial suggestions and he was very receptive. I closely read everything that I could that he had written so that I could mimic his style.

After a while, when I would walk in intending to recommend a change to something he had written, he would wave me away without even looking at it and just tell me to make it say what he wanted. He once said to me, "Petty Officer Green, you know what I'm trying to say, so stop bothering me and just fix it." Talk about building confidence in a wounded duck! After a while, he'd hand me something roughly written and tell me to make it say what he wanted it to, bypassing the administrative officer, my boss. I tried hard to make him glad that he had confidence in me.

The officers on this staff were great to me as well. I had a couple of problems with the chiefs' mess, but I was used to that. I learned a valuable lesson in this job. I had a runner and driver who was assigned to me and would rotate every few months, naturally just as soon as they got the hang of the job. When I got a new one, it would take up to two weeks or more for him to learn his route, his duties, and the whole routine. Often, he'd forget stuff or miss a stop in the route, creating problems. I'd get heat for this from the master chief who ran the temporary additional duty personnel pool. I kept a close eye on the master chief. He was a smoker. More than once, he probed for weaknesses. I thought about the whiteboard Chief Yeoman Brown had helped me set up and came up with a solution.

I finally made an experienced driver write down every single thing he did for an entire week. Where he went, what he did, whom he saw, and what times he was required to be at certain places. He did not like doing this. We refined this over time, and when he was due to rotate, I gave this guide to his relief and told him to follow it, without asking questions. When he couldn't, we revised it for clarity and effectiveness. Using this method, I was able to whittle the turnover process from two weeks to about three days and improved overall efficiency. Not only that, I learned a lot I did not previously know but needed to. I was to carry this lesson forward and use it repeatedly. It was my first standard operating procedure (SOP).

There are good reasons for SOPs and procedural checklists. After having nearly completed the requirements for a bachelor of science degree, I applied for the limited duty officer program three months into this tour. I was getting good at passing these command boards but having less confidence in getting a fair shake. At previous boards, whether spoken or unspoken, the fact that I was Black had seemed to keep getting in the way.

When I received my board results, having just turned twenty-six, I nearly cried. Two lieutenant commanders and a commander, all navy jet pilots with outstanding reputations, who barely knew me, each gave me outstanding marks, and said, among other things, that I had unlimited potential as a commissioned officer. They said I had leadership potential! I could tell by their comments that they had thoroughly reviewed my service record and my application. They didn't care what color the guy who maintained their plane or rescued them was; what mattered to them was performance.

Now I needed a decent recommendation from the commodore. Would he kill this dream? After waiting six long weeks I was in for a big surprise. I was almost afraid to read it when I got it. He said that I would make a resoundingly successful naval officer and that I was most strongly recommended for promotion. I was on my way! Alas, I was not selected. The competition was stiff. I was told unofficially that I was senior enough to apply but too junior to get selected and that I had too many college credits. Overqualified and underexperienced, I was an outlier among outliers. My résumé was a tad unusual.

I kept going to school and considered my shrinking options. During my two internships for my bachelor's degree, I worked with the local community college and also at the local IBM office. The department dean was very encouraging and even tried to fix me up with one of the ladies working in his office. No such luck. The manager at IBM's entry-level marketing program strongly suggested that I apply for a job, and told me with a big smile that he was the one who determined who got hired for that position. I was nearing the end of my enlistment. I decided to try for a commission one more time. I finished my four-year degree requirements and notified Lieutenant Peterson.

Soon after, before I had even officially received my degree, I walked into my office to find almost the entire staff waiting for me. On the table were a big nicely decorated sheet cake, a card, and a nicely wrapped present. Inside the wrapping was a little desk set with a little gold jet (a nice touch) and a brass plaque that included an engraved note of congratulations. Inside the card was another message of congratulations, and every staff member had signed it, even the master chiefs. That was the sweetest cake I ever tasted. The card said, "All of us sincerely hope the future years will bring success in all you choose to do and the best of everything." They were happy I was on their team. What more could I ask for? I had landed in a welcoming village. I never experienced even a hint of racism while I was there. They had enlightened and outstanding leadership.

I next applied for a commission through the navy's Officer Candidate School in Newport, Rhode Island. I decided that if I didn't get accepted—now I had a bachelor's degree and nine years of service—it would be time for me to move on and accept that maybe there wasn't room in the officer ranks for a guy like me. But one year after I had been turned down for limited duty officer (and, before that, the navy's Enlisted Commissioning Program), I was on my third attempt to become a naval officer, on my way to Officer Candidate School. I was going to be an officer of the line, if I could successfully complete the curriculum.

I could feel the genuine pride from the people I worked with, and I received many heartfelt congratulations. This was my first real exposure to members of the naval aviation community, and I have always maintained a profound respect for them and what they do. They worked hard and apparently played hard; I think it's because more than anyone in the navy, to me at least, they lived with more constant danger.

During the year I was at Cecil Field, we lost many aircraft but also several pilots, including a couple of aviators who died in a collision on the airstrip right outside my office. Some of these men were there one day, laughing and talking, and then gone forever. I would read the mishap investigation reports when they came through my office for review and action. This experience would be very helpful to me a few years later. After a brief stint at Attack Squadron Thirty-Seven, a squadron at Cecil Field, I was off to Officer Candidate School. The navy had decided to give me a chance.

I did not know how rare this selection was, and I was too excited to care. I was determined to succeed. I believe that, to more than any other single person, I may owe my chance at commissioned service to a navy doctor, whose name I don't remember, but who took a chance on me. I didn't quite meet the minimum visual acuity requirements to attend Officer Candidate School. My eyesight was very close but not quite there. I wasn't wearing those big glasses as a fashion statement.

When he saw my disappointment, he looked hard at me, conspiratorially, and fudged just a little bit. Was he toying with me? This was the only incident I can say with absolute certainty in my career that was "maybe" affirmative action—unofficially, anyway. I certainly received much help and received many breaks because people wanted me to succeed. This doctor's decision was not formally sanctioned affirmative action, but one shipmate helping another. Was the doctor's evaluation an under-the-table push? I'm glad it happened because it changed my life forever. Why did he do it? God only knows. He had never laid eyes on me before, and he had never even looked into my service record. Maybe he felt the minor difference was just plain Mickey Mouse, like Zumwalt described in his memoir. One chapter he titled "Micky Mouse; Elimination Of." I'm sure Disney executives were not amused. That one decision changed my life. I never saw him again, but I'll never forget him or what he did.

I never had any eye problems as an officer. Another navy doctor gave me perfect vision later via radial keratotomy, after decades of me wearing glasses. He also fudged a bit on the rules to do it. My last navy doctor experience didn't end so well, decades later.

Just one little thing you do can make a dramatic difference in someone's life, positive or negative. Try a good word, a nice card, a little rule-breaking here and there. Remember this story when you're looking at some hardworking, ambitious kid who may need just a little help to achieve what seems like an impossible goal. He or she doesn't know it's impossible, so don't ruin it for that individual before he or she can accomplish it anyway. That person will always remember what you did or didn't do to help. If you're a bully, you may eventually encounter someone you'll never forget. Tearing down the weak is easy. So is being human Wonder Bread, helping build strong minds and bodies. Be a dream maker, not a dream killer. You had dreams once too. Let the young people's futures be full of good surprises when they look back on it—and yours too.

6

Officer Candidate School, Surface Warfare Officer (Basic) School, and Communications Officer School

I had almost achieved the commissioning goal I set for myself. My first enlisted evaluation said that I had officer potential. I was feeling pretty proud that I now had a chance to prove it. Had it not been for people who encouraged and supported me along the way, it would not have happened.

My mother died suddenly in 1983, shortly after I was selected for Officer Candidate School (OCS). I had taken my housemate and younger sister, Tina, to Tennessee to visit my mother for the weekend. I was to get married in a couple of months, to my mother's best friend's only child, Cynthia. It was a long-term wish for both mothers. This dream marriage lasted eight months. It never should have happened: wrong reasons, different expectations, and the wrong time.

When we returned to Jacksonville, Florida, that Sunday evening, my phone was ringing. My mother had suffered a brain aneurysm about thirty minutes after we left her house. Family members tried to contact us before we left town and had also notified the Tennessee and Georgia highway patrols to be on the lookout for us. A patrolman stopped us a few hours later and gave Tina a speeding ticket but said nothing about my mother. I tried to stand up and stretch my legs, and the Georgia state trooper shouted for me to stay in the car. I did.

After learning what had happened, I took a shower and drove, starting at midnight and not stopping until seven thirty the next morning. What was usually a nine-hour trip had taken Tina and me much less time. That little Volvo did us proud.

My mother never regained consciousness, but all five of her children prayed over her as she lay dying in the hospital. She lived long enough to learn that her son was going to be a naval officer, something my sailor father never knew. She was forty-seven. Neither of my parents lived to age fifty. I'm still amazed that I lived long enough to get my first social security check. The effects of stress are cumulative. Ask a doctor or a veteran.

By now, Bill Goss was a naval aviator, a lieutenant. He had gotten his wings of gold a few years before. Years later, he would tell me by telephone how he had snuck into the private office of a captain in charge of pilot training to plead his case and ask for his help. He had been dropped from flight training because of continuing airsickness. He got a second chance after a week of specialized training to help him overcome his problem. When I thought about this, I realized that sometimes the white guys needed a little help too. Both of our lives would have been different had not a number of people helped us achieve our goals.

Initially, OCS was like boot camp, but the classes were a lot harder. In my company, there were about four other minorities, including a female Puerto Rican petty officer who showed up and checked in with a handgun. She was pretty much marked for OCS failure at that point.

After all the pleasantries were over in the first week or so, we had to meet with the company commander. Mine, a female lieutenant, asked if I was interested in a leadership position. I said, "Yes, I'd like to be the company commander." She frowned and quickly informed me that she already had someone in mind for this job and wanted to know if I was interested in any other position. I thought about asking to be the mascot but decided that might mark me as a troublemaker. I said no.

I thought she might be like some of the people who had screwed with me before, based on her nonverbal cues. I started plotting my revenge, thinking about starting a race riot (I'd seen it done). She foiled my plans. The guy chosen was movie star handsome, talented, and Black.

Eric Rivers was, to quote former vice president Joe Biden on Obama, "clean and articulate." He was also a talented artist, and I couldn't draw a decent stick figure. I forgave Eric for not knowing a damn thing about the military and for being prettier than I was. We became good friends. I did everything I could to help him succeed, and he listened. But of course, he made his own decisions. He was a good choice. Through this event, I had it reinforced in my mind that not everything that might appear to be racist is. Sometimes, you have to give people a chance to show where they're coming from.

Besides the company commander situation, there was one thing that had been bothering me since arriving at OCS, or really since being accepted months prior: the celestial navigation exam. Every time I tried to understand the navigation explanations in the welcome-aboard packet, I got a headache.

I wasn't stupid, but I just couldn't get it. The celestial navigation portion of the course teaches students how to navigate by the stars with a sextant and books of star data, an essential skill for a professional mariner. Failure to master this skill would disqualify me from commissioning. Once I started this course, I studied the materials intensely to learn it. I made three-by-five notecards and memorized all the rules and terms, and still, I failed the first celestial navigation exam. I had never before failed a navy exam. Embarrassed and demoralized, I had to attend "stupid study."

Of course, that was not its official name, but that's what we, the students, called it. When I got to stupid study, I was in for a surprise. So many people had flunked that exam that they had to hold "reeducation" in the auditorium. I looked around and saw people who had never failed an exam. They looked just as embarrassed and scared as I felt. They had no excuse, with their quality educations.

I rewrote my incorrect three-by-five cards and buckled down some more. I dreamed about celestial navigation. I scored a perfect 100 on the next exam, and boy was I happy. I wasn't yet proficient, but I knew I could at least understand it. For the final exam, we did a day's work in celestial navigation. This lengthy exam separated the washouts from the survivors. If an individual didn't pass this exam, they got to spend more time with family or went straight to the fleet as an enlisted person. By now, I was doing celestial navigation in my sleep. Even my nocturnal emissions looked as if they had been plotted.

I happily zipped through the exam until almost the very end, and then my final plotted fix wasn't right. I was supposed to have a nice running fix, having advanced a sun line (trust me, you don't need to know any more), but I didn't. No matter how hard I stared at it, I couldn't see the way to fix the plot. I felt this sinking feeling in the pit of my stomach and started getting dizzy. I didn't have time to go back and redo my work. I had been so careful and confident up to this point. I kept staring, but the damn thing would not fix itself. Everything started getting blurry. I heard a loud splash and then another. Then I noticed that there were wet spots growing on my plot. I reached up and touched my face; it was covered with sweat. I was about to pass out right there on the chart.

I had worked for a decade for this, and a stupid line was going to take it all away from me. This was bullshit! Did they still use this stupid stuff? What about satellites? I felt that after all this hard work, I was going to go home in disgrace. I got up and asked if I could go to the restroom before I also pissed my pants. One of the instructor-monitors followed me in, perhaps on the suicide-prevention squad. As I was emptying my bladder, I decided that it wasn't the end of the world, and maybe I should just go back and look at things one more time. I splashed some water on my face and went back, hoping for a miracle.

As soon as I sat down, I saw the problem. My last mark should have been made perpendicular to the way it was. A single error had nearly derailed my officer career. I had let the panic cloud my brain, and the fear of failure was so strong that I couldn't think. I passed. Remember to take a deep breath and a leak if possible when you hit a rough spot. You can think more clearly with an empty bladder.

Much more than celestial navigation was new to me at OCS. Having never served on a ship, I paid close attention to the shipboard organization, afloat damage control and maintenance requirements, and the engineering classes. The weapons, defensive equipment, and tactics and communications classes were also of great interest. I had a pretty quick grasp of the engineering material because it appealed to my logical brain.

Another interesting topic was the maneuvering board classes. Figuring out how to close the distance to a contact of interest was something I had been doing since high school; only the contacts in those days had breasts or, at least, stirrings of them. I had previously never quite realized that this was something you could graph out on a piece of paper. I was mesmerized. I already knew how to open the distance between me and an undesirable contact. I had been practicing that since elementary school.

In OCS, we had to do peer rankings to help the staff determine the top performers and who was potentially unsuitable for commissioned service. Instinctively, I hated this idea. I, with a bit of paranoia, had concerns about these subjective rankings. My past experience with the subjective judgments of others worried me. Was an officer candidate able to judge the potential of another? Would they use subjective or objective criteria? Would personal prejudices or grudges impact their rankings? Were we doing the staff's dirty work? I had reasons to be concerned. I was vocal about not "bilging" your shipmates.

Much to my surprise, I was ranked the number-one officer candidate at each of these rankings. It was truly humbling and gratifying to me. This was much better than being the mascot. I was not the smartest, I assure you. I wasn't even in the top half. If rater bias existed, it worked in my favor. I think they saw how hard I worked to make sure we were successful and that I wanted everyone to be successful. I knew what it was like to have a subjective judgment derail your opportunities. I was determined not to let that happen to anyone else if I could help it. Perhaps some of the leadership classes I taught rubbed off on me. Maybe it was the game I invented during lectures we would sometimes have in the auditorium.

During every lecture, I would break out a piece of paper and start making groups of five slashes as the lecture proceeded. Eventually, people found out that I was keeping track of the number of "uhs" the speaker would utter. That remedial instructor training good old Master Chief Davy sent me to had somehow stuck. The number was sometimes astronomical. The more marks on the page, the sooner we could get the hell out of there. We'd have singles (uh), doubles (uh, uh), triples (uh, uh, uh), and the very popular and highly anticipated inside the park home run quadruples (uh, uh, uh, uh)! If you listened closely, you could hear the not-so-silent roar of the crowd on that one.

These clowns sitting around me would keep looking over my shoulder or asking for the count, all the while snorting, giggling, wheezing, cursing admiringly, or gasping like the juvenile asses they were and making cash bets on the final tally. I couldn't believe it, gambling at important moments like this. It got very distracting sometimes; occasionally, the speaker would look over at the guys around me, pleased to have their full attention, but I never lost concentration. And I never missed an "uh." I can't recall a single word any of them said, except "uh." So, uh, remember this when, uh, you have to uh, uh, speak to a group of, uh, juveniles. They may be listening more closely than you, uh, think.

OCS taught me that I could hold my own with some of the smartest guys I had ever known. They were smarter, but I had experience and common sense. I wasn't afraid to speak up for what was right. I wasn't afraid to work hard. I knew you could succeed even if you were afraid. I knew that you sometimes had to swallow stuff that you knew was wrong. And I knew that if you work hard, do your best, and speak the truth, people will respect you. Usually. Come to think of it, I had been learning all of this since I joined the navy. I think I was just finally starting to believe it.

When I graduated from OCS, I was a happy man. I graduated with a final grade point average of 3.564, a decent B average—almost as well as Mineman A School! It would have been higher if I'd gotten credit for the right answers that they marked as wrong in the naval administration portion of the curriculum. That is my objective opinion, having shown them the correct answers in the directives I taught while I was such a "sucky" instructor when I worked for Master Chief Davy. I was in fact a subject matter expert on naval administration, but that didn't matter to them. I had three As, seven Bs, and two Cs. I assure you, every nuclear power student had a higher average than that. My class standing was 205 out of 320. The picture I took for graduation, my first-ever officer picture, is a picture of the happiest ensign ever to walk the earth, although not the smartest. All you can see is hair, beard, teeth, and big glasses. After OCS, I attended the Surface Warfare Officer Basic

Course and the Communications Officer Afloat Course. I also attended the Communications Cryptographic Materials Security Course (CMS).

When I graduated from the Surface Warfare Officer Basic Course, four or so months later, we had a rear admiral guest speaker, Jeremy M. Boorda. I was not listening too attentively, so I don't remember much of what he said. He didn't use any uhs, so there was no point in paying too much attention. I was dreaming about making captain. I did know that he was enthusiastic, and he was very encouraging. I noticed something else, reading his biography in the program. He had been a petty officer first class, just as I had! A former personnelman! A Tit-less WAVE, just like me! He was living proof of the future Admiral Nimitz had predicted decades before, when he addressed a class at the US Naval Academy, that many future admirals would not have graduated from that institution. Boorda had not attended the Naval Academy. Maybe I too would someday be an executive assistant to the chief of naval operations, as he was. He did it!

Rear Admiral Boorda was probably in his twilight tour, I thought, and he had more than enough reasons and medals to be proud. He had clearly done the nearly impossible; it was time for him to go fishing or something. I'm sure his son, who I'm pretty certain was one of my classmates, was proud to look up and see his father, if that in fact was him. I'm sure the father looked forward to the day when his own two sons, both military officers, would make flag rank. That's how these things tended to work.

My mood sobered when I started attending the CMS school. This school caused me many near-sleepless nights and anxious days. The humorless, grim-faced instructors scared the hell out of us, trying to impress on us that one innocent mistake could get us sent to prison. What happened next was truly dreadful. Near graduation, the FBI arrested a spy, and both the navy and the secretary of defense were in full damage control mode. Retired chief warrant officer John A. Walker, a former CMS custodian himself, had been busily betraying both his navy and his country by selling highly classified documents, equipment, and cryptographic material to the Soviet Union for more than seventeen years.

Secretary of the Navy John Lehman ordered tighter security requirements and procedures in all navy units and strict adherence to the two-man rule for destruction of most classified material. He directed an immediate reduction in security clearances, with a goal of a 10 percent reduction. This was not a good time to be a brand-new CMS custodian. The chief of naval operations at the time, Admiral James Watkins, ordered that any CMS custodian who had been serving before a certain date be relieved immediately. I missed the cutoff by five days. For the next few years, meticulous attention to detail would mean the difference between professional survival and prison or other harsh punishment for mishandling of highly classified top secret material and equipment. I'd spend the next two years daily worried and stressed.

En route to my first ship, despite the trepidation I felt regarding the handling of highly classified materials and the pitfalls that might occur because of that, I nevertheless thought about my past and how lucky I was. My father was wrong, I thought. The "navy" was not racist, even though discrimination and prejudice existed here like everywhere else. I was living proof that a minority sailor could come from the most unlikely circumstances to a position of great authority and respect in the navy, such as an ensign. I, as a surface warfare officer, an officer of the line, would be eligible for command at sea. I wondered which ship they would ultimately name after me and how long it would take for me to make captain. I had to make up for lost time.

At that time, the Black officer percentage had risen from 0.7 percent in 1970 to 3.5 percent, an average 0.2 percent increase per year. I did my part, but many others did a lot more. I had no way of knowing it, but things were about to get a lot harder. I would soon come to know triumph and despair, success and failure, derision and respect.

I thought about my father often as I prepared to assume my place in the officer corps. I often wondered what advice he would have given had he lived to see me put on my shoulder boards. I wonder if he would have apologized to me for doubting that his navy was gone and that opportunities for ambitious young Black sailors and officers were at least available, if not abundant.

I doubt that my father ever worked for any navy supervisor who was not white. In his time, virtually the entire leadership structure of the navy was white and tilted to the southern states demographically, or so I have read. In addition to that, southerners had traditionally been assigned to supervise Black troops and sailors during World War II because they were considered to be "knowledgeable" about the care and feeding (and control) of Black sailors. They lived and worked in closer proximity to Blacks in the South, and northerners were more legally equal but just as segregated in the living arrangements and social hierarchy. This caused a lot of grief for the Black service members who served under them, especially those from the North.

As an officer, I would face problems my father never told me about but might have anticipated. I didn't know any of this yet; however, I had become a bit more seasoned, and I was going to sea for the first time with an open mind and a grateful heart for having the opportunity to serve my country as an officer of the line. I intended to make the people who helped me proud.

Ray holding Reggie, Reuben (far right), Dorothea (behind Ray), Robert (far left), circa 1966.

Author in fourth grade at Kit Carson Elementary School, San Diego, California.

Author's high school photo, Manchester, Tennessee, circa 1973.

Author as a mineman seaman in Charleston, South Carolina, Mobile Mine Assembly Group, 1976.

Author's future wife Ventris Giles (now Ventris Gibson, director, US Mint), preparing for a beauty contest at NAS Sigonella, Italy, circa 1976. She won first runner-up.

Ventris Green pregnant with son Alexander, Guantanamo Bay, Cuba, 1978.

Author and six-month-old son, Alexander, Guantanamo Bay, Cuba, 1979.

Author as discipline yeoman, Guantanamo Bay, Cuba, 1978.

Author receiving a performance award from Base Commander Captain David W. DeCook in Guantanamo Bay, Cuba, 1978.

Author receiving a performance award from Base Commander Captain (future vice admiral) John H. Fetterman Jr. in Guantanamo Bay, Cuba, 1979.

Base yeomen and personnel men and officers in Guantanamo Bay, Cuba, circa 1979.

The base administration department, Guantanamo Bay, Cuba, circa 1979.

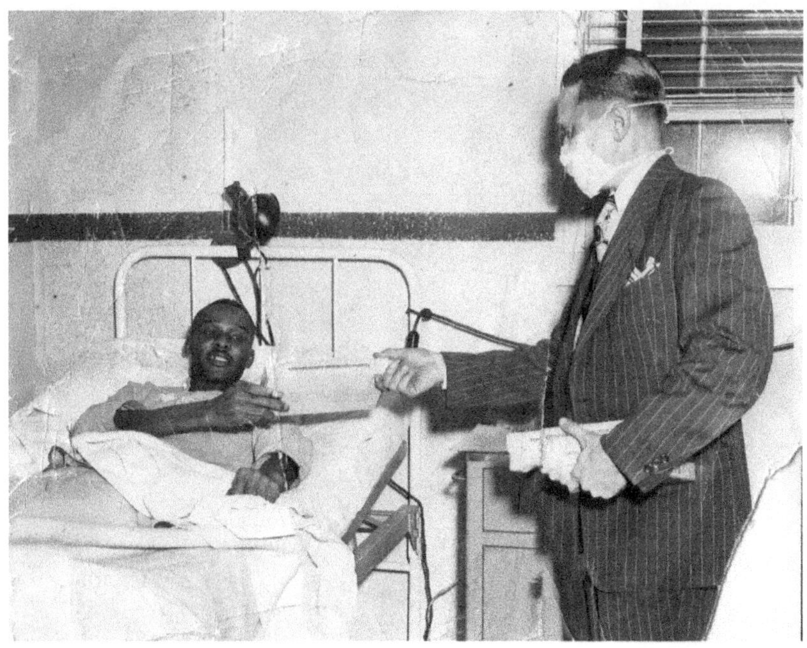

Grandfather Robert Green in a VA hospital in Nashville, Tennessee, circa 1947.

Author's father, Parker W. L. Green, as a third class petty officer, date unknown.

Author's father as boatswain's mate first class, US Navy. Note the army jump wings, a rarity for a sailor. Circa 1970–72.

Author's paternal grandmother, Lucille Daniels, in Clearwater, Florida, circa 1976.

Author's paternal grandfather, taken before military service, date unknown.

Author's father, Parker W. L. Green, while serving in the army, circa 1952–54.

Grandfather Robert Green, World War II, date unknown.

Author's graduating class photo, Defense Equal Opportunity Management Institute, 1980.

Officer Candidate School Papa Company class graduation photo, 1984.

Souvenir photo of USS *Voge* entering Curaçao for a port visit, circa 1986.

Author as executive officer on USS *Gemini*'s bridge, Key West, Florida, 1992.

Author at the start of his engineering department head tour on the USS *Boone*, FFG-28, in Mayport, Florida, circa 1989.

Author and wife Iris Green, stepdaughter Ramona Stallings, and stepson Roosevelt Stallings, 1989.

Author, Iris Green, Ramona Stallings, Roosevelt Stallings, Alex Green, Mickey, and Gidget (rescues), family housing, Newport, Rhode Island, 1988.

Author and Master Chief Dan Ziparo, in retirement, 1990s.

Author at StoryCorps mobile studio, Memorial Park, Jacksonville, circa 2018–19.

Author and Bill Goss, in retirement, at a Jacksonville University event, circa 2019.

Author the day he purchased a large, condemned "white elephant" house (1996) while clinically depressed before retirement. He still owns it.

Author speaking at Jacksonville University to students and faculty about his military experiences.

Author applying mosaic tile to a fountain he built as part of unofficial art therapy following retirement, before seeking VA treatment for moral injury and depression, 2003.

7

Communications Officer, USS *Voge*, the Steam Navy

For my first officer tour, I was assigned to a ship at Naval Station Mayport in Florida. The ship was USS *Voge* (FF-1047), pronounced to rhyme with "Bogey," not like the magazine *Vogue*. I'd been on many ships there, but I'd never slept in one. I officially reported on board for duty on the USS *Voge* on May 22, 1985. I was in my dress blue uniform, and I had my orders and my ID card in hand. The *Voge* was commissioned in 1966. It had pressure-fired boilers—steam at 1,200 pounds per square inch. A Soviet Echo II class guided missile submarine once struck the *Voge* in the Ionian Sea, near the island of Crete. Not many ships can claim that distinction, and none of them want to. By the time I reported aboard, it had seen better days. That didn't mean it wasn't expected to perform. And it did perform, but it wasn't easy.

My father would seldom have entered the wardroom on a navy ship; it would take a while before I felt I really belonged there. I may not have been a "real" enlisted sailor, but he sure as hell was. Maybe there was racism in his navy, but I was now an officer, and I was safe. Or so I thought. I had a house in Jacksonville, Florida, that I had bought on a weekend visit, and I enjoyed a few weeks' leave before I reported aboard. I called the ship and made arrangements with my sponsor to pick up my mail. I told him I would be there shortly and described what I was wearing: a pale yellow shirt (not too loud) and beige slacks.

When I got to the quarterdeck on the ship, I met the leading signalman of the USS *Voge*, Signalman First Class Scott Bell. We would work together for two years, and he was as good as they come. Once, when I asked him about something he forgot to do, I watched him try to split into two to go in different directions. It was comical. Upon retirement, he became a Jacksonville police officer. I would see him occasionally after we both retired, and we would laugh and smile as we talked. Good shipmates are forever. Sadly, he was killed by a drunk driver one night while driving his patrol car to meet his supervisor.

As I chatted with SM1 Bell, he learned that I would be his new boss. He seemed genuinely pleased. He was very helpful in talking about the ship, the schedule, and other topics. After a while, he asked me exactly whom I was waiting for. When I told him, he pointed and said, "That's Ensign Fahrney over there." He sent the messenger over to inform him that he had a visitor. I had been exchanging glances with this guy for a while, as I noticed him look to the quarterdeck occasionally. I knew before being told that he was the one I was waiting for, but I waited to see how things would play out. He apparently didn't see who he was looking for, despite my accurate description of my clothing.

When he walked over to meet his "visitor" and learned that I was the guy who had talked to him on the phone, he blurted out, "You're that guy?" Yes, I was. It had not occurred to him that the guy he had been talking to was Black. Linguistic profiling in reverse. Fooled them again. I knew how rare it was to see a Black officer in those days, but I didn't yet know how rare it was to be one of them. Lawrence "Larry" Fahrney and I would become good buddies. We both liked old cars—me Fords, him Chevys—we both owned houses, and we both were silly. Good match.

Within a few days, the twentieth of May arrest of infamous spy John Walker would begin placing a bright and uncomfortable spotlight on guys like me, and our jobs would immediately get much harder and much scarier. But first, I had to get past the quarterdeck. The officer of the deck looked me over suspiciously and looked over my official navy orders. He looked very closely at my identification card. He firmly asked me if I was a zulu five oscar. I wasn't sure what my ancestral tribal affiliation might have been, but I did know that the Zulus weren't typically captured and sold into slavery. I said no. I didn't know what the hell a Z5O was.

I learned fast, because I would be asked this question many, many times over the next few years. This was the unclassified code word or question that the officers of the deck (OODs) were required to ask anyone suspected of being an intruder who might be formally testing the security readiness of the ship. If, in fact, you were one, you had to fess up. If you weren't asked and you got past the quarterdeck, you were to report immediately to the commanding officer of that ship. When you did, somebody's ass was getting chewed out, starting with the OOD. It didn't usually stop there. The commanding officer would get his ass chewed later, I'm sure.

As Black officers were rare, it was perfectly logical to assume that any one of them who showed up on your quarterdeck might be a fake and trying to get the OOD's ass put in a sling, except for the fact that you weren't allowed to use fake identification. When faced with the choice of pissing off the Black officer standing in front of him whom he didn't know or have a legitimate reason to suspect and embarrassing the commanding officer that he did know and had a legitimate reason to fear, the OOD's choice was easy. This would happen whether I was alone or with other officers. I was the only one questioned as to my legitimacy. The results were painless—well, that is, except to the Black officer in question (i.e., me). The accumulated resentment, frustration, and embarrassment took their tolls, like having a no-shave chit. At some point, it ceased to be amusing. Their suspicion was really a sign of disrespect, and sometimes contempt, masquerading as due diligence.

Sometimes the OODs blatantly laughed as they asked me. They must have thought I was embarrassed at having to dress up like an officer and try to sneak on a ship, where everyone knew I'd be spotted as a fake immediately. I would sometimes reason with myself, telling myself that prejudice and bias had nothing to do with it. I've talked to enough Black officers to know that this was not my problem alone. No matter how impeccable my uniform or credentials were, my legitimacy was in doubt.

People always notice skin color and make judgments and decisions based on it. They may not be conscious of it, but it happens. Decades of research have documented this, and detailed scientific research is showing how this happens and how it affects us. More often than not, however, the Black officer is real. The threat is probably the guy you'd least expect, like John Walker. Treating everyone equally might be what saves your ass. For all the guys who get hassled at the airport, because they look (or don't look) like someone suspicious (think Muslim), you have my sympathy. For each of the three ships in which I served, I was asked this question as I reported for official duty. The more ribbons on my chest, the more suspicious it seemed I became. It was tiresome.

Voge had a lot of problems to overcome. I learned a lot about overcoming adversity during this tour. Within a few months of reporting aboard, we failed our operational propulsion plant exam (OPPE). This is a tough exam for any ship, but for one that's old, nearly obsolete, and difficult to maintain, it is even tougher to get through it.

My first skipper, Captain Paul Nils Johnson, sucked this one up. I've never seen a man look as tired and worn down as he did on this day. He didn't waste any time feeling sorry for himself. One of his first orders after we failed was to have the restricted men's muster and the officers' call at the same time and the same place. This was sending all of the officers a message. We passed our OPPE reexam. Not only that, we went on to win the Battle Effectiveness Award (the Battle "E"), the last pressure-fired boiler ship ever to do so. I was not to have much to do with engineering under

Captain Johnson's tour. The engineer officer requested after I'd been there a while to let me become his damage control assistant, but for reasons I'll discuss later, he said no. Captain Johnson didn't trust anyone with his communications material security (CMS) account but me.

My first executive officer (XO), Commander Dan Ryder—I think that was his name; he left soon after—showed that he was pulling for me. One day, early in my tour, he pulled me aside and told me that I didn't have to be as smart as any of the rest of the guys there. He told me that if I worked hard and did my job, I would do well. I wasn't particularly aware of demonstrating any lack of self-confidence, but maybe he could see it or just wanted me to succeed. I was to have some pretty tough competition in the peer category. *Voge* was top heavy in ensigns, and none of them had my cobbled-together résumé.

One was Ensign Eric Tapp, the top ensign threat. He was the boilers and machinery officer. We called him "the Nazi" behind his back, mostly out of jealousy. He's the only ensign I served with in my entire career (that I'm aware of) who went on to become an active-duty navy captain. Commander Ryder, to show his confidence in me or maybe to boost mine, assigned me to be the liaison officer for a visiting German frigate, the FGS *Bremen*.

I was busy trying to do my job, remember the difference between port and starboard, and learn my way back to my stateroom other than by happy accident. I had been aboard for only two months. In addition, I was not supposed to have any collateral duties as a CMS custodian, according to the chief of naval operations. I knew better by now than to show the XO the instruction that said so or request captain's mast to complain! Give it to Tapp, I thought; he looked like a Nazi. Everyone said so. I didn't want this German liaison job at all. I had seen enough war movies to know that Germans were scary, especially the ones in uniform. I tried to talk the exec out of sending me over there, to no avail. He insisted I was the man for the job.

So, in addition to my regular duties, I had to report to the *Bremen* early each morning and late each evening during the ship's two port visits. If they were surprised at my Blackness, it never showed. What did show was curiosity, but they were too polite to be too inquisitive. They could not have been nicer or more professional. I was constantly being invited on board for a beer, which they served in the wardroom daily. I always said "no thanks." We all learned something about each other, and maybe that was his reason for picking me, *Voge*'s only Black officer.

Commander Ryder also assigned me to assist in the homecoming festivities for an American ship that was returning from deployment. Once, when he saw that I was particularly tired, he gave me some really good advice. He said, "Son, nobody cares whether you've had enough sleep, so you be sure you get enough." I couldn't always do so. For the first assignment, I received a flag-level letter of commendation from Commodore Henry Mauz; for the second, I received a letter of commendation from my own commanding officer, Commander Johnson. Maybe the XO wasn't mad at me after all. Now I love Germans. I have experience.

I soon learned that I loved driving ships, and I got to be pretty good at it, thanks to the expert tutelage of Lieutenant Tom Anderson, my officer of the deck on most occasions, until I qualified myself. I relieved him as communications officer, and he served an additional period as the assistant navigator. He really helped me learn to drive the ship. The smell of the ocean and the feel of the spray on the bridge were things you never forget. I learned to maneuver the ship, make underway replenishment approaches, and run down contacts (close the distance to them) and to love every minute of it. I learned that chicken soup always came back up as a bright pink color when you vomited over the bridge wing or in a trash bag. I learned never to eat sloppy joes if I had the next bridge watch; they didn't agree with me.

We conducted lots of drug interdiction operations in the Caribbean, conducted a lot of small boat operations, and boarded civilian vessels to look for illegal drugs. I loved to grill my watch section on their performance qualifications because I learned something every time I did. They were often training me, but it looked the other way around. Nothing makes a young surface warfare officer happier than the apparent approval of his commanding officer when he does something right or well. The skipper did not miss much.

I was determined to make no significant mistakes; I checked and rechecked everything I was responsible for. External communications for the ship were often the only indication of how we performed our duties at sea. Sloppy communications could indicate sloppy performance and poor leadership. Once, while doing a CMS equipment inventory—required every six months for cryptographic equipment—I found some very difficult to spot, highly classified cryptographic equipment permanently installed in my radio shack that was not on any inventory list. When I called asking for guidance, I was asked how in the hell I had found this stuff and told to send a formal message detailing what I had found. It was not a normal occurrence. I was taking nothing for granted.

Disaster nearly struck anyway. My "you're that guy?" friend, the combat information center officer's people didn't take CMS as seriously as required. I had instilled the fear of God in my people, and they usually toed the line. Others, officers, chiefs and petty officers, did not and paid a steep price. I made a difficult but correct decision once when I was having trouble getting my radiomen to strictly follow the two-man rule concerning the cryptographic material safes.

I was always one of the last officers to leave the ship (this is a hint; I'm stomping my foot), and I would often pop into the radio shack before I left. On one specific occasion, I found something I really, really didn't like. I'm not saying it was a violation of the two-man rule for highly classified cryptographic material, and I'm not saying it wasn't. I am just saying I didn't like what I found. I went to the quarterdeck with a big paper bag I stuffed with innocuous things and ordered the OOD to call the duty radiomen to the quarterdeck. When they got there, I asked them to guess what was in the bag. I'm not saying it was highly classified material that they were supposed to have locked in the two-man control safe, and I'm not saying it wasn't. I can't recall. I have never seen two people melt in front of my eyes before, but I nearly did that day.

Of my two first class petty officer radiomen, one of them, Jan Harris, was selected as my ship's sailor of the year for the ship because of his strong performance, his excellent guidance and advice to me, and my written nomination. The other received a nonpunitive letter of caution from me after leaving the ship one too many times without checking with me before he left, usually on a Friday. This behavior started after he was promoted and moved into the chief's mess, where I assume they informed him that he was able to take some liberties that came with his new rank. Wrong.

After several warnings, I drafted a nonpunitive letter of caution with the assistance of the base legal services office and presented it to him on a Monday morning. It was full of hellfire and brimstone, explaining to him what would systematically happen if he persisted ignoring my direction. I told him that if he wanted to continue wearing those khakis, he better start acting like I was wearing them too. His hands shook as he read the letter. I didn't have any more unauthorized absences after that letter burned his fingers a bit. After that, we got along pretty well.

I got along quite well with the junior radiomen and the signalmen. Some of us were pretty close in age, and I made a point to try to make them feel at ease. I wanted them to be comfortable with me and to feel free to talk to me about any problems they might have. Many of them were Black and Hispanic. I think they were proud to have a competent minority officer lead them, giving them something they could aspire to. Representation matters.

I once interrupted an arm-wrestling contest they were having while in port and loudly announced that I could beat any man there. After much trash-talking on both sides, the biggest radioman, who was Black, accepted the challenge. I, of course, kicked his butt, delighting the few who bet against him. I did not write any report chits for unauthorized gambling. One of the white electronic technicians then challenged me. He was about my size. We went at it for a good while, and he finally pinned me, but only because I had a mild brain seizure and a momentary loss of juice when I remembered that I hadn't yet turned in my spot checks to the XO. That's the way I remember it.

My leading chief radioman, senior chief Gerald Thomas, was a good and talented man; the radio shack belonged to him, and the division belonged to me. I knew he knew that because he told me so not long after I arrived. I was smart enough to know a good deal when I saw one, so I took it. When we disagreed, he would sit me down and explain a few things to me, and I would usually fall back on our original agreement. There is a good reason why chiefs are called the backbone of the navy. Senior chief Thomas had backbone to spare, and he didn't mind showing it.

Once, I had a very loud public shouting match with my leading signalman, Scott Bell, on the signal bridge. He was in a foul mood, and we went at it about something; I don't remember what. We were the same age. Because this was so out of character for him, I eventually just walked away, leaving him to whatever was bothering him, besides me. He soon found me and apologized, and I forgot about it. There was no need to hold this man to a standard that I sometimes myself did not meet. He was one of my best men, and even the best can be shaky at times. I know I was.

I learned in this tour to scrounge and scavenge, officially. I read the ship's instruction binders just for fun and learned a lot. I went to the Defense Reutilization and Material Office (DRMO) on base one day on my lunch break and obtained a bunch of equipment and furniture that we could use on the ship. It was free, like welfare; the instruction said so! When the trucks rolled up with all that stuff, I felt like "Ensign Claus." Lots of it was brand-new surplus equipment that other commands had bought to avoid future budget cuts. This was wasteful but sometimes necessary due to the apparent insanity of wasteful government regulations. Don't let this get out.

We outfitted the operations office and shared with other departments. I got expensive new treads for several shipboard ladders. They looked great during zone inspections. I documented how much money I had saved the ship, and it was a huge ($70,000). The skipper, the XO, and my department head were extremely happy, but I was teased endlessly for being a brown-noser by the rest of the junior officers, which technically was true. My nose was brown. The teasing stopped after the fitness reports came out. I wasn't the smartest, but I was doing the best-est.

When Commander Ryder transferred, I was grateful that he got me started off on the right foot. My next XO on *Voge* was a little tougher to work for. Technically, he was brilliant, but he had an explosive temper. I watched him angrily strike an enlisted man once, on the shoulder, on the ship's bridge, essentially having a hissy fit while we were at sea-and-anchor detail. He did so because the man had requested emergency leave because his wife and the mother of young children had suddenly taken very ill and was hospitalized, and she had no local support for childcare.

I was appalled. This young Black man needed help—not verbal and physical abuse. Early in his tour as CNO, while touring bases and talking with young sailors, Admiral Zumwalt had ordered an immediate transfer for a young man who was in a similar situation, and this young man was Black also. Another sailor stepped in front of the admiral as he was leaving and said to him, "Thank you, sir, for treating us like people." Respect is a two-way street and should be added to the navy's core values.

I don't believe that this XO was racist, just volatile. However, his assault didn't just look bad; it was also illegal. He helped me immensely in obtaining my surface warfare qualifications, and he was an excellent navigator, with an excellent sense of humor. But when he blew his temper, it was legendary. We called him LRMF: little redheaded. . . . You know the rest. I liked and respected LRMF, but I would sometimes pull his chain, gently. Admit it: given the chance, wouldn't you like to poke a sleeping grizzly bear with a long stick, at least once?

One day we were standing at officers' call, and he walked up looking agitated and asked me if I had a paper clip. Why me and no one else, I'll never know. I reached into my pocket and handed him one. Naturally, the rest of the guys started needling me, asking me how in the hell did I "just happen" to have a paper clip and why he had specifically asked me. If I could get seventy thousand dollars' worth of free stuff, surely I might have a paper clip. Using my best James Earl Jones voice, I solemnly informed them that "the very best officers always have a paperclip." My word, the way they reacted, you would have thought I had just claimed to be the Messiah.

While they all stood on one foot and howled like wounded puppies, laughed, or said some very bad and uncalled-for things about me, I kept a straight face, as befitted someone so wise and foresighted, and stared at LRMF, who now had a twinkle in his eyes and this look on his face that said, "Well, you cheeky bastard, you just slammed all of us, including me, and don't think I don't know it." His fearsome reputation would not allow him to crack a smile, but he almost did. I was stupidly playing with fire, and I knew it. If anyone could teach me some humility, he was the one.

I like to imagine that he and the skipper had a good laugh about the paper clip incident when he told him about it later. I am equally sure that there were a lot more paper clips in officers' pockets after that. Every opportunity I got to stand out, without showboating, I took. Funny how something as small as a paper clip can help break you out from the pack. I would eventually feel LRMF's full wrath unleashed, and it was one of the most memorable, humiliating, and fascinating experiences of my life, a true "significant emotional event."

It happened after we had conducted a burial at sea. The ashes of a young Hispanic enlisted man were in an appropriate container in the chiefs' mess. (My father had also been buried at sea, by fellow sailors.) During this official ceremony, everything was completely professional, solemn, and dignified, as always. We recorded a video for the family.

The problem came afterward. Somehow, the short routine burial confirmation message had been either destroyed or misplaced after LRMF had dropped it off in the radio shack for transmission. I had picked it up, read it, and put it back on the shredder where it was waiting to be typed (bad idea), or someone had accidentally shredded it. If anyone knew what happened to it, they were too terrified to say.

I did know that I wasn't going to let any of the radiomen take the heat for this. They were scared shitless of the wrath of LRMF and for good reason. So was I, but I had to face it. It had been a stressful day, and one of his legendary blowups was just one mistake away. Woe unto him who made it. It looked like my number was up. I rewrote the short message from memory as best I could and, full of dread, went to find him. He was on the bridge. The skipper wasn't there; it would have been better for me if he had been.

I tried to hand the message to LRMF and explain the situation, telling him that I had partially re-created it and needed him to fill in the blanks and release it for transmission. We'd done similar short messages before, and they were no big deal. So began the most awful, absolute worst, vein-bulging, spittle-slinging, profanity-inventing, and combination stress-inducing and relieving ass chewing I've ever had in my entire life, and I took it like a man. For a while.

When I sensed him winding down, I tried to hand him the message again, repeated that I was sorry, and asked him to please fill in the blanks and sign it. He kept asking (screaming at) me questions I could not readily answer, like why I was so fucking completely, unrelentingly stupid. Just luck, I guess. This happened at least three times, as he caught his stride and his breath. He was getting a real workout. I could feel my manhood hovering near the point of no return. I wanted to whip a paper clip out of my pocket and stick it in his pressure release valve. (I had some.)

It was deathly silent on the bridge, with watch standers trying very hard to not let the rage-blind, angry red monster notice they were also there. This was a rerun. I forced myself to remain stoic and outwardly emotionless as if I were observing this tirade rather than absorbing it. I was determined to maintain my dignity, if I could. If you've never seen a true screamer in action, it is truly an awesome sight to behold. This man once burst a blood vessel in his eye while screaming at a young sailor. I saw it happen. Now that's passion!

Anyway, he finally snatched the message from my hand and left the bridge. In all this time, he had not even bothered to read it.

Like an idiot, and still probably nearly in shock, I followed him out the door after a moment. I stupidly froze when I saw him standing outside the combat information center (CIC), really looking at the message for the very first time. Even more stupidly, I again apologized. He looked up, glared at me and snarled, "Mister, you better get your fucking head out of your ass," and walked into the CIC. That's when my head spun around three times, and I became an Angry Black Man! I didn't have time to change into my outfit, but the transformation was complete. My abuse meter had redlined. I'd had enough. Where I grew up, it was ass whuppin' time.

I followed him into CIC cursing like a sailor. I don't remember what I said, but it's nothing my grandmother would have been proud of—my father, the sailor, maybe, but not my grandma. I know what my mouth feels like when I'm cursing up a blue streak, even if I can't remember what exactly I've said. It feels like there is a small rancid skunk turd rolling around in my mouth, and I'm angrily trying to spit it out. I didn't have hands anymore; I had fists. I may have appeared a tad disrespectful.

LRMF instantly understood that I had transformed into someone he wasn't quite comfortable with, because he quickly turned around, held his hand up to my face, as if to stop me from abusing him, and quietly said, "Don't say anything more, you've said too much already." Strangely, he didn't seem angry anymore. It was almost as if he'd said, "You're overreacting. You go calm down, and we'll discuss this after you've considered the ramifications of your actions." He turned around and calmly walked out the rear door.

When I could finally see something other than red, I looked around. The entire CIC watch team was staring at me, dumbfounded, like I had a shotgun in my mouth and was about to pull the trigger. Everyone was afraid to move, or speak, and I didn't blame them. Had I really just done that? Were we near the Bermuda Triangle or something? Strange shit was starting to happen. I was probably looking just as stunned as they were, and I'm sure they thought they were looking at a dead man walking. They had not seen the abuse I had endured on the bridge moments before. They had also never seen anyone curse out the XO before. Come to think of it, neither had I.

There was this foul smell in the air, and I didn't know if it was from the filth that had spewed from my mouth or because we had collectively crapped all over ourselves. I wasn't quite as angry when I saw the looks on their faces. Exactly what had I just said? To this day, I still don't know. I left without a word. How could I explain to them what had just happened? My career was surely over. In the Black community, only the weakest and most timid men will allow themselves to be verbally abused or browbeaten so savagely without responding.

It is better to take an ass whuppin,' if you have to, than let someone talk trash to you like that without responding. There is no shame in getting your ass whipped; there is much shame in passively letting someone publicly emasculate you. I'd seen young men push back quasi-respectfully at captain's mast, and it always ended badly for them. I admired them for speaking the truth. Even the strong sometimes respect a person who speaks up for himself. I had responded based on my cultural upbringing, not my military training. Perhaps he had too. Where had he learned to do this? Later, I would be able to take an ass chewing from the best of them. I would learn as I went along. Seldom was it necessary.

A short while later, my department head, Lieutenant Jack Federoff, came and found me. He told me that the XO had told him to "counsel" me, that I was "too sensitive." Apparently, LRMF was offended at being the subject of verbal abuse. Imagine that! Where I came from, when someone talked to you like he had talked to me, they were getting ready to kick your ass, and you'd better get ready, or take action. My fight-or-flight reflex had kicked in, and I was in no mood for an ass whipping.

Lieutenant Federoff would later also have an ugly incident with LRMF. It would occur on the quarterdeck, in view of a large percentage of the crew. I teased him later that he was trying to "act Black." I also counseled him in return, saying, "Jack, you can't be cussing out the XO on the quarterdeck. Remember when you counseled me for cussing him out in CIC, saying that I was too sensitive and I was setting a bad leadership example? Remember that?" We both had a good laugh about it decades later.

People can take this kind of abuse for only so long. Sometimes they take it, sometimes they shut down or quit, and sometimes they lose it. Never bully anyone. No one deserves to be mistreated while serving his or her country by the officers and supervisors appointed above them. If you're being mistreated, you have options. Know what they are. Confidence and being right are your best defenses. Having a little backbone helps too.

Ultimately, LRMF transferred and went to a plum but challenging job, with a warning from an admiral to do well or suffer the consequences: the engineer officer on a US Navy battleship. I heard a rumor that one night, a harbor craft had pulled alongside his battleship as it lay at anchor, idled there for a while, and then slowly departed. LRMF was on it. He had been relieved for cause, after suffering verbal and physical abuse himself, from his XO. LRMF would die of a heart attack after he retired. If you want to know exactly what happened, as told by some of the people who were actually there, I recommend you read *A Glimpse of Hell: The Explosion on the USS* Iowa *and Its Cover-Up*, by Charles C. Thompson II. I quote the following from page 46, to save you some time:

> Fahey accused Ware of being incompetent, pointing to the fuel spill. He said Ware was incapable of leading anyone and had endangered the lives of the crew and crippled the ship at sea while she was in the Middle East. The executive officer liberally laced his accusations with profanity and expletives. Finally, Ware had had enough. "I'm tired of your bullshit!" he shot back. Fahey sprang from his seat and snatched the much smaller chief engineer by the collars of his shirt. Fahey shook Ware like a rag doll and smacked him several times. Kimberlain stood by and did nothing.

What happened before and after this incident is equally disturbing. As I read this paragraph for the first time, and each time thereafter, I couldn't help but wonder if Ware (LRMF) ever realized that he was being treated in much the same way he had himself treated his own subordinates in his *Voge* XO tour. I wondered if he regretted his behavior, having experienced the same treatment himself. At one juncture in the book, he is described as shaken, with his hands quivering uncontrollably. I also wonder what might have happened if he had stood up for himself as soon as this abuse began. He might have kept his job.

I have found that the best way to stop your hands from shaking is to make them into fists. LRMF helped me learn that lesson. I have also found that the best way to keep your knees from shaking, when confronting a bully, is to use those fists, if necessary. Sometimes, you have to show people that you demand to be treated with respect. This is risky, but it worked for me. Usually.

I was doing a good job in my regular duties, but I was greedy. I wanted to get my qualification as engineer officer of the watch (EOOW). This would give me a leg up on my competition for promotion and assignment. The communications officer/CMS custodian was not expected to obtain his EOOW qualifications in his first billet, particularly if he was not assigned to the engineering department.

Secretary of the Navy John Lehman was pushing to build a six-hundred-ship navy, and he was going to need good officers to man it. Captain Johnson promised me I could move to engineering as soon as he was relieved. When Captain Johnson was relieved, Commander James D. Barton happily and enthusiastically assumed command.

Commander Jim Barton loved to drive his ship, and he loved even more to let junior officers try their hand and show their stuff. He was a great ship handler and a great skipper. After a suitable honeymoon period, I asked to be assigned to the engineering department; the chief engineer asked for me again also. This would make it easier for him to kick my ass, and he had earlier threatened to do so because of a memo I'd written to him. He could do it, easily. This was a guy I wanted to work for. Barton promptly informed me that as long as he was the skipper of that ship, I was going to be his CMS custodian. He said it with a smile, as I remember.

Apparently, he thought his career was more important than my unrealistic ambitions. Can't say I blame him. I never did. We'd had a surprise CMS account inspection sometime before that. The legendary master chief Radioman Boatwright, the squadron communications officer, conducted these inspections. He was like a god, a communications god. You admired him and feared him—for good reason. If he wasn't happy, you could get fired. If he was really not happy, you could go to prison. Not jail, prison. The big house. With your own special boyfriend. Guys had been immediately relieved because of the results of his inspections. My number finally came up.

I was standing watch on the quarterdeck as OOD. Master Chief Boatwright showed up and told me to have myself relieved because he was there to do a surprise CMS inspection. I laughed. He didn't. Oh, shit. When we got to the vault, I told him it was completely OK if he wanted to smoke. He didn't. For the first and only time in my entire life, I wanted a cigarette.

A few hours later, he had gone over every aspect of my account with a fine-tooth comb and a magnifying glass. Every now and then, as people would scurry past the vault, he would grunt, slap the side of one of the safes, and yell out, "Who's your daddy, girl?" I would dutifully groan and cry out in my best Michael Jackson voice, "You are, Master Chief Boatwright!" It was very embarrassing, but I didn't care. I did what I had to do to survive. Unless you've ever been a CMS custodian, you have absolutely no right to laugh. You can't possibly understand. You can't handle the truth!

When he was finished, he asked me to take him to the skipper. I'm sure the skipper was having a fit, wondering if he was about to get relieved. Master Chief Boatwright discussed his findings with the skipper. Then Boatwright told him that *Voge* had the best CMS account in the entire Mayport basin, with zero discrepancies. I was not going to jail. This sealed my fate.

Here I began to learn how to fit effectively into wardroom life. It was sometimes difficult being surrounded by guys with whom you didn't share a lot of common personal experiences. We didn't share musical interests, we were attracted to different women, and our cultural upbringings were different. It was often vividly apparent while we were watching the news. Some poor Black guy would be getting wailed on by the police on television—Rodney King, for instance—and we would often see things very differently, if anyone dared to venture an opinion or comment.

Something bad would happen in the United States, and TV people would dutifully interview the most inarticulate, inappropriately dressed person to give the blow-by-blow description of what had happened. You know the people I'm talking about. Colorful. Earthy. Embarrassing. Inarticulate. It would be much easier for me to laugh when these people were not Black. When the person was white, perhaps at the trailer park, it did not reflect on the guys sitting around the room with me. When the person was Black, maybe at the projects, somehow, it always did reflect on me, or I felt that it did. I finally understood my mother and grandmother saying, "Lord, please don't let him be Black." Funny, I catch myself saying the same thing sometimes.

A report of some type of discrimination would flash across the screen, and there would be an uncomfortable silence in the room. I remember once getting upset at something I saw on television, yet another "driving while Black" exposé, and getting up and leaving the room. One of my peers walked out after me, asking me if I was upset. As we talked, he demonstrated a complete lack of knowledge of what it was like to be minding your own business and have a cop pull you over for no reason, other than driving in the "wrong" area, like your own neighborhood.

I have personally had that experience, at two o'clock in the morning, driving home from my second job as an enlisted man. I had to endure the verbal taunting and profane abuse from a white policeman who did his absolute best to provoke some sort of stupid reaction out of me. We were on a bridge over water, late at night, and we were alone. This irate beer-bellied Atlantic Beach, Florida, city policeman clearly wanted to bust my head wide open, yelling, cursing, and insulting me repeatedly with his hand on his gun, and all I had done (so he said) was go a few miles over the speed limit on my way home in my little '69 Volkswagen. When he pulled me over, mine was the only car on the road. If I'd given him any reason, he would have beaten the hell out of me and taken me to jail or worse. I was simultaneously angry and worried. I was lucky to just get a ticket. Army Lieutenant Caron Nazario got much worse, plus emotional scarring for life after being threatened and pepper sprayed during a traffic stop in Virginia. Watching him threatened with the possibility that he would "ride the lightnin'" and the fact that he was related to Eric Garner, of "I can't breathe" notoriety, drove the point home deeper.

I went to the police station the next day, in uniform, to complain, but they wouldn't take a statement from me. That same police department would later get some bad local press when another officer radioed in a report about some "jigaboos" he was engaged with. He made them look bad, but he was just expressing the cultural environment, I suspect. He was young, and just trying to fit in, as I was. My peers in the wardroom had probably never had this experience. I have friends who still do, forty years after it happened to me the first time. It was not the last.

I also learned to be careful at social functions. One particular incident stands out. I was at a wardroom function, and one department head had consumed a few drinks too many—not an unusual occurrence for him. He began to compliment me politely on my clothing, and I thanked him. Then he began to make comments about my stylish gray and black shoes, which looked like they were alligator skin. Most of the white guys in the wardroom wore brown dockers, usually without socks; khaki pants; and a striped shirt of some kind. Black men usually wear socks, hiding the ashy ankles. Lotion only goes so far.

He started razzing me; the conversation quickly became more edgy and pointed, as he finally sarcastically said, "You Black guys can get away with stuff like that." He was getting very close to saying something that we would both regret. I had seen white guys in GQ magazine wearing the same style of shoes but a lot more expensive. I politely laughed, and I made a hasty exit. He was getting close to a line I didn't want him to cross, and only one of us was sober. The rest of the guys could see it, too, and they were looking nervous.

I suspect they'd heard him say things I shouldn't hear. Alcohol loosens the tongue. Race was always there, though seldom spoken about. I learned to be very sociable, polite, and friendly, but I was constantly on guard for signs that alcohol was about to contribute to a situation I'd rather avoid.

On the professional side, I tried to distinguish myself from my peers when I could, even if it was just shinier shoes. We once had excess small arms ammunition, and the gunnery officer was planning to turn it in. He saw only a problem; I instantly sensed an opportunity. I reserved the base firing range and got approval to use some of the excess ammunition for the purpose of qualifying some of the crew for voluntary small arms qualifications and medals.

I put a note in the Plan of the Day informing anyone who wanted to attempt to qualify for small arms qualifications (for medals and ribbons) to sign up. Emperor Napoleon, General George Patton, and I knew what sailors and soldiers would do for a little piece of ribbon. The list filled up quickly, mostly white guys. The Black guys already knew how to shoot, or they apparently thought it was some kind of setup: Lots of white guys I work with having loaded guns? Ha-ha-ha—no, thanks. They may have been on to something. I have it on good authority that there was a racially tinged crew fight overseas after I transferred. But quite a few sailors, including me, were walking around soon after with one or two additional ribbons, and my shipmates thanked me for making it possible. The ship was also better qualified to defend itself because of these additional qualifications, or at least I thought so.

Those two additional ribbons helped me eventually cross a line. Once you had four rows of ribbons, you were a certified navy hero (CNH). I found this information in an obscure, ancient publication on naval lore, the title of which I can't quite remember. Only 13.92175 percent of all sailors ever reach CNH status. This was minimal effort—maximum return.

Since I couldn't get transferred to engineering to work on my engineering qualifications, I started timidly going down into "the hole" on my own, always taking some raw hamburger meat with me. If you plan to befriend a big angry bear or a snarling dog (which some of these guys reminded me of), it helps to have some raw meat as a peace offering. I'd finish my watch on the bridge and then go stand another one in engineering, working on my EOOW qualifications. The engineers or "snipes" were a scary-looking bunch.

These guys looked irritable and tired all the time. One had a tattoo of a skull in the middle of his forehead. I am not kidding. They were hard-drinking and hardworking; smelled of diesel fuel and sweat, even when they were fresh from the showers; and rumored to sodomize with a rusty wire brush anyone caught in their spaces who couldn't explain the pressure-fired boiler combustion cycle. This was a basic requirement to be an engineer.

When I thought that I had learned enough not to be dangerous and passed out enough raw meat to befriend them, I took off my chastity belt and helped out with engineering drills. This more than once almost caused me to wet myself. This could be dangerous work. You could walk through an invisible steam leak and leave your torso behind you as your legs continued ahead. If you suspected a steam leak, you could wave a broom handle in the area.

If a piece of it fell off, you knew where to start looking for the leak. I usually had a broom handle tightly gripped in each hand. I once heard a story about a guy who took an unauthorized leak in a dark space and had a problem, to put it euphemistically. It's probably just a sea story. Once, while we were conducting engineering drills off the coast of some nameless country where bad things were happening, our boiler got "out of specs" for safely operating, and the engineers were having trouble getting it back to a safe operating condition.

We were "smoking white," a very dangerous condition, and I was calculating the seconds left before we were in serious danger of a boiler explosion. Meanwhile, we were drifting in toward shore. People were fighting and dying on that shore. I could see it through my binoculars while standing bridge watches and read it in the message traffic. I didn't want to see it any closer.

The closer we got to a possible boiler explosion, the more ashen-faced the engineers got, and the more urgent the internal communications became, the harder it was for me not to run the hell out of there. If they were getting scared, I was pretty sure I should be terrified. The radio shack, with its air-conditioned spaces and nothing more dangerous than a paper shredder or a stapler, was sounding pretty good about then. We thankfully avoided a main space major casualty.

It did not help that while this was going on, we had a cryptographic security van on our deck, and my CMS account had nearly doubled as a result. I really can't say more because I certainly do not want to have to kill all of you. I didn't want to end up like the spy ship USS *Pueblo*. There are several books about what happened to the *Pueblo*. The captain wrote one, the XO wrote another, and there's the official navy version, shaped by political considerations. The versions do not all agree, unsurprisingly. I never had to write my *Voge* version. Spy John Walker played a pivotal role in why *Pueblo* was seized. He was providing materials necessary to decrypt messages, and *Pueblo* provided the equipment. The Soviets were reading our traffic just as fast as we were. People died, and secrets were lost.

Once I completed my engineering qualifications and stood the requisite number of watches, I had my formal engineering qualification board. Like a proud papa, Commander Barton asked the first question, a lengthy one that began something like "Using your extensive engineering knowledge of this ship, please explain to us in complete detail the following process involving..." I stopped hearing him after the "extensive engineering knowledge" part.

Who in the hell was he talking to? Me? I did not have any "extensive engineering knowledge," certainly not about this plant. I had, at maximum, a rudimentary knowledge of the plant, and I hoped it was sufficient to pass this board. I felt the knowledge draining out of my head. My old friend, fear of failure, hit me right between the eyes. I can remember my mouth moving, but not what I said. I saw big beads of sweat on my arms and felt the sweat beading on my face. It was the celestial navigation exam, all over again!

I recovered, and started slowly talking, not sure if I made any sense or not. I was fearless, steady, and sure under most real performance pressure. I could handle the ship, respond to emergencies, think quickly on my feet, and do maneuvering board solutions as well as and sometimes faster than CIC, but sit me down in a formal setting and fear of failure was my biggest enemy. Commander Barton, sensing that I had choked, asked me a less wordy and less complicated question.

More questions followed, and I relaxed and became more confident. I knew this plant. I passed my board. After it was over and I was notified that I'd passed, Commander Barton sincerely apologized. He realized that his long, winding question had thrown me for a loop and that he'd unnecessarily rattled me. I did get some grief for scaring the hell out of them. Wish I'd seen myself; I bet it looked pretty funny. I laughed with the chief engineer who sat my board decades later when he told me he loved telling that story, and how well I had done, despite the sweat tsunami.

I qualified as EOOW, steam plant, on one of the last ships of its class. *Voge* was decommissioned in August 1989. I was the only crewmember outside the engineering department to qualify. The respect I had for the guys who made this ship run is eternal. Many guys went to shore duty or to a follow-on afloat tour as a division officer.

I went instead to department head school, thereby improving my chances of getting deep-selected for lieutenant commander, but not without the direct help of Commander Barton, who mentored me. I had already been nominated for the Carrier Readiness Improvement Program. This program assigned junior officers with promising engineering expertise to help aircraft carriers get through extensive shipyard periods to prolong their usefulness. The chief of naval personnel strongly encouraged my skipper that I be "counseled" on the benefits of this program and that I be strongly encouraged to apply. But wait, there's more! It was to be a grueling assignment, filled with dirt, dangerous chemicals, extensive repairs and refitting, redneck-looking shipyard workers, and surly engineers—and those were the easy parts. My fingernails would have taken a real beating and my shoes too. Plus, it promised to be a management challenge.

For this program, the chief of naval personnel actually gave you the chance to say no. I did, and instead, I went to department head school with Commander Barton's help and strong endorsement. The six-hundred-ship navy dream had died, but I was still angling for early promotion. The pie had just gotten a lot smaller: "Navy to Shrink Drastically—Women and Minorities Hardest Hit!" The *New York Times* missed this headline. I would have to be both lucky and very successful from here on out.

I turned over my radio shack and my hated CMS account to Ensign Daniel K. Bean. He was smart, inquisitive, combative, and very professional, and had a strong sense of right and wrong. Naturally, he eventually became a lawyer. He had attended Vanderbilt University on a Naval Reserve Officers Training Corps (NROTC) scholarship. If there had been any problems with my CMS account, he would have found them, because he was just as terrified of it as I was. Dan and I would cross paths a decade later when he was a navy judge advocate (lawyer) and I was a lieutenant commander department head ashore. He had attended the San Diego University School of Law on a Navy Law Education Program scholarship. He was the American Bar Association's Navy Young Lawyer of the Year in 1996. He is now a successful attorney at his Jacksonville, Florida, law firm.

I left *Voge* as a lieutenant (junior grade, referred to as a "jaygee") and reported for temporary duty to a regional maintenance support command in Newport, Rhode Island, to wait a few months for my class to start. I worked in the administrative offices, helping the floundering staff get ready for a command administrative inspection. I identified and fixed a lot of problems briefly, reverting to an overpaid yeoman. The thank-you letter got lost in the mail, again, I guess.

In department head school, I was one of only two jaygees there, and both of us were Black. I didn't much like department head school. It was like trying to drink from a fire hose while taking classified notes. I was in the same boat as everyone else, except for one little thing. I wasn't supposed to be there. I was not yet a lieutenant or a lieutenant commander, and I was one of the few Black service members there. There were no Black instructors. Once Black instructors were assigned, I've been told by a retired Black admiral who was involved in that decision, the success rate for Black students improved significantly.

I soon once again felt the tingling sensation that I was sometimes being judged a bit differently in an academic environment. When I'd take certain exams in the combat systems phase, I would write my answers according to how I'd been taught. I knew the material. Often, when the results came back, I did not score as well as I had expected. I believed that some of these evaluations were too subjective, like at Mineman A School. No one asked about fingernails, at least. Nevertheless, I resented when too much subjectivity entered the picture because I often got the short end of the stick.

Remember, the DOD had trained me to recognize and help mitigate bias and discrimination. I just didn't know how to fix it.

As we would review our results, I sometimes saw that my answer to a given question was not much different from that of the guy next to me; however, his answer would be judged less harshly than mine had been, and mine was often better written. When I would challenge this with the instructor, I'd often get additional credit, after sometimes being told, "Well, I understand it when you say it, and it's apparent you know the material, but I just didn't feel like you got it by your answer." There was not much difference between what I said and what I wrote. "Feelings" weren't part of the evaluation criteria.

There was perhaps something else afoot, but I was not then aware of it. Now I can address it with complete confidence. The *New York Times* reported that the chief of naval operations, Admiral Carlisle A. H. Trost, announced in July 1988, while I was attending this school, that an internal navy study had revealed that there was bias in promotion against both minority enlisted and officer personnel. This was a matter of great concern to the navy. Was this bias also occurring for Black students in "subjective" areas of navy schools? The affirmative-action backlash spoken of in the Brookings book *Blacks and the Military*, which I mentioned in chapter 4, was clearly evident by now in the navy, to the point that the CNO addressed it publicly. Whatever actions he did take are unknown to me. That study has never been publicly released.

In 1987, the DOD began to report to Congress the number of resolved formal sexual harassment and other discrimination complaints, based on the request by Congressman Ron Dellums in response to a tour he made of military bases because of the letters being sent to his office from military personnel protesting rampant discrimination around the world. These figures were contained in addendums to the Annual Defense Report. It was an inauspicious beginning. In the beginning of the George W. Bush presidency, the data became no longer available. I asked for it. The DOD ignored my request, for a while.

According to Secretary of Defense Donald Rumsfeld's rules, it was apparently not the public's business how the DOD was handling discrimination and sexual harassment complaints. Eventually, after much back and forth, and my filing a Freedom of Information Act request, I got the data I wanted. It's good and bad that I did. I'll share some of what I learned as we go along. In 1987, fifty-one formal discrimination complaints were submitted, but only three were substantiated, a mere 6 percent. Compare that to a 50 percent substantiation rate for sexual harassment complaints: in absolute terms, out of ten complaints, only five were substantiated. Better?

Why were there so few complaints in this period of rampant bias and discrimination? Institutional denial? By 1988, the percentage of Black recruits had reached 13, while the Black officer percentage had climbed to 3.5. Role models for young Black sailors were still in short supply, especially those role models who effectively spoke out about perceived discrimination. What happened to them? I, better than most, knew that it could be a career-ending endeavor.

By 1988, the navy was still moving in the right direction in many areas, but there were troubling events in others. Without much warning, the relatively new secretary of the navy, James Webb, resigned in protest in February of that year when he realized that sixteen ships were going to be cut from the navy's budget. The plan for the six-hundred-ship navy was now officially dead, and the available coveted at-sea jobs were going to become much tougher to get. The navy was about to start shrinking, and when resources become scarce, the knives come out, even among the survivors. Competition for the remaining available jobs would get significantly more intense.

In fiscal year 1988, the second year for which the data are available, 126 formal discrimination complaints were submitted, and 3 percent (4 complaints) were substantiated. There were 75 more filed than the previous year, yet only 4 of these were substantiated, a decrease of 3 percent in the substantiation rate from the previous year. This meant that 97 percent of the people formally stating that they were being discriminated against were officially wrong. That was roughly the same ratio of white to Black officers. It was overwhelmingly white people who decided whether complaints were substantiated or not, white people who the navy officially reported that same year held biased views of Black service members. Whites and Blacks clearly saw discrimination from different perspectives.

A 30 percent increase in complaints, and a 50 percent drop in validations—now that's efficiency in action. The number of "informal" complaints that were unsubstantiated surely must have approached 100 percent. Statistically, this doesn't appear to make sense. The navy and DOD were acknowledging problems, but then the people sufficiently harried to complain were being told overwhelmingly that they were wrong. Clearly, there was much more work to be done.

Despite my lingering suspicions and growing resentment about rater bias, I passed the tactical action officer exam—a more difficult equivalent of the celestial navigation exam at basic—on the first try. We had one Black lieutenant commander who took it three times. Each exam, he likely suffered the death of a thousand (subjective?) cuts. He eventually passed. Normally, if you failed this exam twice, you were history. He just barely failed it on his second try. Was he getting nickeled-and-dimed too? I don't know why he got a third chance. I bet he wonders too. I wonder if he thought he was being graded differently than his peers also. I don't know if he ever challenged his grading or not. I, at least, felt that I was being nickeled-and-dimed, and I resented it. I developed a habit of challenging low subjective scores, and it helped. I think I made some people think about what they were doing.

After you passed the tactical action officer exam, you were assigned your follow-on orders and your department specialty. If you did not pass, start planning for civilian life. This was the part everyone was waiting for. Lots of us wanted to go to Florida, me included. When the lists of available assignments were posted, there was one ship and one billet that no one wanted: engineer officer, USS *Boone* (FFG-28), Mayport, Florida. The word was that of all the jobs on the list, this one was the "kiss of death."

At the time, the *Boone*'s engineer officer was on temporary additional duty (TAD) to the "fat farm" to lose a significant amount of weight or be forced to resign from the service, and a senior chief on TAD from the squadron staff was running the *Boone*'s engineering department. *Boone* had a history of problems, and there were rumors of personnel instability and other problems in the engineering department. Sailors' talk. In addition to that, the ship would be leaving within two weeks of the department head reporting aboard for refresher training at Guantanamo Bay, Cuba; some of the most dreaded training any fleet sailor had to endure. It would deploy shortly after that for the Persian Gulf.

None of this worried me; I was too junior for this job, and I had not spent one day assigned to an engineering department. *Boone* needed a seasoned engineer, which I was not. There were more senior officers in my class who had served one or two engineering division officer tours and were well suited for this job. I put in for an operations or combat systems job in a Florida-based warship.

When the officer detailers, headed by a navy captain, came from Washington to Newport to give us our assignments, I was absolutely stunned. I had been assigned the engineer's job on *Boone*! My head swam when I looked at the list. Surely this was some elaborate joke the Bureau of Naval Personnel played on the junior guy in every class, and the detailers were in on it. But I could soon tell by the looks on the faces of the rest of the guys that this was no joke. Right about now, I was kicking myself in the ass for having that EOOW letter in my back pocket. I fought to understand why this had happened. Someone knows; I never found out.

Did the navy have such confidence in me that it was assigning me to an engineering billet with no engineering experience? Didn't the navy detailers know about the CNO's reports from a few months earlier? Had I filed some complaint that I forgot about? Was I being set up to fail? No other department head in my class or the one before who did not have engineering experience was assigned an engineering billet. I wasn't even a full lieutenant! Cue the cemetery music and the blowing leaves. Shit.

There were division officers in that ship who would be senior to me. Did the navy assign me this kiss-of-death billet to get rid of me? If I failed in this job, my promotion and retention potential would be next to zero. When the chance came, I approached the captain detailer and said, "Captain, surely there has been some mistake with my job assignment." Somehow, he already knew who I was—name tag, no doubt. I think he was expecting me. He said, "Lieutenant, there is no mistake with your assignment. Those are your orders, and you are expected to carry them out." I wish he had elaborated on why I got the assignment.

Over the captain detailer's head, I could see my father's voice in a thought bubble, saying, "OK, Slick, looks like you outsmarted your own ass. How you like the 'New Navy' now? What did you think the navy was going to do with that EOOW letter, let you use it to just jump ahead in the promotion line? Pin it on your chest like a medal?" I felt sick. What was going on here? I wanted a do-over.

I felt as though I were being set up to fail, and I presume it was because I had in fact been set up to fail on previous occasions. I was getting one of the most challenging jobs available, on a ship with big problems and a very tough schedule looming. Why not kill my career by giving me a dead-end desk job? Oh, I remembered, I had asked to come here. I asked myself, How did the junior Black guy receive the most dreaded assignment? My surprise pity party was absolutely wonderful but had no cake. I was too sick to eat anyway. I was to receive another surprise. At an awards ceremony, I received the Navy Commendation Medal Commander Barton submitted when I left the *Voge*. I was happy to get it, but I didn't feel much better. I would have happily traded it for an operations department job.

By the time I got into the engineering phase of the department head training, which was the phase that followed tactical officer training and assignments, I had developed an even bigger chip on my shoulder concerning the grading policies. Sometimes, over the years, my shoulder was pretty crowded. I also figured that I had really better start paying more attention. I remembered my steam EOOW board. We had a pretty difficult section on thermodynamics. This exam required that you write your answers longhand, and you had to explain your logic. I had learned a lot about the relationships between pressure, temperature, and volume, which are not subjective. The laws of thermodynamics don't fluctuate. You know it, or you don't. There can be little subjective grading. I scored a perfect 100, the only one in my class to do so. Commander Barton would have been proud.

I was roundly congratulated and also received some quizzical looks. Some classmates wanted to know how I had so quickly gotten so smart. I didn't make any bones about my thoughts on that. When I had complained earlier, they thought it was just whining.

Now, maybe they would at least consider the possibility that I had a reason to be skeptical. Unlike the tools and uses test I took as a seaman, no one told me I had to take it again. The entire class of the first Black naval officers had to retake one of their final Officer Candidate School qualifying exams because they scored so suspiciously well. The second time, with a different test, they scored even higher. This is another of your lessons: study hard; success is the best revenge. Right now I couldn't tell you the first law of thermodynamics—I'm not an engineer—but I knew it when I had to.

One of the many things I was to learn during the engineering-specific phase of this course troubled me greatly. We were told that there was not enough time in the day to do all the things we were required to. I didn't believe it then, but I do now. Every fleet engineer knows this to be true. We would have to make a conscious decision each day of what not to do. The navy captain who talked to us, who had decades of engineering experience, didn't pull any punches; he let us know we were all heading for some very tough jobs. I was accustomed to accomplishing everything required of me.

Once I completed this school, I had to attend a firefighting school en route to my ship. I was also tested differently at the advanced firefighting school at the Philadelphia Naval Shipyard. During a live firefighting exercise, the instructor would relieve you when you were manning the nozzle on the fire hose and ran out of air in your breathing device. When my turn came, it took a very long time for me to get relieved, even after I indicated to him several times that I was almost out of air. He had not done this to the guys ahead of me. I had been watching very closely, waiting my turn on the nozzle. I realized that he was trying to make me abandon my post.

Finally, almost completely out of air, I indicated that I absolutely could not breathe. Nevertheless, I wasn't leaving. He could explain why the Black guy suffocated while everybody else made it out OK as far as I was concerned. I kept both hands on the nozzle and hose as I struggled to breathe, leaning hard into him. He pulled my mask far enough away from my chin so that I could get some smoky air, and then he relieved me. I wanted to kick his ass.

I stumbled out, pissed off but proud. I knew better than to file a formal complaint. It was subjective, and I was Black. After finishing advanced firefighting school in Philadelphia, I reported to the *Boone* in October 1988. I didn't know it, but all hell was about to break loose.

More than once during my initial officer tour, I would have some enlisted white sailor casually say to me, with barely concealed contempt, some version of "Mr. Green, the only reason you're an officer is because of affirmative action." Ronald Reagan had set the tone. I would love these teed-up softballs. After explaining how I actually accomplished it, the sailor would sheepishly say something like "Well, sir, I didn't know all that." After pointing out that lack of knowledge didn't stop them from expressing an uninformed, negative opinion, I'd usually get silence. Nobody ever said that on *Boone*. They knew better, and so did I.

8

Engineer Officer, USS *Boone*

I reported for duty on USS *Boone* (FFG-28) in October 1988 in service dress blues, with orders in a briefcase and ID card in hand. By now I looked like an officer but felt like a fraud. Four years prior, I was junior first class yeoman. Now I was about to be a chief engineer, abbreviated CHENG, and I didn't feel prepared. I didn't want to think about the odds of survival. I became a frocked lieutenant two months before.

I also had personal housing concerns. A real estate agent became upset when a homeowner would not allow us to look at her house, even though it had a "For Sale" sign in the yard and was listed in the Multiple Listing Service. The homeowner was sitting in her driveway with some friends, and we were looking at another house down the street. So, the agent stopped and asked if the homeowner could show me the house, as I was in town for only two days. The homeowner said that the house was not "tidied up" and was adamant that we could not view it. The agent left angry. She couldn't fathom the owner's behavior.

After we left, I explained to her that one of my white coworkers revealed that his neighbors had pledged that none of them would sell their house to a Black person when they moved (he didn't agree to this illegal racist pact). I could see my coworker's house from where we stood. Shocked, the agent finally understood why I had resisted looking for houses in this area. This was not my first encounter with housing discrimination in my adopted city, Jacksonville, Florida, and wouldn't be the last.

The problem after finding a suitable house and willing seller (a white pastor) then became the mortgage company. I eventually signed a contract on a larger house, but the mortgage company I was working with declined to give me a mortgage. I had made the down payment; in fact, I already owned two houses, but I needed a bigger one because I had recently married a woman with two teenagers and I was hoping to get custody of my own son. However, the mortgage company determined I was a credit risk because my wife had cosigned a retail store credit card years earlier for her younger sister, who had made a couple of late payments. The account had been paid in full and closed for years.

Both my wife and I had good credit, professional, secure government employment, and money to spare. But this was not good enough for them; the money was the wrong color. My family had already moved in, and I was paying rent until closing. The strangest thing was that the man who processed my application called me and told me that there was "no good reason in the world why my loan was denied" and asked me to call him the next Monday at a new company. He was leaving this one in disgust, and he told me so. His well-coded language let me know what the problem was. I didn't really need him to 'splain it to me. I called him at his new company on Monday, as he had indicated, and my loan application sailed through.

The documents I received when buying my first Jacksonville house included a "restrictive covenant" specifying that only people of the Caucasian race could ever own the house. Finding suitable housing was one of the nightmare scenarios for Bill Norman (Zumwalt's minority affairs assistant), and I was living it more than two decades later. The stress carried over into personal relationships and professional ones as well.

In December 1988, in yet another *New York Times* story, the chief of naval operations revealed that a navy study had discovered that there was widespread bias against minorities in its ranks, not just in promotion, but everywhere. The personnel surveyed for the study freely admitted it! Unless you admit to biases, how would anyone confirm that you have them? The study included seventy-five recommendations, all of which the CNO would accept. I've never seen them. Someone should someday compare the military climate to the actions or stated beliefs of the commander in chief. What if the president's beliefs are different than the military chiefs' and Pentagon officials', as happened during both the Reagan and Trump presidencies? As in any organization, the leadership sets the tone. The conflicts between President Trump and Secretary of Defense Mark Esper are illustrative. Trump fired Esper because he banned the Confederate flag from DOD installations. What signal did that send?

It was in this racial climate that I led an almost lily-white engineering department, in a largely white ship, as the only Black officer on board. There was only one Black chief. Engineering had only one petty officer of color, an E-5. I would be the only minority officer assigned for my entire tour. Color does not matter, I would learn once again, unless you have a smidgen of it.

Meanwhile, in fiscal year 1989, 156 formal discrimination complaints were filed, and zero would be substantiated—that is, thirty more complaints filed than the previous year, in this admittedly discriminatory environment, yet not a single substantiation. You'd have better odds than this at the roulette table. The number of complaints had tripled in three years, while substantiations dropped from six to three to absolute zero. Statistically, this is suspect. A system pressure increase usually results in an increase in flow, not a decrease. If you turn your shower on full blast and only get a trickle, you suspect that there's a system problem, or you should.

I could have perhaps smashed this perfect 1989 record, based on the experiences I would have, but that might have marked me as not a team player. Like many minority officers, rather than risk blowback, I gritted my teeth, worked harder, and tried to outsmart or outwork the people placing obstacles in my way, with varying degrees of success.

I wasn't then aware of these statistics or navy concerns; I had more immediate problems. The *Boone* was a gas turbine–powered guided missile frigate. No major steam leaks from boilers, and less danger of an explosion. Less, I knew, but not zero. I reported for duty, I believe, as the junior surface navy department head in the entire Atlantic Fleet.

Boone needed an experienced engineer but only got me. I was looked at with a jaundiced eye; as a Black ex-yeoman, it was virtually assured that I'd face resistance and adversity. The senior chief temporarily filling the engineer officer billet was not impressed with me. I accepted that. He did not want to relinquish control of this department. This I had a problem with. My orders came from a higher authority than his did.

The second sentence in my first *Boone* fitness report reads as follows: "Stepping aboard USS *Boone* in the midst of a highly compressed, dynamic schedule following a thirteen-month overhaul two weeks before the start of refresher training has not been a simple task." No one statement I ever read about my performance was ever truer than this one. The commanding officer of the *Boone* was Commander Peter R. Smith. He departed *Boone* approximately three months after I arrived. I wish I had served him for a lot longer. We had a rough, rocky start, or at least I did, but he warmed to me and looked out for me later in my travels.

I soon learned disturbing information. One leading gas turbine technician, a qualified engineering officer of the watch (EOOW), was unstable and dangerous. He also had alcohol dependency issues. He'd ultimately be administratively discharged with a diagnosed personality disorder, but not before, among other things, he endangered the entire ship by secretly bypassing some electronic overspeed safety features on both of the gas turbine engines while on deployment in the Persian Gulf, a potentially catastrophic scenario.

In raging desperation, I had a "private counseling session" with him in a fan room while on deployment, told him in my street persona that I was not playing with him, and for him not to threaten to sabotage my engines again. One of us was very close to violence. I never touched him. I made him think I would, though. My main propulsion assistant, my right-hand man, was narcoleptic and prone to falling asleep on watch. There were Polaroid pictures on board to prove it, full of smiling witnesses. I would eventually see the scary reality for myself, more than once. Waking him up at sea, while he was on watch, excited us both. He was excited because he was seeing a side of me that he didn't like or expect, and I was excited because he could have caused a catastrophic failure by failing to pay attention to what was happening to the engineering plant in hostile waters, and with little margin for error.

Some of the senior petty officers in my department were openly disrespectful, in the beginning. I initially did not impress them, which is an understatement; skinny, big glasses, Black, and clearly inexperienced and ignorant. All of that and some other issues would have to be dealt with later. First, I would have to survive refresher training in Guantanamo Bay.

Ships are expected to arrive for refresher training with all major equipment operational. We arrived with one ship's service diesel generator (SSDG) already out of commission. It would be repaired upon our return to homeport if everything went well. It didn't. Disaster nearly struck right away, while we prepared to get underway on the first day of training right after the Guantanamo Bay refresher training team reported aboard. I'd been on board for all of two weeks. I could barely find my rack. I didn't need it much 'cause I wasn't sleeping anyway; there wasn't time. I was not yet qualified to stand watch, and I was trying to get up to speed fast. I could sleep when I had more time. How bad could it be?

The main propulsion assistant was the EOOW, and he was preparing to start the 1A gas turbine engine when lights started flashing on the control console and alarms started sounding. Word was passed from the engine room that we had a fuel spill in the engine room! "Oh, shit!" I exclaimed and ran to the space to see high-pressure jet engine fuel spraying from the fuel pump for that engine and two men trying to keep it contained. They had been reinstalling the fuel pump when the engine was motored (spun rapidly with high-pressure air but no ignition sequence to purge residual fuel and prevent an explosion) before starting it. This was a major problem because they did not have permission to do this maintenance, nor did they have this fuel pump tagged out, properly or otherwise, in violation of standard procedures.

Failure to follow tag-out procedures has gotten sailors killed. To make matters worse, the main propulsion assistant (MPA), the sleepy guy, was unaware that this equipment was being worked on, which he should have been and would have been, if the proper tag-out procedures had been followed. He was required to authorize such work and sign the tags. I ordered him not to start the engines until I said so. Now I had to tell the captain. He'd be pissed.

Engineering was making us look bad, and we'd face greater scrutiny because of this incident. I ran to the bridge and briefed him (as quietly and as discreetly as I could) and said I would notify him when it was safe to start engines. I told him explicitly that the bilges were fouled with fuel and that it was unsafe to get underway. He agreed. Before I could dash back, however, I heard a gas turbine engine motoring. What the hell? Heart pounding, I burst into the central control station (CCS) and asked what the hell was going on.

The MPA calmly informed me that the skipper had ordered him to start the other engine, so he was. Was he really going to start this engine with fuel and fuel-soaked sailors in the bilges, not knowing the status of the other engine's fuel pump? My head, in addition to my chest, was about to explode! I jabbed my finger in his face like a pistol and yelled at him, in all capital letters, "I DON'T GIVE A SHIT WHAT THE CAPTAIN SAID. DON'T YOU DARE START THAT FUCKING ENGINE UNTIL I TELL YOU TO!!!!" He looked at me like I had pointed a real gun at his head and he wanted to hand me his wallet. I was too busy cursing up a blue streak to rob him. "My God," I thought. "Are all these people crazy?"

I had been to the engine room and seen the mess and the chaos; the captain had not. I could still feel the heat on my face when they poured water on a grease fire at firefighting school for our everlasting education. I could imagine a bilge fire, engulfing fuel oil–soaked sailors. They'd be dead quickly, if they were lucky. The skipper, impatient because we had this training team on board cooling their heels, thought it was OK to start the other engine and get underway, despite what I'd just told him. What did I know? I was just the chief engineer.

I was so stressed by this time that I was ready to beat the hell out of somebody, anybody. I was so mad at so many people I truly didn't know where to begin, and they all seemed intent on having a fire on the first day of training. When I ran back to the engine room, I didn't have to tell them to hurry. They actually had the nerve to be upset that someone seemed to be trying to burn them up for no good reason. Was there no respect for procedure around here? Were there loose wires that could create a spark down there?

I ran back to CCS and called the skipper on the bridge before he issued another order. By now, I wondered if maybe he might be crazy, as I was beginning to suspect some of my subordinates were. Breathing hard and fast, I informed him that the bilges were still fouled with fuel and that I had men who were soaking wet with jet fuel down there cleaning it up. I didn't know if there were other hazards from improper procedures. I did know that any stray spark could turn them into flaming, screaming track stars. I told him that it was absolutely not safe to start either engine until I personally told him it was. I could not control the anger in my voice, and I didn't try to. He wasn't happy about it, but he concurred.

I'd barely been there two weeks, and I could already see my career coming to an abrupt and disastrous end. Little did I know the fun was just beginning. Sometimes, I would feel like Danny Glover in *Predator II*. "OK, who's next?" These guys were used to operating by their own lax rules.

We finally got underway and finished day one of training. After we off-loaded the training team, I had a come-to-Jesus departmental meeting, stating that tag-out procedures would be strictly followed, among other things. I showed a lot of fangs. The MPA got special attention. My success would largely depend on him. I did not mince any words with him. The senior chief was pretty low-key, just watching. The next disaster, days later, was also maintenance related and just as serious.

An electrician performed scheduled maintenance on an SSDG and incorrectly reinstalled two wires to the governor because they weren't properly marked. Upon starting, the diesel generator went to full throttle and could not be shut down. Think about starting your car and it going to redline, and you can't shut it off. What would you do? My brave leading engineman, Engineman First Class William A. Duke, climbed on this runaway diesel generator and shut it down with a pair of vice grips. I would learn in short order how dangerous this actually was. I would learn to highly value this outstanding man, who in almost two years never let me down. We now had a serious problem. This diesel generator had oversped and was not safe to run until specific checks, maintenance, and inspections were done. This happened because, again, people weren't following proper procedures. Now we couldn't get underway for training because we didn't have three functional generators. My temper and anxiety level were high and rising. I had to explain to the skipper what had happened. I can still see the look on his face. It said, "What kind of screw-up are you, and why did they send you to me?"

I filed a casualty report and worked to get this diesel generator back online so we could continue training. I soon caught another bad break. Another diesel generator decided to catastrophically fail. It just blew apart.

Oil, fuel, and shrapnel were all over the enclosure. I'm still amazed that there was no fire. I was beginning to hear *Twilight Zone* music. We now couldn't provide our own electrical power. We eventually got enough diesel generators running to train, but the navy had to fly in the reworked rotor for the out-of-commission diesel generator and a special team of repairmen to install it while we fixed the other ones. I was awake and highly stressed nearly around the clock for days.

Because we couldn't get underway, most nonengineering officers would go to the officers' club in the evening, including the skipper. When the skipper would return on these occasions, I'd brief him on the progress and status of the various repairs, and one of those various repair updates, in a memorable incident, was the laundry equipment. During one evening meal, the supply officer mentioned that the ship's dirty laundry had not been done. I knew this because I was recycling underwear. I had told the supply officer about laundry facilities on the base, which were visible on the way to the officers' club, that would need to be used until the ship's laundry facilities were fixed. He had not taken advantage of them. I had assumed he would. I was busy. He also read my casualty reports, which showed the status of the on-ship laundry. No one was uninformed.

The skipper asked me why I had not briefed him on the status of the dirty laundry. I thought his tone was accusatory. This irritated me. I reminded him about my equipment status updates, including laundry equipment, and told him that I didn't know I was also expected to brief him on the status of the dirty laundry. The laundry was the supply officer's job, I reminded him. I didn't appreciate the insinuation that I wasn't doing my job when it was the supply officer who wasn't doing his. I excused myself and left the dinner table, too angry to eat. I wanted to talk to someone but didn't know to whom. No one would care.

I knew I was going to have to take some kind of firm stand if I was going to survive this tour. It didn't help that the supply officer had previously asked me why I was not eating the fine meat that had been prepared for the evening meal. When I told him that I didn't eat pork, I could sense the tension in the room immediately. People stopped chewing and looked at me. Everyone seemed to be silently asking the same questions: "What have they done, sent us a closet raghead?" "Do we even allow Muslims in Guantanamo?" "Who does he think he is, Malcolm the Tenth?"

I explained, as I had before and would again, that I had given up pork as a teenager because it had a tendency to make me sick, but this explanation added another layer of suspicion and curiosity that I didn't need. Just being Black was unusual enough. I didn't have any peer minority I could bounce my perceptions off or discuss the vibes I was picking up in my scant weeks aboard, which would have been helpful. Was past experience clouding my judgment?

A few days later, I was the EOOW conducting engineering drills on the gas turbine engines. We had to do them in port because we were too broken down to get underway. Our engineering training time was quickly going to waste. I was not yet a qualified gas turbine engineer, and these were my first drills on real live engines. I sure as hell didn't want to screw up one of these engines. I had not personally broken anything—yet. I had only done drills on a simulator while in school.

Surrounded by experienced engineers, with my commanding officer and executive officer looking over my shoulder, I could feel the skepticism and hostility in the space as I prepared to perform. My old friend, fear of failure, was sitting on my shoulder, saying, "You're really going to fuck this up and show them what a dipshit you really are. Look around. Do you see any other Black people in this space? You don't belong here. They don't want you or respect you. The word is out that you're a closet Muslim, too."

His two buddies were sitting quietly on my other shoulder: extreme fatigue and stress. They slowly tightened their grip on my neck. I finished one or two of the drills and did OK. I was gaining confidence, but as we prepared for the next drill, I suddenly felt lightheaded. My ears were ringing. Was I hearing things? Hallucinating? I felt myself going down, and I fought hard to prevent it. I remember grabbing the rail in front of me and holding on to it as I squatted down, trying to fight what was happening. I thought I was dying. I remember feeling the back of my head slam into the deck. The next thing I knew, I was looking up from the deck, into my skipper's and the hospital corpsman's faces. I had passed out cold. I don't know how long I was out.

I'm sure the skipper didn't want a dead Black engineer on his fitness report. That might be a black mark he couldn't overcome (no pun intended). I kept saying I was OK and trying to get up, but he wouldn't let me. He asked me, "CHENG, when was the last time you had any sleep?" I looked at him and said, quietly, "I don't know." It was true. I was totally, completely exhausted. I had never been through anything like this. I had failed to take Commander Dan Ryder's advice about getting enough sleep. By this time, it was impossible.

Fatigue, stress, lack of nutrition, overt and covert hostility, and isolation had brought me to a near breaking point. After the corpsman determined that I was OK, the captain ordered me to go directly to my rack, and I slept so long that I was embarrassed when I woke up, determined to make it through this or get carried off the ship on a stretcher or in a straitjacket. I had never before failed at anything professionally, and I wasn't about to start now, if I could help it. I felt like I'd been dealt a bad hand, but I was going to play it. I had gone looking for officer khakis, and I had them.

For a while after that, I would get catcalls as I traversed the mess decks about passing out or fainting, always from some of the Black crewmembers, one in particular. The brothers were smelling blood in the water. I had shown weakness, and they were testing me. It was not unexpected. I understood it. It was a public challenge, a test of my manhood. This problem I knew I could handle.

I ignored it for a while, but finally, I stopped and turned around and announced to the nearly full mess decks that anyone who had something to say to me should be man enough to say it to my face. I said I'd be happy to have a man-to-man discussion with him. I had never run from a fight, and I sure as hell had never passed out in one, if that's what they wanted. It did the trick. I had passed the test. The catcalls stopped. I eventually won most of them over, and I would later reenlist one in front of his family.

I had to address my problem with the sidelined senior chief and my tense relationship with the skipper, who, I thought, didn't think much of me. All I ever brought him was bad news, worse news, and awful news. The senior chief was undermining my authority, and the skipper was listening.

I would inform the skipper of my plans or intentions; shortly thereafter, I'd get called up, and he'd have alternate suggestions or directives, the same ones I was getting from the senior chief. When I didn't agree with the senior chief or he didn't agree with me, he went over my head and behind my back directly to the captain, undermining my authority. We talked about it, and I thought we had an understanding. When it became apparent that we didn't and wouldn't, I went to the skipper and said I wanted the senior chief transferred off the ship. He blew up, yelling and telling me that the senior chief was a fine man and how much help he had been to the ship and that he was not going to transfer him off his ship. I understood.

At this point, I blew up too. I told the skipper that that was fine—the senior chief had done a lot—but the senior chief was going to work for me and quit undermining me, or I was going to pack my bags and put them on the pier and go home because I was the chief engineer, and I wasn't ordered in there to work for the damn senior chief. I was going to run that department, or I was leaving. The detailers had made it clear that this was my job, not his. I was disrespectful. I'd had all the shit I was going to take.

I didn't care if I got fired on the spot. I was going to fix this or leave. Hell, I'd pick up trash on base before I'd put up with this any longer. I don't know why he didn't relieve me on the spot. Maybe it was because despite my inexperience, I convinced him I had some balls. We came to an understanding, and I stayed.

I had no more significant issues with the senior chief. He left after we returned to Mayport. Commander Smith made captain, and he learned that I had successfully completed my extended tour. I never fell to the deck again, but I never got enough sleep. Nobody cares how much sleep you get, so get at least enough to stay upright. Like most sailors, my sleep apnea claim for VA benefits was denied. I wasn't diagnosed while on active duty. My bad.

My next skipper, Commander Mike Newman, from Lubbock, Texas, assumed command on December 27, 1988. His easy drawl at first put me on edge. Tall, thin, and with a shiny strip where his hair should have been, he would be the first to tell you he was not classically handsome. With all due respect, he was right. He more than made up for it by being funny and a superb storyteller. Sometimes, we were too busy laughing to chew our food. He had this uncanny ability to make me laugh no matter how bad I was feeling. He had also been a chief engineer.

During this tour, I saw my first navy hydrofoil on one of the rare occasions I was topside. Those ships were like mosquitoes with sledgehammers. The hydrofoil I'd seen years before in Zumwalt's memoir as an artist's conception was now real. They would fly by us like we were standing still, and they had the same gun we did, plus harpoon missiles.

Between January and June 1989, we underwent a strenuous schedule and got a big surprise. I gradually began to get a hold on this job. Some of these men I won over easily and some I never did. Some didn't hide it well. Commander Newman cared a lot about his people; we sometimes didn't see eye to eye, and that was exploited. I was in a job that required a certain amount of ruthlessness, and he didn't seem to have a ruthless bone in his body. We had various reviews, assessments, training teams, inspections, deployment exercises, and workups. The big one of these for me was the operational propulsion plant examination.

At one point, during the exam, one of my MPA's drills didn't go well. He was our most experienced EOOW, and he was less than stellar. The other was fine, but it looked like I might have to drill in order for us to pass. I had just qualified as EOOW. I'd had almost no sleep in the intervening days and had stood watch as EOOW the previous night after we finished drilling late in the evening so that my MPA could rest before drilling. He didn't do particularly well, and the tension level jumped significantly.

I was the last qualified EOOW, the least experienced, and dead tired. I looked at the executive officer, Commander Rich Maurer, and he looked worried. I had been awake for nearly forty-eight hours, and I was seeing spots. During the drilling that morning, I had closed my eyes during one drill, and when I opened them again, we were on another drill. It was the first and last time I have ever fallen asleep while standing up.

For me to pass the qualification drills like this would probably have taken a miracle. I don't pass, we don't deploy. Luckily, the gods smiled on us, and we passed without me having to drill. I later learned, in a personal letter that Commander Newman sent to my detailer, that no one expected us to, except him. I think he may have fudged a bit, for my sake. Now we could deploy.

During early June, about thirty days before deployment, we were conducting helicopter operations off Mayport with our assigned helicopter detachment. I had been relieved by the MPA as EOOW and gone to the head in officers' quarters. I was sitting there multitasking. Suddenly there was a loud boom throughout the ship, and the ship rose perceptibly under me. A main space fire was announced over the 1MC as I tidied up and washed my hands, of course.

I ran down to the CCS, and the EOOW (my MPA) said we had a class bravo fire in the 1A gas turbine engine and that he had dumped primary halon, the installed fire suppression system. These engine modules are self-contained, with an integrated fire suppression system. Nothing terrifies an engineer at sea like a main space fire, except maybe an active torpedo or a mine.

When I rushed into the engine room, I saw the watch stander spraying firefighting foam on the rear inboard side of the gas turbine module, which immediately flashed to steam, like water sprayed into a hot skillet, as paint blistered and peeled from the module. Holy shit! We were on fire! There was a steady, thick stream of hot, gold-colored lube oil pouring from the main reduction gear into the bilges very near the module's corner, throwing off oil molecules and filling the air with hot, flammable, oily mist. There was yelling, cursing, running, and terror.

The explosion had stretched some reduction gear cover bolts, allowing lube oil to escape. These bolts were about as thick as a hot dog. Pull out a paper clip and try to stretch it. Surely you have one in your pocket, as I had when my *Voge* executive officer (XO), whom we affectionately called Little Redheaded Motherfucker (LRMF), asked me for one at officer's call and I had one to give him, thereby providing me with an opportunity to shine and slam my officer shipmates at the same time. I ran to the module door and saw big orange flames and felt the heat through the glass window. The EOOW announced that the secondary halon didn't extinguish the fire. The installed systems had failed. We were going to extinguish this fire ourselves.

Standard protocol required that the main space fire team fight the fire. I didn't think we had that kind of time. We had the situation under control, but if that lube oil in the bilges caught fire, the people in that space would likely die. I knew how long it took the fire party to get dressed, out, and arrive. The risk of waiting was too great. I decided I needed to break protocol. I was paid to make hard decisions. There were three of us: Hull Technician First Class (HT1) Coles, my leading gas turbine specialist (mechanical), and myself. We all agreed on the plan.

One would open the module door, one would start spraying down the fire, and the other would control the valve. Once the door was open, we would all man the hose or whatever else might be required. I ordered everyone else out of the space. None of us knew what would happen when that door opened. All of us were scared. Flashover was in the back of my mind, if not theirs. When I opened the door, we felt the intense heat but quickly put out the fire. We had trusted each other, and we had saved that engine and the ship from further damage.

These two men went on to very divergent paths. One, the HT1, became a commissioned officer, a limited duty officer. I believe he was the damage control assistant on a ship that had another, more serious main space fire, the USS *Iwo Jima* (LPH-2). The other was made chief petty officer during the deployment but was discharged as a seaman. He was court-martialed after I transferred for failing to come to work and missing ship's movement.

I would recommend to the skipper to discipline him for his repeated alcohol and meanness-driven behavioral infractions ashore during our deployment, including picking fights with and threatening his subordinates, urinating on a police motorcycle while on liberty, and other shenanigans. Early in my tour, he lied to me—to cover up a mistake he'd made as EOOW at sea and anchor detail as we were getting underway—and caused a great deal of unnecessary anxiety for the skipper and me about the state of my propulsion equipment. I questioned him at length on the issue, but he stuck to his story, which made no sense. Many months later, he finally fessed up. He was a problem, but no matter what else, his finest hour was in the engine room that fiery day.

After I briefed the captain on the bridge, we secured from general quarters. He wanted to continue flight support operations, using the other engine. I had to convince him, with the executive officer's help, that this was not possible, due to the reduction gear damage. He then wanted to use the two auxiliary propulsion units (APUs), which would afford us only minimum control and very little speed. Missing a commitment looks bad, but if the failure-prone APUs failed, we were doubly screwed, with few options.

We decided to limp back to port via APUs. We were escorted in by harbor tugboats.

A flash message about a fire and explosion on a ship at sea gets lots of attention, especially one due to soon deploy. The commanding officer of the shore intermediate maintenance activity (SIMA) and other higher-ups were waiting for us pier side. After coming aboard and doing a quick walkthrough, the SIMA commanding officer confidently proclaimed that he would have us back together and ready for sea in a week. He smirked at me on his way out, like I'd made a big fuss for nothing. He was wrong.

SIMA Mayport was housed in the same building that I had worked in as a yeoman first class for Master Chief Davy. Office spaces between the two commands were separated by only a long passageway, and there was a lot of "inbreeding" between the two commands. Some of the same chiefs I knew in that job were now in that command. I would see them and say hello, calling them by name and saying how good it was to see them. Most of them would look at me funny, asking if they knew me. No, but I knew them. I'd say, "Sure, we used to work together." They would almost never have a clue. The astonished and confused looks used to comfort me somehow. Remember Master Chief Davy, my buddy? They were his buddies, too.

I had become a lieutenant chief engineer on a gas turbine frigate in less time than it took for many of them to go from one pay grade to another. I'm sure I smirked a time or two. I hoped that the word got back to Master Chief Davy.

The immediate problem, the main engine fire, didn't look as bad as you might imagine—until you inspected closely. Other ships had experienced this casualty, but with much more visible damage. A seal failure between the engine exhaust plenum, which directs hot exhaust gasses to the ship's stack, allowed oil to leak in slowly and unseen and collect in the plenum. We had just experienced the equivalent of a huge pipe bomb.

The exhaust plenum was badly damaged, the main reduction gear had to have extensive inspection and repairs, the coupling between the engines and reduction gear was totally destroyed, and both the engine and module were significantly damaged. I recall about one million dollars' worth of damage being quoted. With lots of outside help, we worked on that ship night and day for a solid month, trying to deploy on time. At the same time, I managed to convince the navy brass to install a very expensive prototype shaft seal that would prevent the ship from flooding in the event of a failure of the standard version, which was giving us problems.

I wrote Nobel Prize–worthy, very scary-sounding casualty reports, with doom and gloom pervading, because I wasn't going to be sinking in the

Persian Gulf if I could help it. Add another million dollars or so to our cruise preparations. I constantly submitted detailed casualty reports and updates, which were well scrutinized because of our looming deployment date.

The captain decreed that I stand duty every other day, dual-hatted as duty engineer and command duty officer. They each had different duties during an emergency, in different places, and I couldn't be in two places at one time. If things went south, I would be derelict somehow, depending on whether I should have zigged or zagged. Other officers and enlisted personnel thereby got to spend as much time as possible with their own families. My family wasn't going to see much of me anyway. On the days that I wasn't on duty, I would often spend the night or leave late at night. For the month before deployment, I never saw my house during daylight hours. It was June. You may cry here, but briefly.

I was slowly earning the respect of my engineers—some of them. I'd had minor incidents but nothing serious except for a first class who worked for me and was surly, uncooperative, and disapproving in a generally quasi-respectful way. He was also bigger than I was. I knew this game, having played his part, only smarter. One day I hurriedly gave him some routine direction while on the mess decks and walked away. Something told me to look back, and I saw him leaning forward, grabbing his crotch, sneering at me, and flipping me the one-finger salute, jabbing up and down for emphasis. He had a look of sheer hatred on his face. You should have seen the look on his face when he got caught. Uh-oh. I had his disrespectful behind on a silver platter, presented in front of amused witnesses, chewing with their mouths open and enjoying the show.

I could have written a bulletproof report chit. Instead, I invited him in for a little heartfelt talk, in my street persona, using language I usually reserved for less professional settings. I expressed my disappointment, giving him a chance to explain himself. He apologized. So what? No one saw that. But I never again experienced anything even remotely disrespectful from him. I can't say if his behavior was racially motivated. It's never that simple. His counterpart, Gas Turbine System Technician (Electrical) First Class Brian Rolig, was one of my most supportive and strongest men.

The other major personnel problem I had was with the new supply officer. He looked even more girly than I did. He and his chief storekeeper were screwing with us. Maybe he'd heard that I didn't eat pork. Maybe he was trying to establish the pecking order. I had chewed out him and one of his men for violating electrical tag-out procedures, nearly getting one of my own electricians killed. Maybe he just disliked me. Maybe it was all of the above.

His arbitrary and capricious rules and procedural changes when I ordered parts were setting me seriously behind. I was starting to get desperate. I discussed this with him several times, but he always brushed me off or defended his actions and his people. I also discussed this with his Filipino chief storekeeper. He was as antagonistic and belligerent as he thought he could get away with. I learned from books and personal experience that some Filipino service members harbored negative feelings against Blacks. I reread the supply procedures and instructions. I discussed this behavior with the executive officer and the commanding officer. Nothing helped. Work it out, aye. They couldn't be bothered to investigate or mediate.

I asked, and no other department heads were having such problems. I got a 4.0 (perfect) in material management in Officer Candidate School. I understood the supply system; I didn't understand this behavior. My own supply department leadership was hurting the ship's readiness posture and not being held accountable. Yelling didn't help. It probably made it worse.

If this ship did not deploy on time because the engineering department was not ready, no one was going to blame the supply officer. The assholes were even canceling parts needed to fix their own equipment! This was asinine.

My hair started to fall out. I would reach up, pull a plug of hair easily from my head, and look at it in wonder. I could feel my body starting to die from the inside out. I constantly tasted bile and was living on Pepsi, Pepto-Bismol, and chocolate. I was under a lot of stress, which is debilitating and cumulative, I've heard.

Part of the problem was the shipboard parts ordering computer system. This system allowed you to track your parts and the status of the requisitions in the pipeline but poorly. It didn't clearly show the big picture. All you could see was little pieces at a time. Try cutting your phone bill into thirty pieces, mixing them up and spreading them over a table, and making sense of it while arguing with the phone company about an error on your bill. I had to get creative. How could I get the skipper to understand how what was happening to me would impact our scheduled deployment and, therefore, his future?

Listen fast while I tell you; it can surely be of help to you. Petty Officer Duke and I worked all night, creating a brand-new report and a unique format. We made a list of the twenty-five most critical outstanding parts, all necessary for on-time deployment. You previously had to hunt through the existing system and pull out the pertinent information on different screens and in different areas in the system and laboriously write notes. We prioritized them from most to least critical and listed the dates when they entered the system and what happened after they did, including the contradictory requirements, how long they sat before they were reviewed, how long they sat before the parts were ordered, whether or not they were canceled, the reason (if any) given if they were, and how long before we were expected to get the part or whether it was readily available. If it wasn't readily available, we had to submit a casualty report to expedite it but needed supply's input first. When completed, I was dumbfounded to see on paper how systematic this capriciousness was. I couldn't wait for daylight. It came, and we were still working on the report.

When he arrived, I took this report up to my easygoing, laid-back skipper. I must have felt like Zumwalt, testifying at the congressional subcommittee hearings on "permissiveness" in the navy. They didn't listen; would my skipper? As he went through the report, I could see him getting pissed as he grasped its significance. He began asking me questions for which there was no logical answer. He finally understood. This was not incompetence or laziness. This was intentional. He could see that the mission of the ship was being put in jeopardy, as was his future.

He ordered the supply officer to his cabin. We went over the report together. I just happened to have one for the supply officer and a paper clip, nice guy that I am. The supply officer couldn't explain his actions or why his chief was canceling requisitions needed to fix his own damn galley equipment, thereby limiting the menu options. Cut off nose, spite face! He was taking one gut punch after the other while I stood there feeling vindicated.

All I said was, "See? How you like me now, frat boy? Cold busted, you are. Lie if you must, but pay you will." Of course, I was saying this to myself, in the voice of the wise old Yoda. It was not an especially sweet victory. I had been up all night. I was exhausted again. The skipper yelled some very clear orders to my nemesis, and he scurried out and went to work.

His department spent the next several days working overtime to get all my vital parts ordered expeditiously. I was then able to file some high-priority casualty reports that would expedite those parts. Our "forensic analysis" had worked. I wanted to look deeper. The supply officer never explained or apologized. I wanted to know why he was so intent on making me fail. Blacks have lived this story repeatedly. Resource denial is a symptom. We never talked about the underlying issue. This is not unusual. Was it racial discrimination? No charge was made, and no decision was rendered. It was 1989. Not one discrimination complaint that year was substantiated. The skipper treated the symptom, not the problem.

Why was I, the only Black officer on board, having trouble getting the support I needed? A better question: Why did no one seem to care? Who had time to file a damn discrimination complaint and piss everybody off? Was it because they did not believe it would impact them? Had I not created this report, I doubt we would have been able to deploy on schedule. A scapegoat would be needed. I had proximity.

The skipper liked this new report and wanted it updated every day, in addition to the required eight o'clock reports. It made him smarter. He ordered the other department heads to learn from me how to do this new report and to prepare one daily for their departments, which enraged them.

Had they spoken up before, I might not have had to take such drastic measures that ultimately affected them. The supply officer had made it harder for everyone, including himself. Now they all got to see what it was like being the only Black guy, and also extraburdened. The skipper used these reports to keep us on our toes. He would compare the reports from previous days with the one you just gave him.

For a while, I was about as popular as when I got the smoking lamp put out as an E-5. It seemed that the supply officer started serving a lot more ham.

I should have submitted it as a recommended change to the computer system, but I was too busy, sweeping up clumps of my hair. Because of the delaying actions of supply, I wasn't able to get a bulk lube oil delivery. I had to submit a casualty report for barrels of lube oil for my diesel generators, and it was shipped, at great cost, overland by truck from Charleston, South Carolina.

Department heads received a one-hour lecture on command-managed equal opportunity. It wasn't enough, and there was no test (too subjective). The real test would come in the fleet. Would an officer so educated be able to recognize discrimination when he encountered it? Maybe, if he or she was the one experiencing it.

If there was a case study developed to study discrimination, I think my experience with the supply officer should be it. No matter what conclusion the participants reached, they would at least be able to recognize and act when the "minority" sailor was experiencing differential treatment and understand its impact on the organization. Discrimination hurts the organization. I didn't file a complaint; I just outsmarted my nemesis and showed the skipper the consequences of ignoring it. Finally, self-preservation became more important to him than just everybody trying to get along.

We deployed in late July on schedule, with barrels of lube oil lashed on the main deck instead of in the storage tanks. It was embarrassing. We looked like a floating equivalent of something out of *The Grapes of Wrath* or *The Beverly Hillbillies*. I thought about what the other ship's crews must have thought. Within a week, I'd start using that lube oil. We had a diesel generator with a badly leaking oil cooler, but it only leaked when the diesel generator was running (warm). I eventually had to crawl under this running diesel generator to find the leak in order to file a casualty report.

I was one of two engineers thin enough to do it, and in good conscience, I couldn't allow the other to do it. It was dangerous as hell, and if there was a problem and the fire suppression system fired off, the ventilation was going to shut down; in that event, I might suffocate before they could extract me. That would beat burning up. But it had to be done, so I did it—one more adventure in enabling the ship to operate effectively on deployment.

One of the lessons I learned from this entire fiasco was that nothing you say is as important as what you can show on paper. Don't forget this lesson. It would have been beneficial if we had had a sit-down "Lessons Learned" discussion in the wardroom. I wanted answers, and none were forthcoming. This was a lost opportunity, and that's a shame. It's also not unusual.

9

Cruising, Crashing, and Other Disasters

Prepare to get your feet wet; we're going to sea. Put on your life vest, just in case. We deployed in late July 1989. The most exciting and dangerous night of deployment happened before we arrived in the Persian Gulf, courtesy of our helicopter detachment. The pilots flew two SH-60B antisubmarine helicopters (helos), and we all thought the helicopter pilots were a competent bunch. We appeared to be a well-oiled ship. On August 2, 1989, at about 11:00 p.m., something happened that demonstrated the importance of following training.

We were making twenty knots and conducting helicopter operations. I was working in my stateroom. As the helicopter was making its third night approach, five hundred yards astern of us, we lost all contact with it. Instead of sounding the flight crash alarm as he'd been trained to do, the helicopter control officer (my executive officer) sent someone down to officers' quarters to inform the helicopter detachment's officer in charge.

The helicopter control officer recommended the officer of the deck (OOD) throw a smoke float overboard, while he awaited guidance from the detachment officer in charge. When informed of lost contact, the detachment officer in charge had the bridge sound the flight crash alarm, following protocol, correctly assuming that the helicopter had crashed. When I heard the flight crash alarm, I rushed to the helicopter control station, then to the combat information center, and then to the bridge, gathering pertinent information. I learned approximately how far we were from the actual crash site. We had come about and were traveling back down our previous track toward the crash site, but not far enough. We proceeded to where the chart had been marked when the flight crash alarm had been sounded, near where the smoke float had been deployed, and then slowed down.

I thought the helicopter crewmembers were dead. There had been no distress call, no warning, nothing. We soon reestablished communications with them; all three had survived the crash. Now they had to survive the rescue. They could see our lights. We could see no sign of them at all. Throw your keys across your wet lawn in the dark and try to see them.

We needed to work fast in case their wet radios failed. Sharks were a concern as well. We had also turned on our deck and searchlights, so the men couldn't make out our ship's aspect. This mistake meant that the men now couldn't see our profile very well and therefore couldn't guide us, and it hurt everyone's night vision. I had previously done a lot of small boat operations, where we boarded vessels at sea, looking for and recovering drugs. I had been in small boats in weather close to this. We had declined to launch our motor whaleboat in similar weather, during daylight hours, because it was too dangerous.

I was confident I understood the situation, despite not being on watch and having no responsibility to act, so I recommended to the skipper that we increase speed and proceed directly to where the crashed pilots were, while they could still communicate with and guide us. I had gathered information he may not have had, and I felt it my duty to share that information. We could have then used our ship to provide a lee (wind and wave break) for them and possibly recovered them without launching any boat. After getting no response, I continued my entreaties, forcefully explaining where I thought we had erred. It was plain to me that there was no danger to the ship; by now the helo was on the bottom.

The skipper instead decided to come to an all stop and send out the search-and-rescue team in the motor whaleboat. Bad idea. This evolution would take valuable time we could have spent moving closer to the men, and we had better visibility than the boat would have. The search and rescue swimmer, Hull Technician First Class Coles, had helped put out the main space fire weeks before. I ran down to the motor whaleboat to brief him, tell him to be careful, and wish him luck. After the boat was launched, I ran back to the bridge and again began advocating that we close the distance to the men in the water while we still had comms with them. I could hear myself getting pretty loud and nearly pleading with stressed men who would have been justified in telling me to shut the hell up.

Commander Barton, my previous skipper, probably would have done just what I was recommending, as he'd taught his junior officers to do exactly that. We had practiced this many times. The executive officer stayed quiet. A helicopter from another ship had been launched and was looking for them. As if on schedule, our boat's very high frequency (VHF) radio failed. Now we couldn't communicate with the boat crew except by signal flares, and the downed crewmen couldn't talk to them either.

If the boat had any problems, it would be a while before we knew it. We soon lost visual contact and waited. The motor whaleboat eventually recovered the men safely and returned to the ship, with everyone in it exhausted from fatigue and adrenaline, having been roughly tossed around. My roommate had narrowly escaped death. The last man out, he had to cut himself loose as the helo sank, removing his inflatable life vest to escape, and was then snagged by a loose strap he had to cut away, barely making it to the surface in time. His cut leg bled for more than an hour. An hour in colder water might have been fatal for all.

Once the rescue ended, the skipper had me follow him to his stateroom. Uh-oh. I was about to learn what happens when you openly question the captain's judgment on the bridge of his ship during a crisis. I had danced close to some red lines on the bridge. This was one ass chewing I would really deserve. As with disrespectful language, truth would be no defense. Instead of chewing me out, he told me that he wanted me to conduct the Judge Advocate General Manual (JAGMAN) investigation of the crash. He wanted me to include in the JAGMAN investigation everything we did wrong after the crash. I thought that this would put me in a very bad position. I'd have to do that while Black too, and almost all involved, whose actions would be under my scrutiny, were not Black. They would not like this one bit, I thought.

I was still braced for an ass chewing, but I nevertheless said, "No, sir, you don't, because we did a hell of a lot of things wrong." I respected this man, but what he was asking me to do would not reflect well on his decision-making, and it was also wrong. Self-flagellation was not part of the stated purpose of a JAGMAN investigation, as his ex-legal yeoman told him and later showed him in the JAGMAN instruction. (I know so much about this incident because I did end up conducting the JAGMAN investigation, and I obtained a copy of it from the Naval Safety Center via the Freedom of Information Act to refresh my memory.)

Critiquing our rescue performance and the decisions he made, which he plainly knew that I had disagreed with, could lead to problems for him. You could do everything right and still get burned. What happened when you didn't and then informed the world? He insisted I do it his way. When I got back to my stateroom, after briefing the EOOW, I was both worried and relieved. My roommate was sound asleep from exhaustion. I wondered how I would have felt had we not saved them. Survivor's guilt? I couldn't remember our last words. When he awoke and learned that I would be conducting the investigation, we didn't have many more. I had become a problem. Smart people avoid problems; he was smart.

The pilot flying the aircraft refused to give me a statement, be interviewed, or in any way cooperate with my investigation. Having flown a $15 million aircraft into the water, he refused to talk to me about it. He was more than happy to participate in the rescue, but that was it. With the benefit of time and distance, I now realize that the one thing that was then rarer in naval aviation than a Black pilot was a Black surface warfare officer conducting an aircraft crash investigation.

The detachment officer in charge was Lieutenant Commander Michael N. Pocalyko. When Mike informed me that his most experienced pilot was refusing to talk or write a statement, I couldn't believe how calm and matter-of-fact he was. I would have been spitting nails and would have grounded the pilot on the spot. The other pilot's (my roommate) statement was insufficiently detailed. Mike's detailed three-page statement as the officer in charge did not address his pilot's behavior or state an opinion on the cause of the crash. Any pilot would have gone over the flight in detail with his boss, explaining the decisions that were made and critiqued the event. Professionalism and duty would have demanded this.

Mike's final paragraph, the closing argument, stated that the only significant discrepancy in the aftermath of the crash that he wished to note "for the record" was that the failure of the ship's VHF radio greatly hindered the communications from the ship to the crew. This, he said, could have meant the difference between life and death and constituted a significant issue for the JAG. He did not address the failure of one of his pilots to explain to the duly appointed investigating officer (me) what caused this aircraft to impact the water, without which the rescue would not have been necessary, as a significant factor hampering the investigation. He and the skipper continued to allow the pilot to fly the remaining helicopter without a prudent evaluation of his flight fitness. I determined that the cause of the crash was pilot error. I sent the report to the first reviewing authority, a JAG command, listing our shortcomings, and they sent it right back, directing the skipper to do it the way I had told him from the beginning. I rewrote and resubmitted it again, using the time I needed elsewhere, and it passed initial muster. There was still this big gaping hole where the pilot's statement was supposed to be.

The flag officers who ultimately reviewed and endorsed this investigation were incensed that the pilot had not received a field naval aviator's evaluation board, which was clearly appropriate. They concluded that the pilot lost situational awareness, flew the helicopter into the water, and should have had an evaluation of his flight readiness conducted before he was allowed to fly another aircraft. This determination was made after *Boone* had returned from deployment, and it was inappropriate to conduct an evaluation of the pilot's fitness at such a late date. I don't know what happened after that, but I do know that there were some very angry flag officers involved, including my old boss, now Vice Admiral John H. Fetterman. The pilot of the craft eventually advanced to commander. He thrived during this deployment and was protected. My deployment story was different and more like my Scotland deployment. You might be able to detect a pattern.

After we started patrolling on station, things were largely boring and uneventful, outside the lifelines, which is exactly how you want them to be. The Persian Gulf is a harsh operating environment. The temperatures are high at night and higher during the day. One-hundred-degree temperatures can be a daily occurrence in the engineering spaces and often were. You could also suck up stray missiles meant for an oil tanker, enter into a minefield, or have a small boat loaded with explosives come alongside and ruin your day. This has all happened to US warships in or near that hostile environment.

On our first day patrolling, we went to general quarters because we thought we had detected an underwater mine. It turned out to be an oil drum. Lots of us thought it was our last day on earth. I know I did. I was in the central control station (CCS), and there wasn't much chance of surviving a direct mine strike from that location, under the waterline as we were. In addition to mines, we were on alert for stray Iraqi missiles, two of which had hit the USS *Stark* in 1987. They were meant for Iranian oil tankers. I stood both engineering and combat watches, the only officer watch stander qualified to do so.

On one occasion, I was standing watch as the tactical action officer (TAO) in the combat information center. I had to read all secret and top-secret message traffic, the standard operating procedures and directives, any special guidance and directives we received, and keep up to date on the actual or potential threats in the area: air, land, and sea. I had to know what enemy combatants were around and their capabilities, and I was expected to take immediate action should we be attacked and to act with extreme prejudice, if required, until the skipper assumed control.

I constantly monitored the threat environment and combat watch standers and advised or ordered the OOD regarding necessary maneuvers and actions. If I issued a command, anything less than instant obedience might mean someone would soon be dead. I also had to communicate with other ships and authorities and execute changing tasks. There was a reason that the TAO exam was three hours long, and many people failed it.

This watch was usually fairly uneventful, save a few rubbernecking helicopter pilots from the oil companies that flew too close, especially at night.

We were warned against being too aggressive and also warned to defend our ships aggressively. Do I zigzag or not? Tails I win, heads you lose. I nearly ordered a helicopter from an oil platform fired on one night after he ignored our radio and light warnings to keep away from the ship, flying directly over us, showboating. Had he dropped a bomb down our stack, I would have been in big trouble. Had I blown him out of the sky, I would have been in big trouble as well. I didn't feel confident that I'd have had backup in that unfortunate event.

On another occasion, the OOD was preparing to drive the ship closely between two nonmilitary ships transiting the area. In the event of an emergency, this would restrict or limit the ability of our ship to maneuver should they get stupid, nit witty, or attacked by either Iraqi or Iranian missiles. We could be hit instead. We did not have communication contact with these ships, nor did we need to. I spoke to the OOD and quietly recommended that he alter course to avoid this. I had been a member of his OOD qualification board; he was relatively junior and inexperienced. He was tall, thin, and handsome, like the supply officer. He responded that he had everything under control and asked me not to worry. My job was to worry, and I persisted. He still wouldn't follow my recommendation, which gave him an opportunity to save face. Instead, he questioned my authority, since he was the officer of the deck, explaining to me how things worked. I understood the hierarchy; he worked for me.

I finally flatly ordered him to change to a certain course to prevent the ship from standing into potential danger. He did as ordered. This exchange was a little testy and occurred in full view and earshot of both the bridge and combat information center watch standers. Technically, he worked for me, but he wasn't acting like it. I got the impression that he thought he knew more than I did or didn't feel obligated to follow my instructions. Wrong on both counts he was. When we got off watch, I pulled him aside for a teaching moment, explaining the long list of potentially bad things that could have happened. He was gracious.

The next incident was a little more dramatic, and the aftertaste lingered a lot longer. Another TAO watch stander, a lieutenant department head, was having trouble staying awake. To curb this, the leading chief of the combat systems division decided to remove the stool from the TAO watch station, to help his department head stay awake. I didn't realize this until I showed up for watch and discovered there was no stool. No one admitted to knowing where it was. I had the division chief paged to come to combat. When he got there, I told him that I understood the situation but that I wanted the stool to be available when I stood watch. He curtly said he didn't know where it was and abruptly turned away to leave. He was a little guy, with an apparent Napoleon complex.

I called him back, twice, and he ignored me, slowly and deliberately walking out without another word. He'd decided that I would have to stand, for hours, while his enlisted watch standers sat comfortably. End of discussion. This pissed me off, well above the normal tolerance level. The only word I can use to describe how I felt is *rage*: blinding, infuriating rage at this blatantly disrespectful and disobedient behavior. I could launch missiles, fire guns, and fight the ship on the captain's authority, but I couldn't sit down because he didn't think I should, because his boss couldn't stay awake, on his authority? He thought so, with complete confidence. He acted like he thought he was my daddy.

His casual and deliberate demeanor astonished me. He had just all but told me to kiss his ass. At least he didn't call me a "goddam nigger" and hit me in the face, as a drunken white chief had once done to Bill Norman after he had identified himself as an officer, while he was on liberty. I responded appropriately, having the officer of the deck order the chief master at arms (CMAA), also the only Black chief on board, to the combat information center. I told him to place this chief on report for disrespectful behavior toward a superior commissioned officer and disobeying a lawful order and that I would write him a statement.

He looked at me with a knowingly raised eyebrow but didn't ask any questions. These accumulating incidents were making me wonder how long I would have to fight this behavior. Within seconds after the CMAA left, the missing stool miraculously appeared, and I took my seat and started writing out my statement for the report chit, in between my other duties. Having the stool appear only made me madder. The watch standers knew where it was the whole time. I was clenching my jaws so tightly that I was making my teeth hurt. This appeared to be a coordinated act of disrespect and deceit or perhaps a conspiracy. It was time for me to show some fang and demand some accountability.

I wanted to talk to the Black chief, but I was afraid that might start rumors of a conspiracy or a Mau Mau rebellion. The chief's department head asked me to drop the chit. "Hell, no," I said. "I am going to push this through." He understood what had happened, but he didn't care, as with the supply parts issue. "Please, Keith, just drop the chit. I'll talk to him," he said. I refused. This was about my legitimacy, authority, and credibility. I needed to know who my daddy was. Next stop: executive officer. He called me in to his stateroom and told me to work it out with the other department head, as he had done with the supply officer issue before, which neither he nor the executive officer had helped me with—it was not their problem, apparently.

He had no problem chewing on my butt because my maintenance spot checks were late, but he believed this matter did not warrant his attention. This stung more than the initial offense. If the skipper had any thoughts about this, he never shared them with me. Silence. The wagons circled around the white chief, not the Black lieutenant. The chief had shown his entire watch team that he was my daddy, and my leadership had too. Was race a factor? I never raised the issue. In the navy during this time, discrimination was often swept under the rug or minimized, which the navy's own statistics make clear, as I have addressed in various chapters.

Meanwhile, the chief and I had no interaction. I ignored him. He felt wronged, or so I heard. I met with him and his department head, having no choice, and I extracted a grudging apology, a figurative pound of flesh, and let it go. He never explained his behavior. I never knew whether or not the executive officer or skipper even talked to him. I wanted to hear his side of the story. Suppose he or one of his thus emboldened watch standers had decided to ignore an order I issued as the tactical action officer? Danger lurks in disobedience and disrespect. No one seemed to understand the pressures I was under—it was not their problem.

The dangers of disrespect and failing to follow orders were demonstrated in the mishap involving the USS *Fitzgerald* in June of 2017. Lieutenant Natalie Combs, whose father was a navy rear admiral, was serving as TAO in USS *Fitzgerald* when she collided with a civilian ship. There was conflict and no communication between her and the female OOD, perhaps because of disrespect or contempt. Seven sailors were killed in the collision. Combs was recommended for special court-martial until the case against her collapsed, and she was allowed to separate with an honorable discharge. I will go to my grave believing that race was a factor.

I believe that discrimination and disrespect demonstrated toward Black military personnel in all the services can be forcefully addressed. When the navy adopted a zero tolerance policy on drug use, it had a dramatic effect. The same might be true of a similar policy on discrimination and harassment. Making racist behavior a stand-alone Uniform Code of Military Justice offense, as I have recommended in an article published by the Center for International Maritime Security (CIMSEC), would go a long way toward fixing this problem. Being the only or one of few minority officers in a command can be an isolating and lonely experience and can lead to problems for them. Few white people seem to understand this. My life experiences with race were completely different than those of my white peers.

My father demanded to be treated like a man and was charged with inciting a riot. In his day, that could get you sent to captain's mast, or worse. You were expected to fight for your country but invited trouble if you fought for yourself. It was difficult to have someone treat you as less than a man and to have to deal with it intellectually rather than as you instinctively wanted to. It damages both your body and your psyche, or so I've read.

I always made sure that my job performance, or competence, was never an issue. Many of these incidents occurred simply because I was just doing my job. Other incidents caused me to question this command climate. One involved some of my junior personnel who disregarded my written orders not to bypass a troublesome salinity alarm on our water storage tanks. The watch, a Black seaman, fell asleep after wiring the dump valve closed and rigging the alarm to keep it from waking him up, so when the threshold to set off the alarm was reached and surpassed, our freshwater supply became contaminated.

I was fit to be tied, contemplating the death penalty. I knew better by now than to write a report chit. The executive officer talked to the offending watch standers, chewing ass as he thought appropriate, further eroding my credibility and authority, but this time in my own department. He should have done that at the executive officer's inquiry, which I at least wanted. We had to take on fresh water from another ship at sea, after taking salty water showers on the fantail for days. These cascading incidents affected my self-esteem and my mental health. I felt like I was "serving second class," as Zumwalt had described so well in his memoir. Some people thought refusing to cooperate with me had no real consequences, and my superiors seemed to reinforce that.

I'll detail one last incident, and we'll move on. All this whining is exhausting. A junior officer set up a familiar scenario: First, he appeared to befriend me. Then, he became snippy and verbally antagonistic, escalating as he gained confidence. He'd soon publicly and casually threaten to whip my ass, which I ignored. I'd lived this same scenario since high school, if not recently. If he didn't back off, I was going to have to educate him. He escalated, as usual.

I seldom let myself be goaded into action by words, not wanting to transform into the profane, loud Angry Black Man, with bloody knuckles and fiery eyes. I managed to avoid the worst-case scenario. I was walking through the wardroom one day, and he said something threatening to me, which I ignored. We were alone. He was ready to make his move. Normally, in this scenario, I would have been called a racial slur by now, following the playbook, but that would have been against navy regulations. Besides, that would have made it about race.

I was looking at documents, and he reached over his head from where he was sitting on a couch and punched me hard in the stomach as I walked past. I was hurt, but I immediately turned around, leaned over the couch, and punched him in his stomach as hard as I could. He jumped up—surprised, angry, and hurt—and asked me if I had lost my fucking mind! He could not believe what had just happened. Luck was with him; had the couch not been between us, I wouldn't have allowed him to remain standing. I just looked at him. He asked me again if I'd lost my mind but didn't move his feet, a fast learner at last.

Finally, I quietly said, "You hit me, I hit you back. What's the problem?" He glared at me and finally said, "You're fucking crazy." He may have been right. I'm not proud to say it, but I felt better after that. I felt like I had just thrown a brick through the plate glass window at the Hall of Naval Injustice. I didn't get a free TV, though. Not even a six-pack. Sometimes, life just ain't fair. With that, I turned around and walked away. He assaults me, but I'm the crazy one because I retaliated? The chief had clearly gotten away with disrespect, and I guess he figured he could get away with assault. I had no more problems from him. A reciprocal gut punch helped him understand that I was more dangerous than I looked if attacked.

An incident I consider very important but am hesitant to reveal follows. I know what happened; I can only speculate about why. It highlights very clearly what could happen when the forces of bias, necessity, resentment, and trust collide. The incident could have ended in death or disaster. The ship's deck log documents the evolution, but it doesn't tell the whole story. The ship was at anchor somewhere in the Gulf for a rare port visit. We had a small floating platform alongside, and our own ship's brow (gangway) was attached to it. Small craft would ferry crewmembers from the platform. I was the command duty officer on this day, and the senior man aboard, with most of the other officers and chiefs enjoying liberty. I never went ashore during this port visit; I had too much to do.

The wave height increased, and I needed to move the platform because the brow was getting uncomfortably close to the edge of the platform. I had a working party mustered on the main deck, explained the problem, and gave very explicit instructions on how we would conduct the evolution. I asked for questions and answered any that arose. Many of these men had been watching movies, reading, or otherwise relaxing. I was interrupting them. Some of them clearly weren't happy about it. The sullen faces and demeanor told me a lot, but it's just part of the deal. I didn't like it any more than they did, but it had to be done.

I passed out radios and took one for myself to coordinate the evolution from the platform. I felt confident in my men and safe. I needed to be where I could gauge when the platform had been sufficiently adjusted. I gave the order to slack the lines on one side just a bit and then hold that. The next order was for the men on the lines at the other side to take in their lines, thus "walking" the platform to the desired position, at which time it would be secured. What happened next scared the shit out of me. The men who had just slacked their lines, who had been talking to each other, all dropped their lines and walked away, dismissing themselves, and now the platform was drifting away from the ship, putting the brow even closer to the edge.

In a total panic, and disbelieving my eyes, I yelled into the radio for the supervisor to send some of the remaining men to man those lines and call for additional men to come man the lines. A very safe evolution had just turned potentially deadly and very expensive. While more men arrived, repositioned themselves and manned the abandoned lines, I held on to the brow with both hands and pulled with all my might, trying to keep it from falling over the edge. As the platform rose and sank with the waves, it was precariously close to the edge, at times less than a foot.

I was too scared to be angry; I was worrying about dying and losing expensive equipment. I didn't intend to follow the brow into the sea, but I had no idea how I would get back aboard the ship if we lost the brow or how anyone else would either. If that brow had fallen, we would have been in serious trouble. This time, I wouldn't be conducting an investigation; I would be the primary subject of one.

Fortunately, we got everything safely secured, and when I got back aboard, I mustered the working party and started angrily asking questions. Who released those men, in the middle of the working party, and why did they leave in the middle of the evolution? Silence, just as the chief before them had been silent. Nobody released them; they just left. My anger grew as the realization dawned on me; they did it because, in my humble and now paranoid opinion, they didn't like being bossed around by me. I was being sent a clear message by the sullen silence and stony looks on some of the faces. The men who had walked away had acted collectively, with clear intent. After a pretty spirited ass chewing and lecture on military responsibilities, I dismissed them. I explained the evolution to the skipper when he returned, glossing over the significant problems. I figured it was not worth verbalizing my concerns. I didn't expect any understanding. It was difficult for me to feel truly safe after this evolution. I got even more careful.

I have spent years trying to make sense of what happened on that day. The deck log tells one story. I have finally told mine. I think I know what the real issue was. A Black guy was interrupting their well-earned rest, and they resented it. The way they showed it was to abandon their duty at the most dangerous moment and leave me to my fate. They could feign ignorance, and I would bear the responsibility as the "incompetent" officer in charge.

I don't want to believe I am right. Unfortunately, I don't have much choice. At this particular intersection of bias, resentment, necessity, and trust, I had almost bet on the wrong horse. Necessity and trust were almost done in by bias and resentment. Many a junior officer in the Vietnam War learned a hard and sometimes fatal lesson at the hands of his own men. I lived to tell mine. Let us not speak of this again. It is too painful. I still dream about it. Let us not forget the lesson, whatever it may be. If you don't know the name Lieutenant Junior Grade Asante McCalla by now, this would be a good time to educate yourself on what can happen at sea, with no resolution as to why. He disappeared from the USS *Lake Erie* on August 19, 2018. The deck log doesn't tell the whole story. Reading about his death and listening to his mother's plea for information sent chills down my spine. I wrote a tribute article to him on my LinkedIn page. I know the pressures he was under better than most.

A good respite from all the pressure and second-guessing was a port visit we had in Ibiza, an island off the coast of Spain. We pulled into an anchorage and had a few days ashore. Some of the local boats present came out to greet us, and lots of the ladies aboard were waving enthusiastically, wearing bikini bottoms but not tops, as is common on the beaches there. While many of the crew made asses of themselves, running from one side of the ship to the other, frantically trying to ask them for directions to the nearest Christian Science Reading Room, I just sat on the bridge, with binoculars in my lap, occasionally bird-watching. Lieutenant Commander Mike Pocalyko, the officer in charge of the helicopter detachment, and I did take a couple of jogs together ashore, but I never made it to the topless beaches.

One night, I went ashore and had a decent time people watching. I almost always went ashore alone. I walked around Bahrain, during another port visit, by myself, getting away from the tourist areas, looking at the architecture, and wondering if I might get kidnapped and held for ransom. I figured, probably incorrectly, I looked more like an African student or worker than a sailor. I never had a problem. The gold markets, "souks," were interesting. There was more gold than I've ever seen in my life, mostly being bought by women dressed in black from head to toe. I bought a few trinkets and listened to a great Filipino jazz band at a little bar. It was the closest I felt to home during the entire cruise.

When we returned from our deployment, it was both a happy time and a sad one for some of the crew. Relationships had ended, others had begun, and some fathers were seeing their young children for the first time. A couple of sailors had partners who were four or five months pregnant, presenting a math problem. After having managed the enlisted men's club at Mayport for eighteen months, nothing surprised me. Some returned to loving homes, others to empty homes, and still others to no homes. Such is life on the sea.

I still had a wife, a home, two stepchildren, a great many more clothes in my wife's closet, fancy crystal trinkets in the curio cabinets, less savings than I expected, and renewed marital conflict. I was treated at home like I was on the other team. They were a unit; I was a paycheck. This marriage wouldn't last. Getting little respect at both work and home can wear you down to the point of no return. Choose carefully. I was nearing the end of my tour and hoping to get a job close to home, in the Mayport basin, but not another engineering tour.

Shortly before I transferred, we had an engineering mobile training team visit. We had missed two scheduled visits because of various equipment casualties or schedule conflicts. I had one the first few months into my tour, and this would be the final one, when I should have been long gone. I was hit hard during this visit. It was impossible for me to get the necessary training done before this visit. The engineering safety checks were a tightly choreographed routine of starting equipment, checking parameters, and making oral reports to the maestro at the CCS. It was the closest thing you could get to an engineering ballet. It took practice.

You were expected to perform them and then get underway for engineering training. After a week-long "school ship" visit to Newport Rhode Island, for navy students, we had a port visit in Savannah, Georgia. I often necessarily worked my men on weekends. The weekend that we returned was important; we'd only have those two days to prepare for the assist visit that began on Monday. The captain forbade me from working my guys during this port visit. Families were driving up for it, and he wanted everyone to get along and be happy. The squadron commodore had sent out frequent messages about the importance of these safety checks, and he expected compliance.

When the executive officer refused to ask the skipper to change his mind, I contacted the squadron and asked them to move the visit by one week. I told them I wasn't being allowed to perform my safety checks. They laughed and told me to just do the best I could. They weren't expecting us to knock it out of the park.

When the training team walked aboard that Monday morning, Commander Newman confidently announced to the assist team that as far as he was concerned, he had the best engineering department in the Mayport basin. Murphy's law had intervened, however, and we were classified in the worst readiness category, unable to get underway, with two serious casualties. A diesel engine's main fuel line had ruptured, and my propeller propulsion system was contaminated with seawater, due to a seal failure, requiring navy divers days of repairs and testing. Neither casualty resulted from negligence or poor maintenance; they were just normal deterioration. We worked long hours that entire weekend and were exhausted Monday morning. We didn't even "walk through" the safety checks we needed to expertly perform. There simply was not time.

Our safety checks went poorly. We had torn-apart spaces, tired, demoralized sailors, and shore maintenance personnel trying to fix broken infrastructure. We then started going through our admin programs. Those tired sailors presenting administrative programs were also trying to put the ship back together. The results were brutal. I had missed one space reading of one hundred degrees, only one time, while in the Persian Gulf, and didn't do a required heat stress survey. This single oversight occurred eleven and a half months earlier. My heat stress program was judged to be unsatisfactory. I had not been perfect. I had probably been on TAO watch or conducting a JAGMAN when it happened. If this didn't fit Zumwalt's definition of Mickey Mouse regulations and procedures, as he addressed eliminating in a chapter of his memoir, then there isn't one. Declaring an entire program unsatisfactory because of one minor oversight that occurred more than eleven months prior, with no detrimental effects to operations, I certainly consider to be in "Mickey Mouse" territory.

After another administrative program was judged unsatisfactory, for similarly chicken-shit and unreasonable justifications, I looked at the team leader in total shock and disbelief and asked if he was really serious. He let out a big belly laugh and nodded his head, enjoying my misery. My men had done a good job, and I knew it. We had passed our operational propulsion plant exam. We had won the Battle Efficiency Award. I had had no heat stress or other personnel casualties during my entire tour. This "assist" was a demoralizing, humiliating, unreasonable experience that felt like a sadistic massacre, masquerading as "help."

The squadron chief of staff, a captain, spoke with frustration at the debriefing. He said he could understand some of the administrative grading and that it was not his major concern. He said that we'd had a tough schedule and some bad breaks. He said he expected to find problems with administration and paperwork. He got a report like this almost once a week. I was surprised when he said this. What he said he couldn't understand was why we didn't do better on our safety checks after they'd sent so many messages about them.

I felt both vilified and vindicated. I wanted to explain. I started to open my mouth to speak but saw the executive officer looking directly in my eyes, shaking his head slightly from side to side. I obediently shut my mouth, taking one for the team. You could just imagine how it felt to be there, feeling like everyone thinks you're incompetent and can't read. By now, I was emotionally numb and almost too "fried" to care. I had done my best under extremely challenging circumstances, with little command support. Unlike the supply officer, the helicopter pilots, or the disrespectful and disobedient chief, I would be held immediately accountable.

Men on nearby ships, much more experienced than I and with fewer problems, had been relieved for cause or had just thrown in the towel and quit. I wanted to do the same, more than once. I didn't get carried out feet first, either. I simply had no tribe. A few years later, I would be offered the job of officer in charge, Engineering Mobile Training Team, Mayport. I could not believe my good fortune! I could now do to others what had been done to me. I said no.

The abuse I believe I endured on this ship was soul crushing. I often felt like a prisoner. The psychological assault was real. I have come to know a great deal about the firsthand effects of psychological assault. During this tour, I experienced an incident, on average, about every three weeks. That doesn't leave much time to recover before the next wave hits. The stress effects are cumulative.

Commander Newman appeared to agonize over my final fitness report. I still consider this assist visit my only major professional failure. We talked honestly about it. He seemed to be more upset about the results of the assist visit than he was about losing a helicopter on deployment. He awarded those pilots Navy Achievement Medals when they left the ship. In the end, I think he accepted that he was partly to blame. My failing was not being as good an engineer as I needed to be. His decision, in the end, was technically fair.

In my final fitness report, he still had high praise for my performance and future potential but said that my performance was "consistent," which it surely was. Until then, I had always been "improving." I had been prepared to submit a rebuttal to my fitness report, pointing fingers of my own, but I chose not to. "Consistent" really meant "not doing too well" or worse. It was subjective. I was too mentally exhausted to push back. After almost two years, I didn't receive so much as a letter of appreciation for all my efforts. I'd wager that my supply officer nemesis received better. I know the pilots did.

I still have a very high degree of respect for this man, who was both my skipper and someone I thought of as my friend. I accept his judgment. He could have hammered me harder, but he did not. He was a people person, a storyteller, and a good skipper. I wonder if he's ever told stories about me. If he did, I can guarantee you that they were funny. I don't know if I would laugh at all of them, though. I did almost everything I could to survive and succeed. For the life of me, I still can't figure out exactly how. I have nothing but respect for naval engineers. I felt like I once was a naval engineer. I don't ever want to do anything that hard, ever again. So far, I haven't.

Now I was off to the hydrofoil navy, where I hoped things were "clear and bright," like your fuel was supposed to be. I still felt like there was something I could contribute. I had gotten a whole lot tougher, more ruthless, and a lot smarter.

10

Executive Officer, USS *Gemini*, the Hydrofoil Navy

Unless you served in the navy or Coast Guard before July 1993, smuggled drugs by sea, or spent time in Mayport, Key West, or the Caribbean, you most likely never saw a navy hydrofoil. If you did, you'll never forget it. If you ever got to fly on one, you sure as hell won't ever forget that. Mine was the USS *Gemini* (PHM-6).

PHM stands for patrol hydrofoil missile. These were six fast, well-armed, aluminum hulled, and beautiful ships. Captain Al Collins, the only other Black officer I am aware of who served in one, became a limited duty officer (LDO) after his stellar performance on the USS *Pegasus*. The navy assigned him to the ship temporarily, and then his new skipper threatened to kick his ass if he didn't apply for the LDO program. Good leadership that was.

About the time I reported to the *Gemini*, *All Hands* magazine's June 1990 edition had a sea-level, close-up picture of the USS *Taurus* (PHM-3) on the cover. It was screaming away at above forty knots, with ten feet of daylight between its hull and the flat ocean—and looking like it was ready to eat someone's lunch. Many drug smugglers saw this view. All we needed was a pair of big seaweed testicles to hang over the fantail. The men were armed as necessary.

This issue of *All Hands* was dedicated to drug interdiction, and the navy's contributions to the effort. Hydrofoils were a very big part of that. It also addressed the 1980s in a ten-page article about issues of family, operations, equality, readiness, and diversity. The chief of naval personnel was now Vice Admiral Mike Boorda. The article said that Boorda took the lead to bolster the navy's equal opportunity effort, following in Zumwalt's footsteps.

As a young enlisted sailor, he had made mistakes, and people had helped him. Everyone should have to need help now and then, so they remember what it's like. He paid it forward. He said that as of June 1990, the state of equal opportunity was good, but "we have a lot of room for improvement."

I thought it fitting that a former personnel man should end his career as the chief of naval personnel. I thought he couldn't go higher.

This article also said that the *Chief of Naval Operations Study Group's Report on Equal Opportunity* (1988) targeted specific areas where the navy could do better to attain its equal opportunity goals but said that the programs already in place have "realized major improvements in recent years." This study caused the chief of naval operations to admit that there were widespread bias and discrimination and promotion disparities for minority sailors months earlier. I heard no more about it.

These hydrofoils were very expensive to operate. Only top performers were assigned to these ships, officer or enlisted, and they required four or five officers and about twenty enlisted to man them. I was wrung out and dinged by Commander Newman, but I made the cut. These ships had a gas turbine engine, like the ones I had on the *Boone*. They also had two diesel engines to provide propulsion when we weren't flying. Yes, flying. The first ship, *Pegasus* (PHM-1), was commissioned in July 1977, the other five during 1981–82. All were decommissioned in 1993. One, the USS *Aries* (PHM-5), was rescued from the scrapyard and may someday be restored.

From 1989 through 1994, according to a report issued by the Navy Personnel Research and Development Center, African American women in the navy were suffering from a double whammy: being disadvantaged because of race and gender. Boorda knew that well. He tried to fix it. Bullies often look for soft targets, and they apparently settled on Black females in the navy.

Nevertheless, many Black navy women would thrive. Michelle J. Howard graduated from the Naval Academy in 1982. In 1987, she received the Secretary of the Navy/Navy League Captain Winifred Collins Award for outstanding leadership. It inspired me to read about her accomplishments. In 2006, she became the first Black woman to command a ship in the navy. Sailors were seen scraping Confederate flag stickers off their cars on the day she assumed command. She was the first female academy graduate to be selected for admiral.

For fiscal year 1990, there were 168 formal discrimination complaints, with 11 complaints (7 percent) substantiated. During 1991, 171 complaints were submitted with 9 (5 percent) substantiated. In summary, of 678 complaints submitted since 1987, only 27 were substantiated, an average of 4.2 percent. For comparison, the substantiation rate for 2017 was 6 percent. If you filed a formal complaint alleging racial discrimination in the navy, the odds were still overwhelming that it would not be substantiated. My experiences can give you an indication about why. That same year, the Persian Gulf War (First Gulf War) would be the first modern US war in which there would be no significant military racial disturbances reported in the media. An event called Tailhook 91, in September 1991, would have a dramatic effect on the military complaint process, for a while. In 1992, things would be dramatically different.

While assigned temporary additional duty to the hydrofoil support squadron, awaiting my reporting date, I met a white chief petty officer who would quickly make my "bigot radar" lock on. He was the squadron 3M coordinator (supply maintenance related). At first I thought he was just a dickhead. Turns out, he was a whole dick. He walked up to me and asked me if I'd been to a barbershop in the Black area of town, insinuating that I needed a haircut. I told him no but that I intended to. He laughed in my face. His breath smelled like fresh vulture shit, only not as nice. He warned me that if I went there, I better take an assault rifle with me.

I looked him in the eye, through the stinky breath haze, and slowly and deliberately asked him why in the world would I want to do that. He laughed some more vulture shit breath and said something forgettable, so I turned away and ignored him. He was performing for the crowd, insinuating that I would need or want to shoot Black people if I went out in town. I soon sent him some breath mints through the guard mail. He either didn't use them, or they didn't work.

There were several senior enlisted people around, and he was very comfortable with this line of discussion, even with a Black lieutenant that he had just met. He had approached me with the confidence of a sadistic bully. He already had a Black female chief to torment; now he had a Black male officer too! Man, he must have felt like he hit the jackpot. His stature was going to rise dramatically, I'm sure he thought. I decided to keep an eye out for him. I'd dealt with guys like him before (more on him later). When I met the squadron commodore, Captain Ron Berning, he warmly welcomed me, and cautioned me about the hazards of navigation on such a high speed and maneuverable platform, and briefed me about a previous incident in which *Gemini* had run soft aground during a navigation check ride inspection, thereby failing the inspection and damaging several careers. I vowed that this would not happen to me.

Lieutenant Commander David J. Aland was my new skipper. The executive officer carried the administrative load. I was part yeoman, part officer. We relied on the maintenance squadron for most of our major personnel records support. This was a job I was confident I could do.

Like any commanding officer/executive officer team, we had our differences, but we were a good team. He was good cop; I was bad cop—a typical arrangement on board navy ships. I had never had a skipper so close to me in rank. He, I don't think, had ever worked so closely with a Black man before, especially as a near equal. I think we both learned a lot from each other. I've never seen a man who was so clearly happy to be the commanding officer of a ship. I was happy for and envied him. Dave was a short, bespectacled man who looked like a college professor.

A funny memory of him involved one of my old bosses. Shortly after I reported, we flew up to Mayport in order to participate in an exercise involving the USS *Saratoga* (CV-60) and other ships. My old boss, Captain James T. Matheny, was now the commanding officer. He had written my LDO and Officer Candidate School recommendations seven years before. We were in our assigned area when the *Saratoga* turned toward us. Carriers do this all the time, and it always scares the piss out of you when they do. We needed to move! My entire officer career, it had been drilled into me: "Stay away from the carrier! Do not get caught on the bow of the carrier! Do not cross the bow of the carrier! Carriers are big, mean, evil, and stupid!" The law of gross tonnage means that the carrier always wins. In this case, there was a problem.

Dave wasn't going to be run off our assigned station by any stinking carrier. Ultimately, Captain Matheny got on the radio himself and politely asked us to move so that he could continue with his flight operations without changing course. Dave, being a hotshot hydrofoil skipper, was not about to be pushed around by any carrier skipper. He was a skipper too. I listened to this polite radio exchange with both alarm and amusement until I heard Captain Matheny utter a curse and slam down the phone.

I wanted to pick up the phone and say, "Hi, sir, remember me, over?" Under the circumstances, I think it was better that he didn't know that I was there. The carrier changed course. We had the right of way, fair and square. Hydrofoils were special. That's why they built only six of them.

Early in my tour, we were scheduled for a dry dock maintenance period in Mobile, Alabama. I got nervous when I heard that. Mobile, Alabama, was where twenty-three-year-old Michael Donald was lynched in 1981 by members of the local Klan in retaliation after another Black man was acquitted of murdering a white man. Proximity—custody—conviction—ultimate justice; Mobile didn't follow the usual script. I used to talk about this case to classes when I was an Equal Opportunity Program Specialist (EOPS) in Mayport. The Klan bypassed protests and riots and went straight to a retaliatory lynching.

Dave Aland received a phone call from Mobile's mayor, congratulating him on the scheduled port visit and maintenance availability. He extended his desire to make the visit as pleasant as possible. Dave was also puzzled. He told me his honor the mayor had informed him that he understood that the executive officer was a Black man. How had the mayor gotten this information so quickly? Was there an advance warning system that I was not aware of?

We would arrive in time to attend the annual local Mardi Gras festivities. The mayor assured Dave that I would be welcome at these festivities. I'd been to many social functions but was not aware of any calls having been made assuring that I would be "welcome" despite the fact that I was Black. Dave Aland was a US Naval Academy graduate and an Annapolis native. He remembered the separate water fountains, but I don't think he truly understood the vagaries of race relations in the Deep South, based on our conversations. He was, as were many naval officers not from the South, neither expected to understand nor faulted for it. They didn't know what they didn't know, to paraphrase former secretary of defense Donald Rumsfeld. I doubt Rumsfeld understood either. He ended the reporting of formal discrimination complaints to Congress via the Annual Defense Report, around 2007. Given the way the program oversight and administration fell apart afterwards, as I discuss in the Epilogue, this was an unwise decision.

At the official reception, my wife at the time, Iris, and I were the only Black guests. All the help was Black. Everyone was extremely gracious and welcoming, and they seemed to know our names before any introductions. Even so, I felt like a circus or sideshow oddity. While in Mobile, I had also been invited by one of the city's leading Black citizens to attend another event, so I went. None of my white officer counterparts received an invitation. They would not have gone if they had, I don't think. This event was Black. All Black. Not as fine, not as friendly, and nobody knew my name. In my fancy uniform with the little tiny medals, I looked like "the Man."

There was some confusion when I showed up and gave them the name of the man who had invited me as his guest. He couldn't be found, and someone thought that I should have to pay. Hospitality and decorum won out. I had a decent time at this event also, but the contrast was striking. Separate but equal—not quite. Everybody in Mobile knew his or her place, except me, apparently. Being a Black officer can sometimes mean a strange and lonely existence. The year was 1991. It might be different decades later.

After we left the shipyard and I got further settled into my duties and responsibilities in the ship back in Key West and got my hydrofoil sea legs better under me, I found that Dave Aland and I made a good team. There were a couple of things he did, without malice or ill will, that caused problems for us both and ultimately the crew and their families. These problems came about, I believe, because of a lack of trust. On my very first attempt to bring the ship alongside a pier, in Key West, he became a little excited and took the conn (the officer of the deck has the conn when he or she is giving orders that control the movement of the ship from the bridge) from me as I was making my approach. I was a good ship handler with a good bit of experience, the water and winds were calm, and I had the "bubble." The ship was in no danger that I could see.

No one had ever taken the conn from me before. I was embarrassed and surprised, but I said nothing. I stepped aside and let him moor his ship. After we tied up, he called me up to his stateroom and apologized. I didn't think he had done anything inappropriate. It was his ship, and he was responsible for it. If I had been in his shoes and sensed danger, I would have done the same thing. However, knowing what you do about my history, you know I can't just leave it at that.

I am a product of my life's experiences. He had realized that his actions had made me look bad in front of the crew, and he told me he was aware that each person handles a ship differently. I explained to him my intentions, and he said he understood, even though that wasn't the way he would have done it. I chalked this up to jitters. Nevertheless, I never took that hydrofoil alongside the pier again. I never asked to, and he never invited me to. I watched it done many, many times by first class petty officers, and I knew that I could do it. Captain Barton had let me take *Voge* alongside an oiler during an underway replenishment at sea, not bothering to ask if I'd ever done it before. I had not. My primary job on the hydrofoil was navigation, administration, and driving at sea. I stuck to that.

The next incident also involved trust. Shortly after we started our dry dock availability, Dave became curious about the per diem the crew were drawing in addition to their normal pay. This per diem had been paid to hydrofoil sailors under these circumstances since the squadron was established, but for some reason, he questioned it.

When he asked me about it, I asked him to let me check it out in the appropriate regulations and do some research. He knew my background. I believed he was on to something. He agreed to let me do so, but then he called the ensign disbursing division officer at the squadron support activity in Key West that same day and asked him the same question. I would have advised against that.

The results shook the entire squadron. The ensign called the comptroller in Jacksonville, Florida, responsible for our pay and funding, asking him the question. I had learned years ago to know, if you could, the answer before you ask an important question or make an inquiry. If you didn't already know most of the answer, you had not done enough research.

The comptroller put an immediate stop to the pay in question and demanded immediate repayment of these clearly "stolen" funds. This was to put a considerable financial hardship on the sailors and families who used them for travel, phone bills, and child care—whatever expenses they incurred due to the geographic separation. Officers didn't get this pay, only the enlisted personnel did.

This comptroller seemed pissed that we had apparently been cheating the government all these years, and he had finally caught us. I half expected to do the "perp walk" in uniform and on live television, the way he carried on when I called him. He also threatened to retroactively make sailors who had received these funds (subject to the statute of limitations) pay them back. You can imagine the fuss this kicked up in Key West. That ensign was sorry he had kicked over this shit bucket. No one had any idea that there was a problem with receiving these funds. Well, almost no one.

Momma, back in Key West, made her opinion known loud and clear. When momma ain't happy, nobody is happy. "None of this happened; everything was fine, until *Gemini* got that damned new Black XO. He can't even drive the damn ship. My husband said the skipper won't let him." I could just hear them in my head. A scapegoat was needed, and I was the most logical choice.

Needless to say, we weren't popular for a while. I had to submit paperwork for each individual sailor, signed by each of them, requesting a waiver, and boy, did I get an earful. Both ears! I eventually convinced the comptroller to let me submit one form with everyone's name on it. Although this system made more sense, it was easier on me, so he resisted it for a while. It was easier on his people, too, but that didn't matter. We had no idea whether the waiver would be approved, but it was eventually. When you start screwing with a sailor's pay, he loses focus on his work. I know I did.

This long-term arrangement, right or wrong, had been terminated forever. Commodore Berning, the hydrofoil squadron commander, made no effort to hide his displeasure. When I asked Dave why he had not given me time to look into it, he didn't really have a good answer. Again, I felt like it was a trust issue or maybe a competence one. I had to deal with it. He didn't yet know that I would never knowingly steer him wrong.

When things of this nature happen, and you're a minority, especially one with my tortured history, sometimes, you just can't help but wonder. The average minority, who rears up at some perceived slight or questioning of his or her competence, is dealing with not only that particular incident but also a lifetime of them. We eventually got through it, but it was stressful.

Our maintenance support activity had an administrative division that was headed by an officer and a master chief yeoman. Master chiefs still made me wary. I would ask this one to do certain things, and he would invariably challenge me, saying that I was wrong. After he'd research it, he'd inform me that I was right, and that he'd take care of it. I'd never ask him to do anything that I wasn't absolutely certain was right. He had no problem telling me I was wrong without checking it out first. He was, after all, a master chief.

One of our biggest battles involved my crew's service records. I created a customized checklist for my officers to use in reviewing the crew's service records, starting with their own. We did drug interdiction operations, and the drug runners were not the nicest people. Accidents happen as well. Over the years, I had seen incidents that resulted in funds going to the wrong person, because the members had not updated their records.

There are common misconceptions about what paperwork is required to ensure your dependents are taken care of as you might wish. I've seen a sailor's sweetheart or ex-wife or girlfriend get his life insurance proceeds or back pay rather than the current wife and children. None of my men had a will. Many were quite surprised to learn that their inattention had been a ticking time bomb. Being an ex-yeoman in this job was a distinct advantage.

These checklists resulted in a significant workload for the support staff, and they weren't happy, even though these errors were things they should have already fixed. They checked the records when each member reported for duty, but things change and things fall through the cracks. At my request, the base legal office set aside blocks of time to get wills completed and signed by all my people, including the officers. The master chief yeoman initially thought I was trying to make him look bad; I was only trying to take care of my men. He ultimately came around. He later sent out a message to the entire squadron, using my checklist, telling the ships to review their service records and to make sure all records were up to date.

He said that this was a great initiative but somehow forgot to mention that *Gemini*'s ex-yeoman XO was the one who developed the checklist or that my ship had already done what he was now directing the entire squadron to do. This would appear to be his initiative to the squadron commander. We eventually got to the point where he wouldn't immediately challenge me. Again, there were no overt racial overtones present, but I have my suspicions. I was the squadron's only Black officer; the only other Black senior person was a chief petty officer, and she was catching hell, too.

This chief storekeeper was also the only female chief in the squadron. The one person who could easily make her life more difficult was the Maintenance and Material Management System (3M System) coordinator,

Vulture Breath. He controlled access to the system that allowed her to do her job. He took a special delight in making her life miserable and stressful. He controlled access to the system passwords. She was a decent, married woman on an unaccompanied tour; she was alone in a sea of testosterone. Her nickname, which delighted Vulture Breath, was "Doofus." He purposefully withheld information from her to make her look bad. I'm sorry to say that I would sometimes see the squadron commander heartily laugh when he was told of some "prank" played on her. Mission effectiveness took a back seat to sadistic entertainment and abuse, and this was a national security issue. Hydrofoils needed those parts fast.

I would occasionally tell her to hang in there. She was not an assertive personality, and she was suffering. I didn't know how badly until the command's equal opportunity person, a Black first class petty officer, asked me if he could speak to me about her situation. He thought I might be able to help. If not me, who? I suggested that they come to my room ashore later that evening. When they did, the truth came gushing out.

Overwhelmed with anger, frustration, and despair as she shared her story, she soon collapsed in a heap, crying uncontrollably for a long while. She was clearly near the end of her psychological rope. Sitting there watching her cry, and trying not to cry myself, was the only time I had ever been ashamed of being a sailor. Other sailors were doing this to her. I knew it could happen, having lived through it, and I became quite angry myself.

This abusive behavior had trickled down to junior personnel. A person under fire tends to lose allies and support: ask any whistleblower. She had, however, been amassing documentation, and she was now ready to fight back. Over the course of several evenings, I helped them write her formal discrimination complaint. It's not what you believe; it's what you can prove. There was a tremendous amount to work with.

She was smarter than they thought and tougher too. She had a pretty good wheel book. As I helped them over several evenings, I learned that there was a pervasive discriminatory environment at the command, which I had some inkling of already. The person sent to investigate her complaint was a Black first class EOPS. He made my day when he told me that on the morning he arrived, while having breakfast at the mess hall, he listened to Vulture Breath laughing and bragging about how he had changed Doofus's password again so she could not do her job. Important parts for important missions be damned. Hilarious he thought that was.

No one else laughed; they all had figured out who the new Black petty officer was or were smart enough to keep silent. Vulture Breath viewed Blacks as potential targets, hence his assault rifle recommendation to me seconds after introducing himself to me and warning me about the local Black inhabitants. The wheel book–derived evidence soon buried him. Vulture Breath went to captain's mast and had his wings clipped, and his mouth washed out with industrial strength bigot soap. Shortly after, the female chief was medically transferred permanently out of the command by the naval hospital commanding officer.

Commodore Berning, who I personally saw laughing and commenting about this chief, was the individual responsible for administering the punishment. He did not need an EOPS to come down and tell him what was going on; he could see it every day. The irony of this still bothers me. He treated the symptom, not the problem. What, exactly, was the problem? It was systematic, institutional, condoned discrimination and harassment, not simply the actions of one lone individual. It was poor leadership as well.

I would still have occasional debates and hear snide comments about affirmative action from white sailors and officers who were picking up on the clear signals being sent from the highest levels of our government and often parroting them. These comments and signals have consequences. Even well-qualified and top-performing minorities like me were harmed by them, not because they necessarily benefited from affirmative action, but because of the "perception" that it was affirmative action, not qualifications, that got them the job in the first place. Affirmative action was designed to overcome past discrimination and give qualified individuals a chance to compete. Changing the discussion to diversity made it more acceptable in the years to come, but similar resistance has grown over time.

Despite the challenges to my knowledge and authority from certain members of the support squadron and the conflicts and challenges I had when dealing with my second commanding officer, I thoroughly enjoyed my hydrofoil tour. One of the highlights of hydrofoil duty was harassing warships in the Caribbean for exercises and training before deployment. We would be assigned as opposing forces, with orders to test their defenses and independently simulate attacks to help them prepare for real attacks they might encounter in hostile waters. The hydrofoil was an excellent platform for this.

We would drift among the small fishing boats, sometimes altering our lights to make ourselves as inconspicuous as possible, licking our lips and waiting for them. On radar, we looked like a small boat, not a warship. We'd quickly go from a five-knot fishing boat to a screaming fifty-knot predator, raining in simulated missiles and gun rounds on a powerful foe.

In darkness, they were in big trouble. All we were missing was the hockey mask and the scary music. It was not unheard of for a hydrofoil to contact one of these target ships by radio, pretending to be a distressed helicopter, declaring an in-flight emergency, and requesting an emergency landing. If they went to emergency flight quarters and turned to receive us on their deck, rather than rescuing a distressed helicopter, they'd suck up a bunch of simulated missiles or gun rounds in their fantail. After we'd kick their butt, we'd moon them by flashing light as we zoomed around them once or twice, celebrating and gloating.

In a real-time hostile environment, these ships would have been deadly. We soon had the opportunity to spank the USS *Boone*, my previous ship. It was like taking candy from a baby. We would spare the engineers but not the supply weenies. We made them surrender all their steaks, ice cream, and watermelon and throw all their pork products overboard, including the bacon and especially the pork rinds.

After we'd spanked them, Dave Aland had a great time pretending to be a vessel filled with terrorists, holding as hostages the closest relatives of Mike Newman, still *Boone*'s skipper. I had listened to him regale us with tales of his Texan father, whom he called "the Giant," and his brother, whom he called "Crazy Louis," for so long I felt kinship with my own crazy family. The laughter you could hear on the radios of both of these ships as these insulting exchanges between COs took place was something that still makes me smile. Newman left his poor relatives to their fate. War is hell. I'm sure the other ships in the area got a big kick out of it too. After they finished harassing each other, I talked to him; he wished me well and sent me a very nice personal message, which I still have.

Led by Dave Aland, *Gemini*'s crew had become a well-oiled machine but not like my frigate was. We excelled through a series of major inspections, seized millions in illicit drugs, and helped recover four Cuban nationals trying to escape Cuba on a rubber life raft. If this had been at night, we'd most likely have killed them instead. We were heading straight for them. Traveling at night, at more than forty knots, we'd often hear something go bump in the night and not know what it was—a log, a little rubber inner tube, a bale of marijuana or cocaine, who knows? I tried not to think about it.

I had complete confidence in these men, and we were a great team. We'd meet all our commitments and take many for those ships that could not. Sometimes, we would have to get underway on just a couple of hours' advance notice and be gone for weeks at a time.

Typically, during drug interdiction operations, we'd be directed to an area where intelligence sources believed drug activity was occurring. We'd intercept or run down suspected vessels and then, if it seemed prudent, send armed members of our Coast Guard law enforcement detachment in a rigid-hulled inflatable boat to board, inspect, and secure the craft. For larger vessels, we'd wait for the arrival of a bigger vessel (navy or Coast Guard) and hand over the detained craft and crew to them. There were lots of firearms involved (at least on our side), but we never had to use them. We were really too small and not sufficiently manned to take aboard detainees.

One night, we had an aircraft fly directly above us and drop bales of cocaine next to us, thinking we were the drop vessel. After they flew back over us and shined lights on us and realized that we were a navy hydrofoil, nearby boats started scattering like waterborne roaches. We recovered all but one bale, and the aircraft was followed back to Columbia by a Drug Enforcement Agency aircraft. I never knew if the pickup boat was detained; we were busy seizing drugs. Sometimes, the intelligence was pretty good, sometimes not. Either way, it was tiring.

I tried to not think about the large fish and marine mammals I'm sure we occasionally sucked up (instant sushi) into our water-jet propulsors, hydraulically connected to our jet engine, which enabled us to fly foil borne. If lucky, the sea creatures could hear us coming, but luck ran out for one whale and one hydrofoil. In 1991, USS *Aquila* (PHM-4) hit a whale at forty-five knots, cutting it into three pieces, and received a blubber bloodbath and a million dollars' worth of damage. The unfortunate skipper slammed face first into his stateroom metal door and then spent three days strapped in his seat on the bridge while he directed damage control and rescue operations. His door had a perfect face-sized dent in it. He had a broken back. This incident helped bring an end to the hydrofoil navy—and one whale.

Because a navy hydrofoil was so unusual, nearly everywhere we went, we'd have to do a demonstration ride for local dignitaries, military and civilian. These dog-and-pony shows were very annoying after a while but were great public relations for the navy. You want to see a bunch of grinning people? Hydrofoil ride! When Dave Aland detached, he was in the good graces of the commodore and went on to command another ship.

Lieutenant Commander Robert (Bob) M. Wall relieved him, and it showed that he had been an admiral's aide and was clearly planning on being an admiral too. Things quickly changed. I would like to say that Bob Wall was like a lot of officers I've known, but he wasn't. Bob Wall was in a class by himself. He had self-combing hair and self-polishing teeth, his breath smelled like polished brass, and he had a set of big brass balls. You could hear them clinking when he walked up the brow reporting aboard and every day thereafter. When he stepped off the brow, they made a sound like a gong.

The first time he stepped aboard, the officer of the deck (OOD) announced him: "Ding-Ding, Brass Balls Wall, arriving." Well, he should have. Wall exuded confidence and authority, his uniforms too intimidated to ever get dirty. Every time he poured himself a cup of coffee, it stayed steaming hot and at least half full. He was tall, slim, fit, extremely smart, aggressive, competent, and driven to succeed. He was only one pay grade above me, and he was the scariest boss I ever had. Bob Wall was something else. He could look right into your brain, pinpoint the target areas where you were plotting to destroy his career, and then commence rapid firing. Collateral damage was your problem, not his. I checked his ID when he reported aboard. Under blood type, it said "Tabasco." I didn't ask him if he was a zulu five oscar. Nobody did. If he didn't make admiral, it would not be from lack of trying. Like many new bosses, he intended to ride in hard, whip us into shape, and ease up after we improved to his satisfaction. This was a good, battle-tested plan, but there were a couple of problems with it, from my perspective, as his slightly seasoned second in command.

First, we had being a hydrofoil crew down to a science. Dave Aland had whipped me into shape, and I had passed it down. The passing on this ship went both ways. Under Dave's leadership, we had excelled in everything we had done. It ain't bragging if it's true. Second, Bob Wall had a little problem letting up. Zumwalt said that he didn't believe a tight ship had to be an uptight ship. Bob Wall was very tightly wound. Third, he left the impression that no one, including me, quite measured up to his standards.

Under Dave, I'd assumed the "bad cop" role. Sometimes, I'm sure my guys hated me. Many XOs can relate. I once made them all come back to the shipyard, leaving their nice Hotel Alabama dinners, after they'd paid for them, to clean up the ship to my satisfaction while it was undergoing shipyard work. Despite my warnings, they tried me one time too many. I had to make a point. For a while afterward, I thought about hiring a bodyguard, a big white one named Cletus. I was, after all, still in Alabama. Sometimes, I forgot.

The crew later saw the wisdom of my approach when we received a surprise visit from the commodore, who left very happy and impressed, and I later fought off an attempt by the shipyard contractors to leave their huge mess for us to clean up, saving them money. Not happening on my watch. I had also relentlessly made the crew document every single minute discrepancy on the ship during zone inspections, much to their disgust and amazement, especially the engineers.

Having gone through a bunch of inspections, including a Board of Inspection and Survey (INSURV) inspection, not much escaped me. I made them re-create the previous INSURV report that had largely been purged and document any outstanding discrepancies, again to their great disgust. We'd then clear the ones we could. When we passed our INSURV inspection with the best results a hydrofoil had ever achieved, their attitudes improved. They quit asking me where all those bite marks on my ass had come from too. Dave Aland listened to me and let me do what needed to be done.

Bob Wall saw each of us as potential weak links and didn't truly trust any of us, including me. He once kept me awake for so long that I briefly fell asleep late one night on watch as the OOD, at sea. He did this by making sure I was on watch while he was asleep and that I was beside him when he wasn't. Dave Aland once asked me if I ever slept; Bob Wall made sure I didn't, at least for a long, long while. The bridge watch standers had let me sleep in the OOD chair, knowing I was exhausted. When he "found" me, he prepared to chew my ass after he got me in his stateroom. Being acquainted with French and Raven's five bases of power, which I had taught to sailors and junior officers years before, I knew how to address this coercive behavior.

I fought back.

Rather than be contrite, I called him on his behavior, which was trying to diminish me in the eyes of the crew. I asked him if he couldn't function without any sleep, how did he expect me to do so? Having no logical defense, he knocked it off, picking a softer target. There's a reason that old adage exists about how if your primary tool is a hammer, everything pretty much looks like a nail. I gradually became "good cop" and crew confidant.

Unfortunately, my combat systems officer did not survive this treatment, even though I tried hard to help him. It was distressing, watching him keep trying to measure up. I watched this already slim man drop about twenty pounds before he was transferred from the ship for psychological reasons. He privately shared with me the verbal abuse, physical threats, and unwarranted criticism he'd endured until he couldn't. The CO of the hospital had him transferred before he wound up dead. I don't know what happened to him after that, but I've never seen a man so happy to leave a ship, all the while looking like he was in shock. I kept checking my weight. I had one of the Haitian ladies living in town make me a voodoo talisman, but it didn't work.

The combat systems officer's department chief, my only one, soon left the ship and went to see the base chaplain for counseling, for a time refusing to return to work. He was traumatized, having seen what happened to his boss and knowing he was next. He was one of my finest men. I had to visit him at home and convince him, plead with him, to return to the ship. He was willing to throw his career away, as my father had done, rather than return to that toxic environment.

My quartermaster was a fine young first class petty officer who was responsible for preparing our navigation charts and records. While we were preparing for our precision anchoring qualification, we both nearly crumpled under the pressure. I eventually told Wall I believed he was destroying his crew. Morale had crashed, and it wasn't because our high level of performance had changed; it was because the perception of our skipper had.

When I told him that I hated, absolutely hated to come see him, I think I finally made an impression. He understood that the rest of the crew felt as I did. This was one of the toughest, scariest, and most necessary conversations I have ever had. I risked my job to do it. I'm pretty sure the commodore got wind of what was happening, perhaps telling him to ease up a bit, but I have no proof. I believe Bob Wall would have considered racism as a personal weakness, and therefore beneath him. There was only one other minority assigned other than me (an E-5). If he was prejudiced against anyone, it was someone whom he thought could harm his career.

He eventually encouraged me to become an admiral's aide myself, but I wasn't then interested. I didn't want to act like him. He told me a Black surface warfare officer with his shit together like me could go far. I never wanted a job because I was Black and good but just because I was good—unless maybe it was the Supreme Court. I could adapt my principles and my behavior to fit the circumstances. I knew that I couldn't keep a smooth face every day, due to PFB and genetics. I didn't want to risk going to work for the wrong admiral. I'd never met the wrong admiral, but I've sure met the wrong captain or commander. More on that later.

When Bob Wall gave you his respect, or his blessing, you were sure you had earned it. When you were under suspicion, you knew that too. After he assumed command, we flew to Puerto Rico on drug interdiction duty. As often happens, we came into port for a short stand-down period to on-load supplies, do our laundry, take care of maintenance, and relax.

As often happened, we received a radio inquiry from headquarters regarding our ability to get underway on short notice. They had just assigned us a stand-down period, and it was probably a bored watch stander just making radio talk. Wall informed them that he was ready and able to get underway.

My initial reaction the first time this happened was the same as Bob Wall's; get ready to get underway! My crew and Dave assured me that this was no cause for excitement, and I learned the routine. In this case, nothing I said could convince Wall that we weren't about to get tasking, and he wasn't about to look bad because of our lazy, sorry asses. I understood what was happening, and I tried to prevent it.

We made all necessary preparations, and when the radio call to get underway didn't come, he inquired about our tasking and was told there was none. It had played out just like it had many times before.

Wall called me into his stateroom, and he told me to inform the crew what a good job they had done in preparing to get underway. Then he floored me with a two-by-four between the eyes, telling me to inform them that he now expected the ship to be able to get underway on one hour's notice. He did not want to miss any tasking if the call came. This meant that no one could go do laundry, get a haircut, make a phone call home, jog or work out, nothing.

I was expected to go tell them as a reward for their outstanding performance, they were now pretty much restricted to the ship. I tried to dissuade him. He told me to follow my orders. I left and returned a short time later. Issuing these orders would be devastating to my crew. I desperately didn't want to add to the tension that he'd already created. I walked around for a few minutes and went back and again asked him to reconsider. He now clearly felt that I was challenging his authority. I was questioning his judgment but not his authority.

I was a slow learner, again tiptoeing around a minefield, but trying to help him, as I had Newman on *Boone* during the helicopter crash. What would I say if he asked me later why I had not pushed back harder? That I was afraid of him? I had something he didn't have just then: experience in this situation and knowledge of my crew. I knew that every man on that crew would have done whatever was necessary to get that ship underway on time if ordered. He didn't. He again told me through tighter lips to follow my orders. No compromise. After agonizing a few more minutes, I went back to his stateroom a third time.

By now I was beginning to get questions from the crew, who knew I was clearly having a difficult time about something. They were beginning to suspect what was going on. They were sharp, and they'd been through turnover before. When I entered his stateroom, Wall was now visibly upset: red-faced, pissed, and clanking. I told him I was about to go execute his orders but wanted him to understand he was making a terrible mistake.

I told him that he was about to send an unmistakable signal that he didn't trust his crew or his officers and that the morale repercussions were likely to be long-lasting. I told him that the morale of the crew would hit the toilet and probably stay there. As I was leaving, I heard this low voice say, "OK, XO, we'll do this your way, but I'm going to hold you responsible if something goes wrong. Do you understaaand?"

I was afraid to turn around and look at him, and it suddenly was very dark and very cold; I heard the clock on the wall stop, waiting for my answer. Maybe it was my heart. I hadn't been this scared with a shotgun pointed in my chest or with LRMF screaming at me like a fiery dragon. I'd heard that voice and that breathing before (in a Star Wars movie), and I knew what I would see if I turned to look at him, so I quickly said, "Yes, sir," and got the hell out of there. The way he said it was truly frightening. Message: if you screw me on this, I'm going to have your balls for breakfast—raw and freshly harvested.

I was nevertheless relieved. I gathered my leadership and told them that the skipper was "a bit jittery" about the liberty and to minimize the time off the ship to the absolute minimum. I also told the men to make sure someone on board the ship knew where they were and how to reach them at all times, and that my ass was riding on their total compliance. My trembling voice did the trick. These men were superb. They had seen me go to bat for them, help them load supplies during underway replenishment, occasionally wash dishes for some of them so that they could watch movies (which they got a big kick out of). They also knew I'd ride their ass if necessary. It seldom was. They weren't going to let us down. We never missed any commitment or tasking.

The one time I couldn't sway him involved a visit from James Webb, the future senator from Virginia and presidential candidate, who was not visiting in an official capacity. He had previously resigned as secretary of the navy. We were soon spitting and polishing all over the place. We were to take him and other dignitaries out for a hydrofoil ride and precision maneuvers with other hydrofoils, and Wall ordered me to conn the ship during this visit. Being the best ship, we got the dignitaries, of course. Why else would we? I was a good ship handler, but not the best hydrofoil ship handler on board, and I told him so. We practiced these maneuvers, and I nailed it on the practice runs. On the appointed day, we welcomed aboard our dignitaries and got underway.

We went through our practiced maneuvers, and I was less than stellar. The precision of the day before was gone, probably overtaken by nerves and fear of failure, my old friends. I've always hated the spotlight, and this day was no exception. Senator Webb was not especially impressed with my station-keeping ability; it was pretty easy to read his stony face. All was not lost, though. Senator Webb was given the helm of the ship, and he dutifully executed the several maneuvers that I, as OOD, ordered him to complete. I suspect I'm one of the few men he's taken orders from and executed them immediately, without question. He did a pretty good job, for a former jarhead. Actually, he did very well.

After off-loading the dignitaries, Wall called me up to his stateroom and informed me, looking amused, that we had done a good job and that these dignitaries seemed to fuck with me. He even laughed. He was right. I reminded him that I told him I wasn't the best ship handler on board, but he didn't listen to me.

I was surprised that he was amused—this was a big day for him. But it seemed he had realized that a minor hiccup wouldn't stop him from making admiral. He had softened up a bit, and the change was a good one. We still had some rough spots, but they were minor for the most part. Our styles were very different. In my next job, I'd host a visit he made to our area as a detailer, and he'd thank me for helping make it a success. He made captain. Like my *Voge* XO, Jerry Ware (aka LRMF), Wall would die of a heart attack shortly after he retired in 2010. He was younger than I was. Think about that if you see yourself in either of them. I have.

From my time on the hydrofoil *Gemini*, there's an important leadership teaching moment I want to share. The *Gemini* running aground during a navigation check ride, specifically a precision anchoring exercise, conducted by Commodore Berning, had happened years before my arrival. The primary cause of this grounding was the action of the commanding officer in silencing his navigation team while anchoring because they were distracting him. Everyone from Dave Aland to Commodore Berning to my quartermaster had discussed this with me when I reported on board. This wasn't going to happen to me.

Within a few weeks of reporting, I discovered that my bridge team was not listening to me when we were in a high-speed transit in the Roosevelt Roads channel, headed in port to Puerto Rico. They were standing into danger, but they were visually misjudging their position by the channel buoys. The USS *Spruance* had been run aground because a Black OOD misjudged where he was and didn't listen to his quartermaster. I informed them that if they did not land the ship immediately, we would be aground in less than two minutes. I didn't say "maybe." If they were going to run us aground, at forty knots, I was going to be on tape as being against it, as the navigator.

Dave Aland immediately landed the ship, and he wasn't happy with me. But after he came to the combat information center and looked at the electronic navigation chart, he realized I was right, and his face went white. They weren't seeing what they thought they were seeing. These experienced, confident guys were wrong. My navigation team had saved his career. He thanked me, with true gratitude. We never had any such conflict again.

I never liked high-speed, shallow-water transits. Our communications were recorded, and our charts were electronic ones, with paper for backup. You couldn't possibly do standard chart navigation under these circumstances, and you run out of navigation room fast at forty knots. Several of the other hydrofoils ran aground, which ended careers. Afterward, the commodore ordered a navigation stand-down and a squadron-wide thorough and complete navigation assessment of each ship. When the report was released, we on the *Gemini* were specifically singled out for our safe, cautious approach to high-speed navigation. Shortly after that, high-speed restricted-waters navigation was severely limited, which made me happy.

Bob Wall was very concerned about navigation. Before I left, we were to have our navigation check ride inspection. We practiced for this event carefully, and I was very satisfied. He was not, particularly with the performance of my quartermaster, a relatively new, junior first class petty officer. This petty officer also knew the skipper wasn't happy with his performance, even though he was doing a very good job.

I had been in his shoes. He was just shaky conducting the briefing because of the body language and tone of the questions coming from his commanding officer. He was beginning to crack, and his stress level was reaching a breaking point. Fear of failure I knew well. I pulled him aside and told him, "From now on, the only person who matters to you on this ship is me. You direct your briefings to me, and you look directly at me when you're feeling stressed." I told him that I would debrief him on his performance and to not even think about what anyone else said and that he was doing a great job. I told him not to even make eye contact with the skipper if he didn't want to. I also asked the skipper to ease up on him. I'd lost an officer and nearly lost a chief and now was worried about losing my only quartermaster.

During our check ride, the entire crew performed flawlessly—except for Bob Wall. As we approached the selected anchor spot, we were required to make constant updates to the bridge on the range and location of the spot selected. This necessary information, coming from several sources, can get noisy and confusing. At some point, Wall called down from the bridge and ordered me to belay (stop making) my navigation status reports.

I wanted to immediately request he reconsider. This was exactly what led to the grounding of *Gemini* before. Instead I said, "Belay my reports, aye, sir," and immediately turned and jabbed my finger in the log so hard that I hurt it, saying, "Log it!" We all knew he'd just made a big mistake, and we were a pretty grim and somber bunch. Nevertheless, I was not about to question him, especially with the commodore standing right next to him, which is where I assumed he would be, on the bridge with the captain.

What I didn't realize was that the commodore was standing right behind me. I should have; after all, I was the Black guy. When I turned and saw him, he didn't say a word but turned and climbed up to the bridge. After we successfully anchored, the commodore invited the skipper up to his stateroom. When they finished talking, the skipper called me up to his stateroom. The commodore was gone. I walked up full of concern. We had nailed the anchorage. What was coming?

I wish I'd heard commodore Berning's comments. For the first time, Brass Balls Wall seemed rattled. He apologized, said he was wrong, that he should never have given that order, and that we had performed flawlessly. He said that the commodore made it plain where the problem was and that it wouldn't happen again. He told me to challenge him if he did something like that again. Yeah, right.

He informed the crew that they had performed superbly. The remainder of the check ride went exceptionally well. The lesson: when you make people fear you, they may not try, or be too afraid, to save you if needed, or they may let you hang yourself. This is dangerous, in the long run. Wall learned this lesson, I hope.

My last hydrofoil night was spent guarding some smugglers we ran down after breaking up a drug transfer. They were in a fast cigarette boat and trying to outrun us and off-load their cargo before we apprehended them. Not a chance. We could see with our night vision goggles that they were tossing bundles of cocaine as big as hay bales over the side as they maneuvered. We were more interested in apprehending them than obtaining the drugs, so we kept on their tail. Outmaneuver us, yes, but outrunning us was impossible.

When they surrendered, we took them into custody and warily guarded them all night, later handing them over to the Coast Guard. This operation caused me to miss my flight back to Key West, but I didn't mind.

As Bob Wall gave me my fitness report, he told me he thought I would go far if I stuck around. He kept telling me to give him a write-up for an end-of-tour award, but I resisted. When he persisted, I told him that I honestly didn't feel like I had performed to his satisfaction, and I didn't feel like he thought I had earned a personal award. I also told him that I had never before written up (and never would write up) an award recommendation for myself.

Surprised, he asked me why I felt that way, and I explained why, with examples. We both learned something. I eventually gave him a list of my accomplishments during the entire tour, but no flowery stuff, and soon received another Navy Commendation Medal for my *Gemini* tour. I got orders back to Mayport, Florida, where my family was living, as a squadron safety officer, a brand-new billet. But first, I had to check out of the squadron.

We flew to Puerto Rico, and I caught a flight to Key West, where I had my departure interview with Commodore Ron Berning. I was surprised to hear him say how happy he had been to have me in his squadron and how highly he thought of me. I swelled with pride when he told me that I was the best executive officer in his squadron. Ah, the "goodbye kiss."

I wasn't supposed to tell anybody. It would be our little secret. I resisted the temptation to ask him if he said that to all the girls. He asked about my career plans, and when I said I wanted to go to another executive officer afloat tour and command my own ship, he delicately informed me that I was a little old. He knew I was a mustang and seemed to be trying to let me down easy. He eventually asked me how old I was. When I told him, it was his turn to be surprised. He assumed I was older. Joining at age seventeen had its advantages. He said I wasn't too old after all. I wasn't much older than my peers who joined right out of college and well ahead of my year group in at-sea experience. Most of my peers were on their first department head tour. I was going to my third. I had punched my engineering ticket. He only needed to look a little closer, a little deeper, to see what I really was.

11

Training the Fleet

After three demanding sea tours, I needed a break. It was July 1992. In February that year, the chief of naval operations (CNO), Admiral Frank B. Kelso, signed the Department of the Navy Strategic Goals, part of his new Total Quality Leadership initiative, which was built on the work of Dr. W. Edwards Deming, who developed a system of ongoing process improvement in an organization. He had done wonders for the Japanese automobile industry, while the American business community had largely ignored him, until Toyota and other Japanese companies started eating their lunch. I would be involved in that during my next two assignments. Not everyone would be on board.

Something very dramatic and unprecedented happened a few months after I arrived in Mayport, though it occurred with no fanfare. The number of formal discrimination complaints filed in fiscal year 1992 was 297, the most ever reported. The 233 of those substantiated (an astounding 78 percent) was astronomical compared to the previous years. Since 1987, of 678 total complaints, only 27 had been substantiated. The average number of substantiated complaints jumped from 4.2 percent to a whopping 78.0 percent in just twelve months. What caused the huge jump? These numbers still astound me, and while no explanation has ever been given, I have my own theory. At the 1991 Tailhook Association convention in Las Vegas, a large number of naval aviators were involved in the sexual assault and harassment of women, which resulted in years of negative stories about the navy; congressional inquiries and investigations; and many careers either ruined, promotions placed on hold, and other general unpleasantness. I believe the men and women filing these complaints were possibly emboldened by the reaction by the President, George H. W. Bush, various congressional representatives, major news organizations, and others to the '91 Tailhook scandal.

A statistical anomaly of this magnitude screams for an explanation. I believe that the answer lies in the official files of Admiral Jeremy Boorda. I suspect he issued some directive about the previous failures to substantiate formal discrimination complaints. A 74 percent increase in the substantiation rate for these claims defies explanation. The navy isn't talking, especially to me. Like Zumwalt, Boorda was under tremendous pressure for the cultural changes he was trying to make.

I next became the safety officer at Destroyer Squadron Eight, Mayport, Florida. Captain Stephen A. Jarecki was the squadron commodore. Mine was a newly created billet, created following a series of accidents, fires, and other incidents that indicated safety was not a top priority. No one was sure what this job entailed, which I hoped to use to my advantage. This time would be useful toward completing a graduate degree.

I was again the only Black officer in the command, except for the doctor. I started getting my office and programs together and trying to have a meaningful impact. I had no subordinates. The chief staff officer, Captain Robert H. Rankin, called me to his office about sixty days into this assignment to "talk." He talked, I listened. I talked, he didn't really listen. He said he wanted me to take over the in-port training department.

I politely informed him that I was happy where I was, that I had enrolled in a graduate degree program, and that I was not interested in taking on the busiest and most contentious department on the staff. Since I had been paying attention, it was pretty clear to me that this job was trouble. The incumbent, a white lieutenant commander, spent a lot of time dealing with pissed-off ship commanding officers (COs), getting hammered for putting them on report to higher authority for fouling up some training exercise, formal schooling, or other event. I was a Black lieutenant; I could only imagine how much worse my hammering would have been.

They were all trying to get promoted, and the incumbent department head, wasn't making it easy for them. He was the point man, and he was sucking up a lot of rounds. My own future was a factor; going to work for any of these guys after beating them up would not be pleasant. People have long memories.

I was by now more keenly aware that I am an INTJ Myers-Briggs personality type, which stands for introvert, intuitive, thinking, judging, and we constitute about 2 percent of the population. The portion of that 2 percent who are Black males is very tiny. Such individuals are ambitious, eager to learn, strategically minded, and not especially fearful of authority figures. Colin Powell was one. We are inclined to be rule breakers. I could get into a lot of trouble in this job. Not being fearful of authority isn't considered a beneficial survival trait in a Black man. It sometimes gets confused with arrogance, and previously with "uppity." I felt I'd be safer where I was.

Captain Rankin was unmoved. He firmly informed me that he'd been watching me and thought I'd be good in this job, and whether or not I "volunteered" to take it, I was probably going to get it. After he "allowed" me to go home and sleep on it, I came in the next morning and "volunteered." You were expecting another result? He was a big guy, a good ol' Florida boy, and built like a bull. He'd just given me the best job I ever had.

After listening in on the brutal exchanges between the incumbent and some of the skippers, it was pretty clear to me that some changes needed to be made. This brutality was one way and not pretty. We were talking to one cruiser department head one day about some training the ship had screwed up and, unbeknownst to us, his skipper was listening in.

All of a sudden, he unleashed this long profane tirade about how we squadron guys didn't understand the pressures the fleet was under and how we needed to get off our sorry asses and get out to the "real" navy. The incumbent was silent, accustomed by now to sucking up this "informal counseling." I spoke up, informing this irate skipper that I had only been there for a couple of months, having come from three consecutive ships, and I had much more of a fleet perspective. I said that I'd be happy to visit him and see if we could eliminate the problems. I silently hoped he would chew me out too and call Captain Rankin, who would give me my old job back. No such luck.

I went to see this angry skipper the next day, and he could not have been more gracious. I don't think he realized I was Black until I showed up, and he seemed to be a little bit "spooked," so to speak. He was much calmer in person. Once the turnover process was complete, it was time to make some changes.

There was one other lieutenant, three chiefs, and one first class petty officer permanently assigned to this department as well as rotating fleet personnel temporarily assigned while waiting to report or return to their ships. One of the individuals was a Black master chief boatswain's mate named Wilbert Calloway.

Calloway was the only one I had to recalibrate—gently. Early on, we had a discussion, and I think he forgot I was a lieutenant—or, at least, he hoped I did. I don't think he'd ever worked for a Black one before. I realized almost immediately that he was testing me, as I'd been tested many times before, although usually, the testers were white. I'd have to talk to him in language we both understood.

After a minute, I informed him that I didn't like the way the conversation was going and that I was going to go buy me a so-dee pop, and when I got back, we were going to start this conversation over. Never raised my voice, never accused him of anything, and I walked real slow. This is where

I gave him time to wonder if I was going to my car to get my piece. This is also where he started to wonder if it was time for him to get his hat and ease on down the road.

When I returned, I had one so-dee pop for me and some Skittles in my pocket. I bought the bag of Skittles and tried to rearrange them so that they looked like a handgun. I walked back in real slowly so that my Skittles wouldn't make any noise, trying to look like Darth Vader or Omar Little from *The Wire*. I didn't yet know Skittles could get me killed. This was before Trayvon Martin and he-who-shall-not-be-named.

Master Chief Calloway, as I slowly began putting my hand in my Skittles pocket, apologized, and we started over. After he left, I happily ate that whole bag of Skittles. He was still a master chief, and he now saw I was a lieutenant. I had passed his test. We began a long and very successful relationship. Very often, when I would look at him, I would see what my father could have been. He was a boatswain's mate, too, like Carl Brashear, of *Men of Honor* fame, and Calloway.

I'd tell everyone I introduced him to that I worked for him. When I watched the PBS documentary *Carrier*, with its Black command master chief, full of wisecracks, knowledge, and confidence as well as piss and vinegar, I smiled a big smile. People who had just blown me off would get a call from him and give him everything he wanted, including what they'd just moments before said no to me about. He looked out for me and made sure that I knew what the hell was going on around there. He was a very big part of the success we had.

The other chiefs were great too. One was selected for limited duty officer, and the other was promoted to senior chief. The first class petty officer, a white guy nearing retirement, was about to get canned due to an alcohol-related incident in his service record before he reported to the staff, which disqualified him from staff duty. This was the first test of how much support I would have. I was convinced he could do most of what I was already doing. I was far too involved in the day-to-day operation of the department. Petty officers and division officers should have been working these problems out. I was more interested in improving the training than putting people on report. There were bigger fish to fry.

Captain Rankin told me he was going to have the first class petty officer transferred. I asked him to let me keep him for a while; I said that I would be responsible for him, and that if he caused any problems, I'd take the heat. I'd reviewed his service record and watched him work. I still remembered that if a navy doctor had not bent the rules for me once, I might still be a first class petty officer or a bitter former sailor.

Captain Rankin agreed to let me keep him, breaking the rules for me. When this man understood what had just happened, he was grateful and eager to perform. It took him a while to understand how much power and freedom he actually had. The first couple of times he came to ask me if it was OK for him to leave for the day, I told him that if he wasn't sure whether he should leave, then neither was I and that he should go back to his office and think it over. He soon stopped asking me if he could go home; he'd just say good night on his way out. Often, after that, I'd have to tell him to go home. He became Mr. In-Port Training, and he was perfect for the job.

The guidance he received from me was to lower the temperature on reporting discrepancies in training and to work with no one higher than a division officer if there were problems. He was now listed as the point of contact on the training messages, but I was still getting calls from irate senior officers over some perceived slight or legitimate airing of dirty laundry.

When I'd get these calls, I would listen and then inform the callers that these issues were now being handled at the proper level. I told them that I would like for their division officers or leading petty officers to work with my training petty officer, the official point of contact, to handle them and that we were working on revamping some of the training, including what was being reported. As long as they didn't completely fail to conduct the required training, we'd usually handle it at a lower level. I didn't ask how.

It took a while for this to get across: handle everything at the lowest level possible, without hurting command effectiveness. Essentially, many of the problems were communications related. These junior officers, chiefs and senior petty officers formed a tight-knit group who knew how to handle problems within their own group and knew how to make it painful for slackers without getting the bosses involved or telling the whole world. This helped calm down the senior khakis. This involved counseling, extra training after hours and off the books, informal lessons-learned reports, peer pressure and recognition, and less trepidation if mistakes were made. All of this led to better, more consistent training and lower temperatures. Taking off some of the reporting heat also led to greater cooperation. The emphasis shifted from reporting discrepancies to actual training. Unlike the infamous engineering mobile training team, we were focused on improving training, not reporting discrepancies.

I'd still have occasional unpleasant conversations with some of the skippers. One captain informed me tersely that I needed to watch how I spoke to senior officers, after I held my ground. When I pressed him for specifics, asking him if I had said anything to offend or disrespect him, he informed me that no, it was just my bedside manner. I apologized (fake) and stated that I was only doing my job and I did not intend to offend him. He was angry and surely wanted to call me arrogant or the "U" word. When I later discussed this with Captain Rankin, he listened and then said, "In other words, you just didn't kiss his ass enough?" I said, "Apparently not." He said, "OK, carry on." I did. Carefully. Captain Rankin always had my back.

Meanwhile, in 1993 there were seventy-five formal discrimination complaints, with thirty-eight substantiated (51 percent) The number of complaints substantiated would continue to drop to near previous levels. The 1992 year proved to be an unexplained anomaly. The Obama years' statistics have never been made public. The 2017 substantiation rate was 6 percent, a return to the 1980s levels.

My little training department personnel focused on our own problems. When we'd go to a command or ship to set up or discuss training issues, I was clearly the senior person there, as the other lieutenant was junior, younger, and had just a couple of ribbons. By then, I had a chest full. I was a Certified Navy Hero, with four full rows of ribbons on my chest, a total of twelve. We would watch as all the questions and comments got addressed to him, and I would always just watch and listen, at first. He would tell them that I was the department head, and they'd often look at me like they were seeing me for the first time, despite the fact that I'd usually started the discussion.

We'd sometimes have an uncomfortable laugh about it. Once after we left a particular meeting my lieutenant division officer turned to me in exasperation and asked why this kept happening. Master Chief Calloway gave him a very succinct, revealing answer. He'd been in the navy a lot longer than the rest of us. He told him that it was because Lieutenant Madison was the white guy, and everyone expected him to be in charge. This was a revealing teaching and learning moment for all of us, seeing how the Black boss was treated.

Other issues were more contentious. We were responsible for ensuring that team training of various types was conducted, but we did not control the quota assignments by these training organizations. There were numerous instances of someone from one ship calling up, pretending to be from another ship, canceling training for that ship, and then calling back and scheduling the newly available training for their own ship. Sailors can be very resourceful! This had to stop. I decided to try to take control of the scheduling of training for the ships in the Mayport basin that was being conducted by certain fleet support activities, primarily the Fleet Training Center. No one willingly gives up territory or responsibility unless there is a compelling reason or an order to do so. There was strong resistance. After a couple of disasters, we got them to listen to our proposal at the CO level.

After a couple of contentious meetings in his office, he agreed to let me take temporary quota control of two of the most vital classes. Before long, we had permanent control, and they were soon asking us to take over quota control for other training as well. We did. The results were outstanding, and greatly improved efficiency.

We did some things to make the training more diverse, visible, inclusive, and enjoyable. Every month during Surface Warfare Training Week, known as "Sweat Week," ships would conduct multiple training exercises, and at the end of the week, we provided a combined message report on how well each ship did. Before I got there, this was often brutal. We expanded this tremendously and made it fun too.

We added events that included some of the ships' crewmen who were seldom seen but were vital to the success of the others. We established competition between the cooks and ship's servicemen on the ships. For the finale of Sweat Week, each ship would pick a country of origin, prepare cuisine from this country, and present it at the enlisted club for judging. This got the supply officers and food service officers involved. Many of these cooks were very talented and from diverse immigrant backgrounds. They welcomed the chance to participate and show their stuff. They'd have volunteers help them with their entries and presentations. Senior officers present would judge the entries.

These guys went all out, with regional dress and costumes, flags, indigenous displays, brochures, music—you name it. The vast array of food prepared was amazing. It smelled wonderful, looked fantastic, and tasted great! You could see the immense pride in their work. We would award prizes for the first few places, and you could see the pride in the winners. After the judging, the food would be consumed by the sailors present. This was done on a Friday afternoon; it wasn't unheard of for a beer or two to be consumed. There was a lot of good-natured ribbing. Everyone loved it.

The only person who knew for certain who was absolutely ahead at all times was the training petty officer, and I kept it that way. He would announce the winners, not me. We designed and had made a grand prize, which was the Sweat Week flag, to be flown by the winning ship until the next competition. Symbols matter.

The ships' commanding officers, who once hated this Sweat Week, were now smiling and drinking beer and networking. In this sea of khaki and dungarees, one skipper would be talking to another ship's cook about what he'd prepared and commending him for his efforts. Each was sizing the other up for future reference, I suspect. Networking vertically, as well as horizontally, they were. This transformation of Sweat Week from a hated time to an award atmosphere and networking opportunity for all is one of my proudest accomplishments.

And now comes the ugly part. I had enrolled in a master's degree program in human resources development at Webster University, which had extension programs around military bases. In one of my first courses, the instructor informed us, looking right at me, that he had once lost his job to a Black man because of affirmative action. "Oh, boy," I thought. On my first paper, I received the worst grade I ever got in a college class, or a military one, except for the first celestial navigation exam at Officer Candidate School. I got a seventy, one point away from failing.

As I looked at his slashing, sarcastic comments in red, I could see his anger leaping off the page. It would have been impossible for me to address his comments or questions in the length allotted for the paper, and we both knew that. I still have this paper. It virtually screams racism. He all but said I was too stupid to understand what was required to pass this course. This guy was pissed, and I was his target. I kept my own counsel. There was nothing wrong with my paper. I was exceptionally diligent and exact for the remainder of the course, and I still nearly got lynched academically. I wasn't dumb; I was Black. For our final project, we worked jointly, completing a project, sharing our research, but writing our own individual segments for a given subject. After I had turned in my project, I got a call at home, and it was this instructor. He asked me a series of questions, and I answered each one promptly, truthfully, and without hesitation. I knew something was afoot, but I wasn't worried.

I asked him what the problem was, and he said that he was not at liberty to say. I persisted, saying that I had answered all of his questions and had a right to know what this highly unusual call and line of questioning was all about. He finally told me that there was a problem with my work. What was the problem, I demanded to know. He told his version. One of the guys with whom I had shared my research (as was allowed and encouraged) had simply turned it in without paraphrasing it or putting it into his words, as was required. Sections of our final project were exactly the same. This was clearly a problem. It wasn't the biggest one, I soon learned. I was.

I volunteered to bring my computer disk, my research notes, and my source documents over to his house immediately, so that he could verify that I had indeed done all of the work on my report. He said that would be "unacceptable." Now I was really getting a bit worried. I told him that he clearly knew my writing style, and I asked him if he had spoken with the other individual involved. He said that he had not. So I asked him, point-blank, what he was telling me.

I was flabbergasted when he told me that I would probably not get any credit for the entire course! He was going to fail me, and he had not even talked to the other guy! In his mind, I was the criminal, and there was nothing I could say or do to convince him otherwise. He couldn't hang the Black guy who took his job, so I would have to do! I had proximity and fit the description. The other guy was white, but that is just a coincidence. As far as I knew, he had no intention of talking to him, just me. I was the only Black student in the class. John C. Stennis would have been proud: no torture or beatings, but a conviction based on real evidence!

I switched clothes real fast and became the Angry Black Man because this was an emergency. I verbally unloaded on this instructor with an angry, profane tirade, and I told him just what I thought of his bullshit deductive reasoning. I all but called him a racist bastard, and I also told him that I was well aware that he was taking out on me his resentment about his job loss to a Black guy, based on his ongoing blatant and veiled comments throughout the course. I said I was not going to take this shit lying down, particularly since it was going to harm my reputation and my pocketbook.

I told him to do what he thought was best but that I would be fighting back, not taking his crap as I had for the entire course. I filed a written complaint the next day, with all the supporting documentation, and explained what had been going on to the college representative, who was a very nice, fair, and intelligent woman. I also pulled no punches in explaining exactly what I believed was fueling his clear animus toward me.

The guy who had turned in my work as his own immediately owned up to it; he said he had simply run out of time. He apologized, in writing, and he failed the course. I, on the other hand, received a written apology for the way this incident was handled and the assurances from the adviser that I would not have any problems or be stigmatized by this event. I had done nothing wrong, and that was made clear. I didn't talk to the instructor who tried to academically lynch me. I knew for certain that I would never, ever take another class from him. Had I not hit back hard, I would have paid dearly. I would fight a similar battle thirty years later as a TRICARE patient after a navy doctor accused me of lying to get a biopsy appointment and patient misconduct. He was wrong too and lived to regret it.

Shaken, angry, and more than a bit distrustful, I took a break from classes for a while, trying to figure out whether I would fight this battle again and if it would be worth it. Quite a few Black and minority students enroll in college but never finish. I would have to fight another battle with another biased instructor, and I would win this one too. I would eventually complete a degree but not until several years after my retirement for reasons you will soon learn.

Having partially mastered the military style of writing, I was frequently tasked with writing things for the commodore, and he would often tell the other department heads to have me look at stuff they'd written for his signature before he did or to let me assist with something they were preparing for him. People who worked for me had the best track record of getting promoted or selected for commissioning programs because of my great care and effort in making sure that their evaluations and paperwork submissions were top-notch.

It annoyed the affected department heads to have to let me look over or correct their writing, but they wouldn't challenge it—except to me. Take it up with the commodore, I'd say; I was just doing what I was told. The commodore took to publicly calling me "the Golden Pen," causing me both grief and pride, and would publicly tell people who asked him to review their applications for commissioning programs to let me look at them first. This was a double-edged sword at times.

Most of the ship commanding officers knew that I was writing a lot of "Personal for the Commanding Officer" messages (ass biting, usually) regarding training screwups, and some of them appeared to take it personally. I walked into Captain Rankin's office one day, and a senior captain was there. Captain Rankin casually told me to write a "personal for" message to that same captain about something his ship had screwed up.

Looking straight at me, the captain said to hurry up and send it because he'd need to take a dump as soon as he got back and he'd need something to wipe his ass with. He wasn't happy, he wasn't smiling, and I didn't dare smile. Now, it's time for the really ugly part.

Two things then happened at pretty much the same time. One was that I was assigned responsibility for a damage control training team that had previously been assigned to another command. The team consisted of four guys, as I remember, led by a first class petty officer. The second thing was that the mobile damage control wet trainer we occasionally used was discontinued due to funding cuts. This trainer was out of state, and it was expensive to transport it, staff it, and set it up. Now we had no mobile wet trainer and had an underutilized training team. So, naturally, we decided to build a wet trainer from scratch. We called it the War Wagon. This idea came from the leading petty officer, Damage Controlman First Class (DC1) Long. He thought we could build our own.

I listened and thought how hard could it be? I had rebuilt car engines and carburetors. A big metal box should be a piece of cake. We got busy. When

I told Commodore Jarecki during a staff meeting that we were building our own wet trainer, it got a few big laughs and some snickers, mostly from the engineers. I just smiled. We had, however, bitten off more than we could chew. I eventually asked the commodore to persuade the Shore Intermediate Maintenance Activity to finish the job, with our personnel helping out; their skipper agreed, but he wasn't happy about it. I assigned DC1 Long to bird-dog the construction. Progress was slow. The chief warrant officer responsible for the work didn't want the job and was jerking us around. I went to see him, several times, and I finally made it clear I wasn't expecting any more delays. He canceled the work the next morning, without explanation. I knew our next chat would be different from the one before.

When I walked into his office early the next morning, he grinned and propped his feet up on his desk in a "boss man" posture. I asked him why he'd canceled the work we had agreed on the previous day, and he said, "I don't have time to talk to you right now, just have a seat and wait for me to get back." I said, "Fuck you, you worthless son of a bitch, you're going to talk to me right damn now." He jumped up out of his chair, surprised, and said, "You can't talk to me like that, sir!" He eased past me, looking panicked, but I was right beside him, cursing up a storm as he tried to outwalk me. As we walked, I fed him a steady stream of curses, telling him what a piece of shit I thought he was and some other not nice things. I was seeing those faces on the sailors we passed that people make when they're not sure if what they're seeing is really happening.

He burst into the conference room where his boss was having the morning staff meeting and told him that he didn't appreciate how I was talking to him and that I was acting crazy. As I started explaining the problems I was having to the commander maintenance officer, he cut me off, telling me he was busy fixing ships and that he didn't have time to worry about my little box. I profanely and very disrespectfully informed him that I didn't give a damn about what else he was doing. As far as I was concerned, there was only one job he had and that was the one I was there about. We exchanged more harsh words and I left, after looking at the now-grinning warrant officer. He looked confident that I'd just screwed myself. All the witnesses worked for his boss or were his buddies.

On the way back to my office, I wondered what was going to happen to me. Lots of people had seen this ugliness, and I was on their turf. Chief Staff Officer Captain Rankin soon called me, having had his ass chewed on about me. When I explained, he told me to meet him outside my building; he'd be right over to pick me up. Captain Rankin was a southerner, from north Florida. I didn't have to explain to him why this was happening. He knew. Southerners understand each other. It's easier to understand than to explain.

When we walked into the maintenance organization's captain's office, he was loaded for bear. He was a good ass chewer, having had lots of practice. He was talking to Captain Rankin, but he was often looking at me. I was his real target. I wondered if he was thinking about the Good Old Days, when Negroes knew their place. He was likely a southerner too. I soaked up everything he said, preparing my defense. Other than what he said I had done, nothing else he said was true. Captain Rankin listened silently, and when he spoke, he said, "That's not true. Keith?" I opened my War Wagon wheel book and demolished the story he'd been told. I kept pieces of paper and made excellent notes. Calmer now, he asked me why I had not come to him if I was having problems, and I told him I was following the chain of command, as I was taught in boot camp. He called the maintenance officer and told him to meet him at the War Wagon with the warrant officer in tow. On the way, he stopped and spoke to people he trusted and who knew shit from Shinola.

When he got to the War Wagon, now more enlightened, he started asking some hard questions, in a deceptively easy manner. Incredibly, he was lied to again, repeatedly. When he asked the warrant officer if he had all the parts he needed to finish the War Wagon, the answer was "Yes, sir." I immediately asked about the four parts he'd told me were on backorder, looking at my notes, and he looked at me and said, "We got them stashed." One of those answers was a lie. I looked at his skipper, who was staring at him intensely.

The bull elephants walked away and talked briefly, and then Captain Rankin and I left. He told me not to worry and that the War Wagon now had the skipper's personal attention. He told me to come see him if I was ever to have any more problems like this. This event happened on a Friday, the start of a three-day holiday weekend. That maintenance facility worked double shifts all that weekend in an effort to get that War Wagon finished. That captain had decided it was time for some ruthlessness. When elephants fight, it is the grass that suffers, it is said. The War Wagon was completed in short order.

We would roll it up on a different unsuspecting ship every week, after hours, and their duty damage control personnel would practice their skills on it, preparing patches and stopping flooding and simulated hull damage within it, without trashing their own ships or damaging electronic equipment. We incorporated the War Wagon into Surface Warfare Training Week.

We were the only East Coast squadron with its own War Wagon. Ships, including visiting ships, would call up and ask for it. To see what one looks like, look up Mobile Damage Control Wet Trainer on the internet. This self-help accomplishment was written about in *Surface Warfare* magazine, and my commodore received great recognition for this significant accomplishment. The maintenance facility was also mentioned for their great production assistance. Before Captain Jarecki retired, he placed me front and center before a true legend.

While I was fighting these battles, I was having others as well. My third wife, Iris, and I did not see eye to eye on finances, education, ambition, and raising children. I was buying properties to rent, and she was spending money on clothes, purses, shoes, trinkets, and cars. In addition, she told me I was too ambitious. I asked her to name another Black man she thought was too ambitious, but she declined. I suggested Colin Powell. Silence. A Black wife tells her Black naval officer husband that he is too ambitious while she spends extravagantly; no marriage counseling could fix this one. There were also typical teenager problems with her boy and girl and my own son, who was living with us then. She found it easier not to deal with those issues and said she was sick of me and the children. We were not a good match.

More things had changed. In February 1994, the *New York Times* named Admiral Jeremy Boorda as its man in the news, identified him as a mustang, and called him the "People's Admiral." Retired Admiral Zumwalt said that same month that the navy needed a surface warfare officer (SWO) as CNO, citing morale issues, and I'm pretty sure he had someone in mind. The navy officially closed the Tailhook investigation, but not before the military judge, a captain, hammered the CNO, Admiral Kelso, for "hindering" the investigation. He retired two months early. Admiral Boorda, an SWO, became the second-known Jewish CNO in March. The 1994 discrimination complaints were 72 percent substantiated. The 1992 seismic shift had heralded a new era, but it would not last.

After the War Wagon fiasco, the commodore decided to put us in for a Meritorious Unit Commendation, and each department submitted a list of its accomplishments. I was shocked to see how much our training department had accomplished, including taking control of numerous quotas, assuming chairmanship of the regional training board, expanding the scope of training, identifying serious problems with electronic multiport training from outside activities, more efficiently utilizing the training dollars available by taking control of and combining multiple funding accounts, starting a conditioning program for prospective search-and-rescue swimmers, revamping in-port training, and a lot more. Oh, yeah, and don't forget we built our own War Wagon too.

Our accomplishments were quantifiable, verifiable, and represented clear dollar savings and significant efficiency improvements in multiple areas, in addition to being well beyond the scope and breadth of what we were tasked to do. I had taught my guys to be ready when the boss needed a paper clip and to keep a good wheel book. What made all of this easier was that we had developed a standard operating procedure (SOP) for each desk in the office, at my insistence, which spelled out who, what, when, where, and why for every responsibility we had.

I went through and utilized each of these SOPs myself, to be sure. I wanted each man to know how to do each job in the department. I remembered the value of my very first SOP. I would send them all away for golf or a long lunch and man each desk myself. If I got a call and the answer wasn't in the SOP, I would put on my so-called frowny face. Any toddler who has seen the disapproving look of a parent because of their misbehavior knows this face. I would exaggerate mine for effect. We had assumed so much responsibility and added so much complexity that we needed those SOPs for consistency, continuity, and redundancy.

The senior department head (operations) responsible for compiling the recommendation said openly that if we received the award (we didn't), it would largely be based on the strength of the training department's input. I am convinced that we were able to do so much because the level of authority had been pushed down to those who knew what needed to be done to make it better, and who had great leadership and backup. Our little training department's accomplishments did not go unnoticed by our extended chain of command.

Captain Jarecki had asked Vice Admiral J. Paul Reason to attend one of our morning meetings while he was touring the Atlantic Fleet bases and facilities, of which he would soon be master. He also spoke at the commodores' change of command and retirement ceremony. Jarecki informed me that morning to casually feed him items on the exceptional accomplishments we had achieved in the training department so that he could elaborate on them to Vice Admiral Reason. There was quite a bit to cover. I brought a big spoon.

When Jarecki finished, Vice Admiral Reason looked at me and said that he wished that everyone in the Atlantic Fleet conducted training the way we did it in Mayport. I swear, I faintly heard that Abraham Lincoln music they play on PBS! I can hear it again now as you read this.

Hearing that comment from Admiral Reason was definitely my proudest moment in the navy. Here sat this soon-to-be-four-star admiral, accomplished, Black, and proud, telling everybody in the room, my peers and my superiors, that he was proud of me. He had no idea that just a few of months before, I had been on the verge of possibly getting punished for insubordination and disrespect.

Our new squadron commander asked me to take over his admin department rather than take the orders I'd just received to lead the base telephone office at Naval Air Station Jacksonville. He could make it happen. He had made it clear at his first staff meeting that he would not tolerate people on his staff with what he called "Assholic Tendencies." He was surely my kind of guy. Unfortunately, I'd be reporting to his new chief staff officer, a ship's captain from within the squadron whom I didn't have a warm and fuzzy feeling about—and for good reason. We had tangled before.

I wasn't taking any chances. Also, I had pretty much run an admin office as a first class yeoman. Before I left, I made sure that the first class petty officer whom Captain Rankin wanted me to fire when I assumed this job, but he let me keep him and accept responsibility for any problems he might cause, pinned on his shiny new medal I had recommended for him and that he had surely earned. He retired with pride and dignity, having done a phenomenal job.

Little did I know the next two years were going to be the most difficult of my career, by far, not physically or professionally, but psychologically. I would soon learn, once again, that you could be a golden boy in one command and a dipshit in the next one, even as an officer. It mostly depended on the leadership style and personal beliefs of the person(s) you served. Even after all I had been through and with my good performance record in challenging assignments, I would be targeted. I never expected it to happen to me—again, that is.

12

Sailing Second Class

I finally went to work for the two wrong guys. The first was my boss for three months and the second relieved him. I felt pretty confident walking down the corridor at my new headquarters building, the Naval Computer and Telecommunications station in Jacksonville, Florida, in May 1995. I was the incoming department head for the base telephone office. I could dial a phone with the best of them. The incumbent was a lieutenant commander, and we had spoken by telephone just minutes earlier. There were no problems that I knew of, but that changed within seconds of meeting the executive officer (XO).

Commander Jay Caler, an aviator, approached me in the corridor as I talked with several people who were introducing themselves. He set the tone for my tour. He informed me that instead of taking over the telephone office, the captain had decided that I would instead be relieving an ensign, whose only job was implementing the Total Quality Leadership (TQL) initiative in the command. She had two part-time civilian subordinates, both with other full-time responsibilities. My challenging job, and with it my future chances for promotion, had disappeared in seconds.

She was the junior officer on staff, and I was quite surprised and confused by this. What had happened in the last few minutes, I wondered? Unlike my Mineman friend Jimmy, I didn't have to tell them I was Black, but apparently, it mattered a lot. Caler walked me back down the way I'd come to this tiny office. It looked like a converted closet, with boxes of files sitting on the floor and barely room for one person to set up shop.

I asked Commander Caler why I was being given this job vice the one the chief of naval personnel had ordered me in to take. I don't remember the answer. I do remember that he would not make solid eye contact with me. I had an overpowering sense that this change had happened because I was Black. Not "sounding Black" on the telephone before had led to confusion for people I eventually met, only this time there appeared to be immediate and damaging consequences. This "linguistic profiling" is common.

When I met the commanding officer later that morning, he didn't elaborate on the situation, and I didn't ask. He was polite but distant. I decided on a wait-and-see approach. I learned I would be reporting directly to Mr. William "Bill" Whitman, the comptroller and a prior enlisted marine. Instead of being a department head, now I would be reporting to the supply officer as his subordinate. I felt like a massive door had slammed in my face. I soon read the skipper's official biography. Commander James "Jim" Booth, my new skipper, was born, raised, and educated (in an all-white college) in the great state of Alabama—Auburn, class of '71. He was in college when Martin Luther King Jr. was murdered. He had previously served on the USS *Spruance* (DD-963).

Six years before we met, in January 1989, *Spruance* had been run hard aground by a Black officer of the deck who ignored warnings from his quartermaster and used poor judgment. He was subsequently dismissed from the service and killed the careers of his leadership. I'm sure Booth was aware of that, as I was, having talked to people who knew the quartermaster involved. I was only three months into my engineering tour when that grounding happened, and I talked to people who knew people who were on the bridge. I remember praying, "Lord, please don't let him be Black." Based on his background, and this abrupt behavior, I think Booth may have considered me a threat to his own career. His biography helped me understand what might be going on. The principle of Occam's razor applies to this situation.

I flipped the script and made my own subjective judgment. Soon after, at an all-hands meeting, all the officers sat on stage as Booth talked about the command goals and direction, and the coming TQL initiative, my new "job." I waited for someone to introduce me. When I realized as things were wrapping up that no one was going to mention anything about this new Black officer who was sitting on stage, I stood up. It was like I was invisible or unimportant. I made my first stand.

Having been on the TQL executive steering committee at my last command, I was well versed in its goals and objectives. I introduced myself, stated that I was the coordinator for the effort, and was looking forward to working with each member in the command. This appeared to irritate Commander Booth. He was making frowny faces. I was pissed at not having been acknowledged or introduced. Something didn't feel right here, and the visual was just as bad.

My new department head, Bill Whitman, the ex-marine comptroller, showed his contempt early. I needed cabinets to put all the TQL materials in, and he had a warehouse full of them. I asked for some, and he told me to put in a requisition. I did, but he didn't approve it, mimicking *Boone*'s supply officer. I realized he was screwing with me, supply officer–style. I didn't know if I'd ever get them, so I bought file cabinets from a thrift store and transported them in my personal truck. I was used to being resourceful and getting around obstacles. I'd have plenty of practice here. He would blatantly continue this pattern of denial of resources for the remainder of my tour, with no consequences.

At my eventual welcome-aboard interview with Booth, weeks later, things became clearer. Normally these interviews are conducted almost immediately, but this one was not. He did most of the talking, giving me his command philosophy and such, and then he asked me a startling question: Had I had considered going to department head school? For a moment, I was dumbfounded.

Why would he *think* I had not already been? He'd read my orders to a department head billet, and he'd had access to my service record for weeks. As slowly and with as little emotion as I could muster, I informed him that I had gone to department head school seven years earlier, immediately after my division officer tour, and that I'd completed three back-to-back department head tours before reporting for this one, my fourth. Where did he think all those ribbons on my chest had come from? Could he see them?

I told him I believed I wasn't serving in a shipboard XO billet because the pipeline was so backed up with more senior people awaiting those jobs who didn't have my experience. None of this would have surprised him if he'd bothered to open my service record or had not been acting on racial prejudice. As I schooled him, his eyes widened and his jaw dropped open. When I finished, I asked, "Didn't you review my service record?" The answer was a sheepish no. I resisted the temptation to ask him why not. I had almost immediately read his biography, trying to understand him, yet he had not even bothered to open mine. I knew why. Southerners understand each other. We have deep experience.

As the 1945 Chief of Naval Personnel Admiral Jacobs said, assigning people on the basis of theories of racial differences could be a serious waste of human resources. Days after our talk, Commander Booth proudly announced at a staff meeting that he had decided to assign the fine, talented, experienced "superstar" surface warfare officer (me) to run the telephone office and that I would be taking over the facilities department as well. I went from no real job to two important ones.

In other words, he was going to give me two departments to run but only pay me for one. Any Black sharecropper who'd ever seen a mule would recognize this tactic. I'd have twice the opportunity to fail but no more hours in the day to do it in while being under resourced. By then I was pretty disgusted. Again, I'd had no clue that any of this was coming. I learned it when everyone else did. I had gone from an undertasked division officer to an overburdened department head in the blink of an eye, with no warning or notice. What I wanted or thought didn't matter either way.

Where and when he grew up, you didn't ask Black people what they wanted; you just told them what they could have and expected them to be grateful. I was not accustomed to being treated this way by my boss, and I resented it. When he mentioned that he had not discussed this with me or asked me how I felt about it, I couldn't help myself. Barely hiding my disdain at this treatment, I said, "When you get around to asking me, I'll let you know." This didn't go over well, and I didn't care. If his daddy had heard an "uppity" Black man talking to him like this, he would have been in big trouble. The guy I had been sent to relieve snapped at me, "He's asking you now." He'd had nothing to share about why I had been reassigned initially, and now he was defending his boss. His fitness report was due soon, as was his end-of-tour award. The tension in the room was thick, so I flashed him a "fuck you too" look, gritted my teeth, and stayed silent.

I don't expect many people in the room understood the dynamics of what had just occurred. They probably saw me as arrogant and ungrateful. I was being treated poorly, and I seemed to be the only one who cared. Not a good beginning. It wasn't long before Commander Booth assumed command of our headquarters and was promoted to captain. Before leaving, he assigned me to investigate an inspector general complaint submitted by a white petty officer at a subordinate overseas command. I soon departed for Puerto Rico to investigate the complaint the sailor filed about unfair treatment by his commanding officer and at the counseling and assistance center where he was sent for treatment, which he did not believe he needed. He also alleged that the counseling center personnel were violating his privacy rights by recording him without his written permission, in violation of their own procedures and command directives. He also alleged that he was the victim of retaliation.

After I introduced myself and showed my credentials, I asked for the relevant directives from both command's representatives. The next morning, I was escorted to the base commander's office, where I started receiving quite the ass chewing. He didn't want me there and immediately tried to intimidate me, accusing me of using "Gestapo tactics" on his base. It got pretty ugly and a little loud. I stayed completely calm. I had seen this fear-based tactic before.

I had absolutely followed proper protocol. Someone at the counseling and assistance center had called him, complaining about the questions I was asking, and they knew they didn't have good answers. They were scared. I informed this angry captain that he should be careful making such accusations, because the petty officer whose complaint I was investigating had said similar things about his treatment and he had received an involuntary mental health examination. His mouth suddenly snapped shut, mid-rant, and he calmed down a bit. It was true.

After completing my investigation, I briefed him on issues relevant to him, and he sincerely thanked me for exposing significant problems that could have led to serious pain for him professionally. The people using "Gestapo tactics" worked for him. I think one of them was named Karen. He would now be acting on what he knew, not on what he believed, as had happened with the previous captain in the War Wagon fiasco.

The commanding officer of the young man who formally complained wasn't happy with the investigation's outcome, but I reported the facts, all thoroughly documented in writing. Once people realized that I was seeking the truth, they started pouring out what had been going on, especially some of the senior khakis. A brave junior division officer spoke up, in writing, defending his subordinate who had filed the complaint.

The commanding officer I was investigating pretty much hung herself. The documentation told a story that didn't match hers. I was so sure that she would perjure herself that I contacted the inspector general's legal staff for guidance, and they mandated that I have a JAG lawyer present when I questioned her. I was specifically told not to read her her rights. In retrospect, that was probably helpful to her. Before I interviewed her for the last time, I structured my written questions to her to get at the truth. I did. I even gave her a typed copy of the questions I was going to ask her, in order, and she had them in front of her as we went through them. No ambush, no surprises. As I expected, she lied, irrefutably and fully documented. After I submitted my report, which said "failed" a lot, I never heard about it again.

After he read the report, Commander Booth had a change in demeanor toward me; I could sense a chill. He gave me a look but said nothing to me about it. I had once been a young petty officer who was being treated unfairly, and I sure as hell wasn't going to help whitewash the mistreatment of another. I believe that if you're willing to misuse your authority, you should face the consequences. He apparently did not.

My next commanding officer was Commander Thomas D. Goodall. He assumed command in July 1995. Initially, we got along fairly well. He was only eight months older than I was, and we were both surface warfare officers. I'd been in the navy three years longer than he had. Our experiences were similar, but our perspectives and leadership styles were worlds apart. I had grown up with a bully, a violent one. He'd written a paper about gunboat diplomacy, an appropriate topic for a bully. The mindset and behavior appeared almost immediately.

Once we started having TQL implementation meetings, things got ugly. As I pushed to do something meaningful and productive, he pushed back. Getting confused, I went to talk to him about it. That's when he told me privately that neither he nor Booth supported the navy's TQL initiative. I finally understood why Booth had put me in charge of the effort; he valued me less than the ensign who had the job. Goodall also said that he believed what he did at sea was the only important thing. Both he and Booth were likely the kind of officers who Admiral Jacobs had warned about in 1947 when he said, "The efforts of the commanding officer to apply all the techniques of good leadership will be of little value if the junior officers under him destroy the effect of his work through actions resulting from disinterest, lack of knowledge or personal prejudice." They represented a double whammy.

Only lip service to the TQL initiative was evident. The leadership was simply going through the motions with no real commitment to the principles of the initiative. The lack of any measurable goals and objectives was a source of constant friction and annoyance, primarily because I kept pointing it out. I didn't know how to just "pretend" that we were trying to do something meaningful. It was not in my nature. I kept raising issues with our process (as the process encouraged) and was subsequently singled out in writing after one meeting for "special counseling" for my insistence on trying to do something meaningful and productive. I was working for a man who cared less about his command than I did. I tried to shut up.

After a few more contentious meetings and dueling emails, I went to see Goodall. He told me I was the problem. I asked to be removed from the TQL executive steering committee. He refused. I asked about the special counseling mentioned in the previous meeting's minutes, and he feigned ignorance. His behavior made no sense. He wanted me at these meetings but had actually stormed out several times because he didn't like what I said. I had expert power but was supposed to stay silent or agree with him. This was a catch-22 situation.

People continued to tell me negative things he was openly saying about me, but when I engaged him, he'd say everything was OK and that he was just frustrated. I began keeping a little file of what was happening, when, and by whom. Something was afoot. It was time for a special wheel book to be created.

In one of my two department head jobs, I provided telephone service for military commands in Jacksonville, Florida, and outlying areas. We handled all things telephone. The real brain was Lee West, my number two, who was retired enlisted US Air Force, and he knew his stuff. We got off to a rocky start because he had been a master sergeant, so I bought a bag of Skittles, we had a little talk, and things settled down. We set up a pretty good system: he got the credit and I got the blame; it worked pretty well most of the time.

The telephone switch we were installing had been rescued from the Philippines following the Mount Pinatubo eruption. Our operation would have been lucrative for any commercial provider, and they sought it for years. Lee West had listened to and carefully analyzed numerous proposals. He briefed me thoroughly. When one company realized that a new Black guy with no telephone experience was in charge, they got creative.

They bent the ear of the base commander, Rear Admiral Kevin Delaney. He was the senior naval officer in the US Southeast region, and he knew it. He was a highly decorated 'Nam helicopter pilot. Someone had evidently been reading Machiavelli's *The Prince*, and the plotting was thick. They convinced Delaney that we were goofballs who were obstructing capitalism and likely said that we were Communists or Marxists as well. Lee was fat and white and working with minorities, and I was skinny, four-eyed, difficult, and Black. We fit the description.

It got ugly fast. Delaney ordered me and Lee West to his office to "discuss" our plans for upgrading telephone service to his commands. He wanted us to turn our operation over to a particular civilian company (though he gave no explanation why), went into "Admiral Mode" when we resisted, and told us that we didn't have any credibility and didn't know what we were talking about. My polite, respectful response was "Sir, with all due respect, just because you believe that doesn't make it true." This was the safest way to tell him that he didn't know what he was talking about. He then got very quiet. I was making friends both inside and outside my command.

We soon briefed the admiral and his staff with an extensive slide deck brief at our headquarters command in Norfolk, Virginia. Everything went well, I thought. The next day, he ordered a Performance Audit of the existing telephone plan from the Navy Audit Service. The long knives were coming, and Goodall pretty much told me I was on my own. After a weeks-long audit, having evaluated three separate takeover proposals, the audit team sided with us.

They briefed Admiral Delaney, many base commanding officers, and our other customers on what they'd decided. Neither Lee West nor I was allowed to attend. (I asked if we could; Goodall said no.) He went instead, now that the coast was clear. If things had not gone well, I'm sure I'd have been there, and he'd have written me a special fitness report. Sometime afterward, I was near the admiral's office relieving myself in the head (known to landlubbers as the restroom or toilet) when he walked in and stood next to me, relieving himself too. My bladder seized up immediately.

I had never before peed on an admiral's shoes, and I sure as hell wasn't going to start with this one. He asked me what I was going to do when I retired. I croaked out, "I'm not sure," trying as I spoke not to dribble terrified urine from my mouth. He said to come see him when I was ready to look for a job. I never did go see him about that potential job.

I had continuous and fairly serious conflict with Goodall. The telephone audit and phone switch installation were wearing on his nerves. He started to verbally abuse members of his staff, and he was casting about for more targets. Our safety officer, a civilian, suffered sustained public and very harsh verbal abuse from Goodall. It was absolutely disgusting to watch. I felt sorry for him and angry about it. Goodall would smile after doing it.

On one occasion, Lee West and I were in a staff meeting about telephones, and Goodall snapped at me in a nasty fashion, catching me by surprise. I was just simply reporting the status of certain issues. I was too embarrassed to react. I just listened and continued on with what I was saying, looking him in the eye. The bully I'd recognized many times before in my life was back.

I considered my hard-won experience with bullies and decided not to turn any more cheeks. I forewarned Lee West not to be surprised at my response if Goodall did it again. The command leadership attended these meetings. I wasn't going to be a target child. When Goodall erupted again a week later, I waited for him to finish talking. When he did, I calmly asked him why he was yelling at me. Now he was surprised. He had no good answer for this simple question, so he started yelling again; I cut him off. I asked my question again but didn't wait for an answer. I told him that I had not done anything to deserve being talked to that way, I didn't appreciate it, and I wasn't going to tolerate it.

He wilted and was speechless, looking confused and embarrassed, and I hadn't even punched him in the mouth. Caler, the XO, tried to rescue him by saying that it was just that these telephones had everybody so upset and that was the problem. I said that the telephone is an inanimate object and that everyone needed to remember that. By now my collar was hot, and my jaw was tight; my fight-or-flight reflex was about to kick in. As Captain Robert Rankin would say, I was getting to the part of meetings he liked the most: where we pointed fingers at each other and called each other "motherfucker."

From that day on, I was a marked man. Goodall would follow Master Chief Davy's retaliation playbook, only more openly and with powerful allies.

It got a lot harder for me after that. He would at least not adopt the pretense of trying to "help" me—exactly the opposite.

One of my janitors, a Black man and military veteran, was encouraged to file a discrimination complaint against me by the president of the union, who had previously worked for me in the TQL effort. He received the lowest performance mark in his group for this performance period from his facilities department supervisor. I went over the ratings with his supervisor and submitted them. I didn't change any of them; I trusted his judgment. Afterward, I went over each man's performance with him, discussing what he was doing well individually, what the team was doing well collectively, and my desires for the future. None of their performances was rated as unsatisfactory, but I was accused of improperly lowering his marks. I was easily able to rebut this because I had submitted them as received before I talked to him. His supervisor confirmed this. I still had to go through a formal investigation. The investigator asked, "Whiskey tango foxtrot (WTF)?" since I clearly had done nothing wrong. I kept silent.

Goodall, following the comptroller's lead, refused to release the necessary funding for new furniture for the new telephone building. There was plenty of money available; he just wouldn't release it. He gave no explanation, just wouldn't do it. I had previously given him a nice credenza for his office that I obtained from defense reutilization facility as I had done as an ensign while assigned to *Voge*. Caler also refused to allow me to move the furniture from my other office, the facilities department, again without explanation. He gave that furniture to a junior officer who worked for a chief warrant officer in another department. This was humiliating to me, but I said nothing, stuffing my wheel book instead. I directed that what money we did have go to where it was most needed. I wanted nothing for my office. This caused consternation, as I would have no furniture and I led the department.

After the big move, I sat in my big new office that Friday afternoon with a computer and a black plastic trash can. You could see the somber, pitying looks from my subordinates. What none of them knew was that I had lots of furniture and antiques that I bought and stored in a very large house I had purchased in the Riverside area of Jacksonville, a historic district, with the intention of renovating and making it my home. I had other rental properties as well. When Monday morning rolled around, things had changed. They were happily surprised to see how busy and industrious I had been. A couple of days later, the XO came to see me.

He walked into my office speaking but stopped midsentence, doing a full 360 turn, all the while staring with his mouth open. He couldn't believe my office transformation. I had US Navy–themed oil paintings on the walls, a mahogany conference table surrounded by the type of wooden office chairs you see in jury boxes, a mahogany office desk, telephone handsets from the 1920s, antique radios and vintage typewriters in an old oak bookcase, and two ancient adding machines on tables for good measure. I had an oak drafting table with the building blueprints for ongoing work atop it. An antique wooden coatrack sat near the door. It looked like an old movie set and smelled like money or revenge. Goodall didn't have to buy me furniture. I had my own.

Caler asked me where I got this stuff from. I told him it was stuff I had lying around in one of my unoccupied investment houses. Goodall soon came to see for himself. He was surprised. My office was much nicer than his, which he blurted out with clear annoyance. He could only blame himself—and me. People from all over the base would often come and ask if they could look at my office. I happily obliged.

The comptroller stayed true to form. He let my important requests linger or ignored them. When I complained to Goodall, he'd take notes, but nothing changed. Needed government work went undone, a national security issue. I kept a file of emailed update requests, making sure both of them got these. The cell phone I ordered for myself as head of the telephone department never made it to me. He gave it to another department head and said he'd order me another one. I never got that one either. We had an equipment casualty once, and I had to coordinate repairs and efforts from several locations using my personal cell phone, racking up personal charges that went unreimbursed.

The biggest issue I had with him was the uncompleted and unsigned support agreements between our organization and many of our customers. He had supposedly racked up extensive overtime while building his dream house, but he was too busy to do these vital agreements. This impacted my funding, as some commands decided that they didn't have to pay for service without a valid signed agreement. This had been impacting our revenue for years, and when I began poking around and asking questions, I was told in writing by the comptroller to keep my nose out of financial matters, with Goodall copied on the email. He didn't say he was going to fix this, however. Goodall seemed to be afraid to make him do his job, as I was urging him to do. When pressed on this, he informed me that the comptroller had an "unusual management style." I thought that was bullshit. This was going to cause Goodall a bigger headache than the telephone audit had.

Two of our major Naval Station Mayport customers, lacking these support agreements, were not paying their telephone bills. I pushed Goodall to get this resolved. The comptroller's brilliant solution was to convince

Goodall to terminate their telephone service and stop ordering their telephone equipment. Resource denial was his specialty. Even more brilliant, he convinced Goodall to have me send out the letter informing them of this—so much for keeping my nose out of financial matters. He said he had the backing of his boss at headquarters, but I didn't believe him. I wanted no part of this crazy plan.

Since my name was going to be on the letter, not the comptroller's, guess who was going to face the blowback? Wasn't this a financial matter? I didn't want to enrage a whole basin full of captains and the admirals they reported to. Important military commands with no phone service?

When Goodall called me in to discuss the letter, I told him that he was making a big mistake. I also felt that I was being set up. I told him that he had no documentation proving the support of his own boss on this and that the only one who was telling him to do this was the comptroller, whose negligence brought it all to a head. I told him that he was about to kick over a hornet's nest and once he did, everybody was likely to get stung. Since everybody meant him, I got his attention.

I requested that he obtain written verification that headquarters supported this action before I drafted this letter. I wasn't signing anything without it. He did and promptly learned that the comptroller had lied to him, as the War Wagon warrant officer had lied to his boss. He was advised to make the comptroller do his job. He told me that they needed two detailed, succinct point papers detailing the two separate financial issues in order to attempt a final resolution by higher authority. Now I could get back to my own job, I thought.

The next day, Goodall told me to draft the needed papers. I flatly refused. I told him that it wasn't my job, I had not created this mess and that I wasn't familiar enough with the terminology, the history, or the financial directives. I wasn't responsible for support agreements, the comptroller was. I pointedly reminded him that he'd told me in writing to keep my nose out of financial matters. Goodall ordered me to do them. I had just saved him from turning a disaster into a catastrophe, and my reward was to be ordered to clean up the mess the lying comptroller had made. I felt like he was adding insult to injury. I was wrong; that would come later. He was pacing himself.

It took me a while and a lot of work, with a steep learning curve, to complete this extremely complex task. When I had finished, I forwarded the draft point papers to the XO via email and then went to his office. When I got there, Caler was forwarding them to Goodall without making a single change. He was thrilled. We went to Goodall's office to see what would come next.

Shortly after we got there, Goodall handed me a draft email to read. He looked quite pleased with himself. He was forwarding the point papers I'd prepared to his boss, Captain Booth, my previous skipper there. Caler sat down, looking disinterested. I read the draft email and got more furious with each word. In it, Goodall was informing Captain Booth what an outstanding job the "XO" had done, "using his vast Pentagon experience and expertise, in distilling this complex financial information and issues into such succinct, easily understood point papers" and how this would likely resolve these long-standing issues. The XO sounded like a superstar.

Raging inside, I realized that he was going to give Caler the credit for what he had ordered me to do and was asking me to bless it! I was being written out of the story. This was after I'd done the work of the comptroller, who had blatantly lied to him, and had been doing everything he could to undermine my success. I had just saved his ass, twice, and he was treating me like I was just a fucking proofreader. I felt like I'd just been slapped in the face.

Refusing to acquiesce, I quietly told him that I didn't mind Caler getting credit, but that I had written both of those papers and that I wanted to be included in his email as part of the solution. When I handed this email back to him, he snatched it out of my hand with a look of pure fury on his face and snarled, "Well in that case, they're UNSAT because they're more than one page!" The XO looked up and asked what was going on, acting like he had not been paying much attention.

I'm still surprised that a very pissed-off alien monster didn't burst out of my chest and start dispatching him immediately. I don't think I've ever felt such unbridled hatred for anyone before in my life. Abuse wasn't enough; he wanted to humiliate me as well. I could see myself snatching him from behind his desk and throwing him through the second-story plate glass window. I'm sure my arteries were straining mightily to contain the blood that was threatening to burst out like an alien parasite. Not before or since have I felt such hatred for another human being.

I had previously started exhibiting physical manifestations of the stress I was under. Lee West had insisted that I go to the naval hospital when in a staff meeting I showed him how my left-side chest muscles were quivering like Jell-O; you could see it through my shirt. He thought I was about to have a heart attack. We walked into the emergency room (I ordered them not to call 911), and I was rushed by wheelchair into a room and hooked up to everything important. My heart was fine. They asked me if I was under any stress. I laughed. Lee did not. He was worried that this abuse was going to kill me. I had already talked to a civilian mental health professional about what I was enduring. I didn't trust that the military medical system had my best interests at heart. I would later learn how right I was.

Anyway, Goodall rewrote his email and again handed it to me to read. I had to unball my fist to take it. It said these papers should resolve the situation, without attributing authorship to anyone. As far as anyone knew, the comptroller wrote them. I handed it back to him and left. I remember thinking that this must be what slavery felt like. Booth was a kind, benevolent master compared to Goodall. I asked myself where he had learned to treat people this way. What had been done to him to make him behave this way? What would Booth think about this?

It was around 1700, quitting time. I sat down and started typing. When the sun arose, I was still typing. I'd had no sleep or food. I was running on pure hatred and cortisol. Goodall had never seen my fangs, but he was about to.

I stayed in my office for days, typing my own special project. Now I was working for myself, not for him. He had destroyed any loyalty I felt to him. I went to no meetings and sent no representatives in my place. We were in separate buildings. I was at work, but I was intentionally invisible. I ignored calls to my office phone and my cell phone if it was CO/XO/secretary. I treated my personal pager the same. It wasn't government issued, because the comptroller had blocked that request as well. I wasn't going to spend any more of my own money talking to people who were treating me like shit. I ignored their emails. I hoped they would come to my office and confront me. Neither did.

Master Sun Tzu wrote, "What causes opponents to come of their own accord is the prospect of gain. What discourages opponents from coming is the prospect of harm." Lesson: If you are afraid to approach someone you've harmed, you probably have good reason to be afraid.

When I went to Admiral Delaney's office a few days later to brief him on the status of the telephone switch work, both Goodall and Caler were standing outside, frowning. It was the first time I had seen either of them since the humiliating point paper perfidy. When Goodall asked me if I was ready to brief the admiral, I said, "Yes." Not, "Yes, sir." He snarkily said that he'd never gone to brief an admiral before without knowing what he was going to tell him.

I looked at him with disdain and said, "I had other priorities." I've never seen anyone's demeanor change so quickly after such a simple statement; I saw fear in his eyes. He'd had time to evaluate his behavior, and he was now dealing with someone he didn't recognize. As the navy had taught me, I was going down fighting, if at all, but not before inflicting maximum damage. I was channeling the spirit of Commander Ernest E. Evans of Taffy 3 fame.

Master Sun Tzu wrote, "To be violent at first and wind up fearing one's own people is the epitome of ineptitude." Lesson: If you're afraid because of the psychological or physical violence you have sanctioned or done, which you didn't have to do, after they've helped you, you should be expecting a response that you deserve.

I believe it was the next day when Caler came to my office and told me Goodall wanted to see me in his office. I told him I didn't have anything to say to him over there. In a pleading tone, he asked me to please come over and talk to the captain and said that this had gone on long enough. He said we should all sit down and try to work this out.

Master Sun Tzu wrote, "Those who come seeking peace without a treaty are plotting." Lesson: This one is self-explanatory. It was time to see what the plotters were up to. I wasn't going seeking peace. I knew I was at war.

I decided that if he wanted to talk, I was ready. The conversation was going to be on his turf, but it was not going to go as he expected. I had been mistreated enough. He didn't know that I'd spent the last several days going through my treatment under his "leadership," pulling together all the documentation I'd been keeping. My wheel book was packed. He'd probably forgotten most of it, but he was about to get a reality check. I had irrefutable, overwhelming evidence that I was being discriminated against, and I didn't know why. I intended to get an answer. I got more than I bargained for.

They were waiting for me. I walked in and was told to sit down. I did. In a friendly, fatherly way, Goodall said that he wanted to put this behind us or words to that effect. I didn't hear anything that remotely resembled an apology or explanation. I said, "You've been fucking with the wrong guy." They weren't expecting this. Neither was I. I don't know where it came from, but it was what I felt. He squirmed and looked a little confused. I was just getting warmed up. "You've been fucking with the wrong guy," I repeated, looking from one to the other. Silence. In the past, when I said something like this to a bully, someone reconsidered their behavior, started to bleed, got kicked backward into a ditch, or quickly went to sleep. Luckily for him, he had legitimate power, one of French and Raven's five bases of power. I had expert power, which I was about to demonstrate. I told him, "OK, you want to talk, huh, so let's talk. I've got some things I want you to talk about."

I had my firing solutions locked in, so I started launching torpedoes. I had a bunch of them. He immediately started zigzagging, but it was useless. I questioned him on his consistent behavior with laser-like precision. He couldn't answer with anything resembling logic. I had prepared well, and he stumbled, trying to find good answers to questions he'd never even thought about. He had none. There weren't any. I stripped away all the bullshit to get to the truth. I told him when he would rather give no one credit for vital work that I'd done, writing me out of the story, that was personal.

Eventually, he was dead in the water, full of direct hits, but refusing to list or sink. He didn't have to; he was the captain. As I got more and more emotional, I finally revealed the pain he had tried so hard to inflict. Despite his inability to defend his behavior and the detrimental impact it had on his entire command, he seemed unconcerned about the impact of his behavior and pleased that he had caused me so much pain and confusion. He enjoyed me sharing my pain; he wore a little half smile and said, yes, deep down, it probably was personal. Feeling confident and seeing that I was hurting, he tried to deepen it. Once I had revealed these emotions, nothing I'd said seemed to concern him. He was in bully heaven. If he'd had any idea of the lessons I'd taught bullies much bigger and meaner than he was, and the thoughts of violence racing through my head, he likely would have been concerned. Leaning back in his chair, twirling his pencil, this man looked at me and asked me, with fake concern, and dripping sarcasm, "Do you feel like a second-class citizen?" The smirk said it all; he was happier than I'd ever seen him. Caler only spoke when I addressed him directly. A person under fire tends to lose allies. Caler had nothing to gain by being mine. I hope he was ashamed.

Now I ask you, when someone asks you if you feel like a second-class citizen (surely you've been asked that question), what's the first image that comes to your mind? For me, it was the iconic image of the striking Memphis garbage men, wearing the sandwich boards that said, "I AM A MAN," the ones Martin Luther King Jr. got his neck blown open and his spine severed for, in believing all men were equal before the law and the Lord. That question was really a declaration of belief. It's likely the dumbest thing Goodall has ever said.

Now I understood. What I quietly told him was that no, I didn't feel like a second-class citizen, but I felt like I was being treated like one. After I said this, I calmed down. I now had an answer, and it was a gift. I had never, not once, interjected race into our conflict. Goodall essentially told me why these things were happening to me, and the gift was the freedom to use it. Just like the marine colonel Jessup in the movie *A Few Good Men*, he wanted to tell the truth. Only after I showed him my vulnerability, my pain, did he feel confident enough to speak the truth. This bully wasn't just apparently bonkers but also dangerously culturally stupid to boot. I got up and left his office. The future was going to surprise him.

The next big day was May 11, 1996, a few days before my thirty-ninth birthday and after the anniversary of my twenty-first year of service.

I had been in the navy three years longer than I'd been out of it. I had taught for years how people were to be treated and what would not be tolerated. I had taught many sailors and officers how to lead, direct, and manage people. I had experience. I'd investigated transgressions and abuses. Now I was going to have someone investigate my complaint. I marked a mail routing slip "Action" by the CO and "Information" to the XO, and I personally handed the slip to Caler. It said, "ROUTE SHEET PREPARED AND DELIVERED BY LCDR GREEN TO CDR CALER WITH CORRESPONDENCE."

The attached five-page, single-spaced letter detailed eighteen specific items requiring redress. Each item was one that I had sufficient written documentation to prove. I have read discrimination complaints. Never have I seen one that was as thoroughly documented or provable as this one. Even if you threw out half of it, I still had enough to bury him.

Filing a discrimination complaint against your commanding officer is serious business and is not to be taken lightly. Even if you win, your career is most likely over. Most people don't advertise the aftermath of their attempts to obtain justice. Your feelings are irrelevant. If you haven't done your homework or you have insufficient documentation, you should expect to have a hammer come down on you, probably from somewhere you don't expect. Retaliation is real, it is likely, and it is as illegal as discrimination. Both usually go unpunished.

I hoped that the last paragraph would strike terror in Goodall. It read:

> 4. Redress requested. Because of the extensive nature and complicity in the wrongs I have alleged, I request your concurrence in forwarding these complaints to the GCM [general court-martial] authority for resolution. I am not confident that you can fairly assess these matters or provide appropriate redress to me regarding this matter.

My reading of Article 138 of the Uniform Code of Military Justice and Article 1150 of the United States Navy Regulations (1990) indicated that my complaint should go to the general court-martial authority in my location. That would be Admiral Delaney. After our adversarial encounter about the direction the telephone service on his base should take, and the audit service taking my side, he had become much more friendly and respectful toward me. He knew by now I was professional, dedicated, and unafraid to look him in the eye and speak the truth. He also knew I could back up what I said. I couldn't wait to talk to him. Captain Booth talked to Goodall regularly. I never spoke to him at all. God only knows what they discussed about me. I'll give you one guess whom Booth was likely going to protect.

I could have called the navy inspector general. I could have called the media. I could have called Al Sharpton or Jesse Jackson. Hell, I think Clarence Thomas, former head of the Equal Employment Opportunity Commission, could have found merit in this one. I knew people just a few miles away who would have vouched for me and helped me, powerful people who were much better men than the ones I was working for and a hell of a lot more senior.

The Tailhook scandal was still fresh, and the highly popular and much beloved (by the junior enlisted, anyway) Admiral Boorda had committed suicide on May 16, 1996, five days after I filed my complaint. The navy was getting some bad press and didn't need any more. I didn't want to bring any unnecessary negative attention to the navy, but how could the navy explain why something like this was happening in the climate of TQL?

Things happened pretty quickly after the XO got my letter. Goodall had been scheduled to leave the next day for a week's worth of temporary additional duty visiting our tenant commands, but he canceled the trip. Master Chief Davy only canceled classes for one day, so the threat must have seemed bigger to Goodall. As word spread, I suddenly became radioactive. People looked at my shoes instead of making eye contact with me when I walked by. I understood.

From the moment I filed my complaint, I didn't miss a meeting, forget to cross a *t* or dot an *i*. I flossed every day, and I stayed in the crosswalks. I kept my hands visible at all times. If I had to fart, I went out and did it in my truck, with the windows rolled up. I knew how this game was played. There was now genuine trepidation in this place; I could feel it. I was alone in a hostile environment, with no allies of consequence. I soon got a nice call in my office from a navy JAG lawyer, an upbeat, cheerful female lieutenant. She said she had received my complaint and assured me that "they," meaning Captain Booth, my previous commanding officer there, and his legal team, were going to be taking immediate action on it. She was calling from Norfolk, Virginia. Headquarters. This phase of the game is called "Stall and Betray."

If they'd had a nice Black grandmotherly lawyer who sounded like Claire Huxtable, the attorney mother in *The Cosby Show*, call me, it might have worked. I wasn't buying it. I knew that as she spoke to me, there were people desperately looking for something to use to discredit me, and like most of us, if they looked long enough, I'm sure they would have found it, planted it, or made it up. It happens. I politely told her, and whoever was listening on the other line, that "they" weren't going to take any action at all on my complaint.

She was calling on behalf of Goodall's boss, Captain Booth, trying to cut Admiral Delaney out of the process. As wrong as he clearly was, they were trying to protect him and themselves. Race trumped right. Tribalism trumped duty. Wrong trumped right. Nevertheless, I explained to her how things worked so that she could tell "them," meaning Booth and whomever else might be listening in to the conversation.

I explained to her that I had not sent "them" my complaint; I had sent it to Goodall, and it was going to the GCM authority in this area—Jacksonville, not Norfolk, Virginia. We were all going to follow the rules, not just me. I didn't know anyone in Norfolk, Virginia, except Admiral Reason, and I wasn't going to bother him. This would have looked like one Black man crying to another about the injustice of it all. Besides, he was worn out from dealing with some of the Tailhook scandal participants. They were likely as miffed as Goodall was that accountability for assholic tendencies was on the horizon.

I also informed her that my complaint was not complete, that I had more than fifty enclosures that would be appended to it once it was returned from Goodall. I'm pretty sure that while "they" were listening to this, the blood was draining from their faces. I soon after called Admiral Delaney's office and spoke to his chief staff officer. I let him know what was coming, and he listened politely; then he strongly urged me to handle this within my own command. This was in direct contradiction to the official directives, but it didn't matter. I have a suspicion that Goodall had called him to give him a heads-up and to enlist his help in saving himself.

Delaney's aide, Lieutenant Commander Jennifer Carroll, was a Black female mustang, and I thought Delaney might at least run the potential merit of my claim by her once he received it. I also thought about confiding in her about what I was going through but decided against it. I didn't want her to be potentially accused of "colluding with the enemy." That can get you in big trouble. She would later be elected the first African American female lieutenant governor of Florida, serving Governor Rick Scott, a former naval officer. That did not end well. She has written a memoir about that and her struggles as a Black woman facing discrimination and harassment in the navy. Anyway, it was clear that they wanted no part of this mess, and I can imagine that I would have been found to be the problem somehow, documentation or not. So much for following navy regulations. Many sailors have learned this hard lesson.

It was then I realized that I was up against the weight of my own commander, his boss and legal arm, and the indifference of the general court-martial authority. This was a lot of opposition to overcome. After all,

all I had was twenty-one years of exemplary performance, and the truth. In terms of what this could do to some powerful people, I was expendable.

I was not surprised. I remembered the plaque on my first skipper, Captain Cyrus R. Christiansen's desk, which said, "Old age and treachery shall prevail over youth and skill." By now, the fight was draining out of me. I knew that I was now a marked man. It was a matter of time. I decided to retire. My father had left the navy with a bitter taste in his mouth, and it looked like I would too. I put together a plan that would save us both.

I was never going to command a ship. I had gotten to fly a navy hydrofoil. Not many men can say that, Black or white. In the days following my complaint, Goodall never said anything to me about it. He didn't want to talk any more. He just sat on it, desperately looking for a way out. He had help. Have you ever had a lawyer who worked for your boss's boss call you, offering to help you with a complaint you had filed against your boss? I look stupid sometimes, but that doesn't mean that I am.

The first time I ever felt ashamed to be a sailor was when I understood what was happening to the Black female chief in Key West while I helped her with her complaint. The next time was when I understood what was happening to me. My father, who had been dead for fifteen years by now, would have been amazed at how far I had come in the organization he tried to keep me out of. He would also have not been surprised at how much racism and discrimination I had faced, if that's what it was. Almost never had anyone openly called me a name or stated any personal racial animus toward me. Only Goodall had come close, dancing as close to the line as he could.

After about ten days, eight days after he was required to answer my complaint, I sent Goodall an email, telling him that I intended to retire on April 1, 1997. I did not desire to be there after January 1, 1997, which would require his concurrence and some "extra" leave time, known as "basket leave." I told him I would be willing to withdraw my complaint if he concurred. He immediately agreed. He returned my five-page complaint with a three-paragraph reply, stating that my complaint was "inappropriate." He also advised me, a former legal yeoman and equal opportunity specialist, where I could go to get help filing a "real" complaint. He couldn't help himself. His response also included copies to his boss and the legal officer of the boss, with whom I suspected he was colluding and were assisting him. I had been right about who the lawyer was working for, and it wasn't me. Goodall probably doesn't realize it, but I think I saved both of us. Once again, I took one for the team.

Goodall had a nice change of command ceremony, officiated by Captain Booth, who read Goodall's Meritorious Service Medal Citation, which was filled with praise for the good job Goodall had done with the challenging telephone switch installation, completing it on time and under budget. He talked about the innovations that the telephone office had made, with many of them adopted by other commands under his authority. Goodall sounded like a superstar. What a proud moment it was for him, like it was for Mineman First Class Lemieux when he got credit for my work in Sicily. I thought about that as I listened to Booth praise "Goodall's" accomplishments.

When Booth approached me and extended his hand, I could see the wariness in his eyes. I was still just as Black as the first day I met him, but something had changed. He had protected and rewarded the man he knew beyond question had abused me and harmed his command's, and therefore the military's, effectiveness. National security be damned; this was tribal. They were from the same tribe. I was not. He now knew for sure that I was dangerous to his career but not like he initially thought. He never said a word to me about my formal complaint. He didn't have to. It wasn't substantiated. Officially, it never happened. I interacted with my new commanding officer as little as possible for the next few months, which was fine with him. In early January 1997, I took off my uniform for the last time. After what I'd been through at this command, I just wanted to leave, quietly.

I have attended lots of retirement ceremonies, and each one was touching. You envied the person who was leaving after decades of honorable service. I had no ceremony, by choice. I wish things had ended differently, and they probably would have if I had taken the admin officer job. The devil you know and all that. Neither my grandfather, my father, nor I had a retirement ceremony. I'm the only one who ever collected a military retirement check. My family has more than one hundred years of service in the military, with my father and his sons accounting for half of that and my uncles and cousins the rest. We weren't always appreciated or rewarded. Like all veterans, we were necessarily expendable. A lawsuit has been filed against the Veterans Administration for discriminating against Black veterans for decades. I'll be watching.

I wish I had gone to sea again, as a skipper, but that was not to be. I learned to love the sea. There have been many fine Black officers who followed me, and I don't know what their experiences were like. Someday, we all may learn. Let's hope that they start to tell us. There may be some lessons still to be learned. There's bound to be a great sea story or two they can tell.

Goodall and perhaps Booth's parting shot to me was to reduce my end-of-tour award recommendation submitted by one of my subordinates (without my knowledge) from a Meritorious Service Medal to a Navy Commendation Medal, my fourth such award. I forget who left it on my desk.

As the loyal, treacherously betrayed, and enslaved fictional Roman general Maximus Meridius said (in the movie *Gladiator*) to the cowardly, murderous, bullying, and unbalanced Emperor Commodus, standing defiantly on the blood-soaked ground in the Coliseum, unbowed and unbroken, "I will have my vengeance, in this life or the next." And so he did.

Epilogue

Thomas D. Goodall next commanded the USS *Thach*, a frigate homeported in Japan, and made captain. He escaped accountability, like the skipper of the USS *Shiloh*, dubbed a "prison ship" by the media. It's harder to escape the judgment of history. Some former *Thach* sailors shared their memories of Commander Goodall on a website (navybuddies.com). One said that the "Kane (Caine) Mutiny" seemed to play a lot when he was captain. Another asked if anyone knew what happened to him and said he was the worst commanding officer he had in eighteen years of service. I can top that by four whole years. They would recognize the man I have described.

After suffering in silence from the results of moral injury for twenty years, I began critiquing the military, particularly the navy, primarily on LinkedIn, regarding ongoing discrimination; the failed formal discrimination complaint process; beard and facial hair policies; poor, toxic, and failed leadership; sexual harassment and assault; injustices in the judicial system; and lack of accountability for all of the above. After I selectively revealed some of the dismal statistics I found in the formal discrimination complaint reporting and encouraged people to study them, all the historical reports were stripped from the archived Annual Defense Reports on the internet, at the hands of persons unknown (to borrow the appellation historically used in newspapers to describe participants in unsolved lynchings). I subsequently filed Freedom of Information Act (FOIA) requests for updated statistics directly to the Department of Defense (DOD). I got responses two years later from the army and marines, which both provided limited and insufficient data. I received no consolidated data as had been previously reported as part of the Annual Defense Reports to Congress.

The Coast Guard ignored my FOIA request, despite engaging me in phone and email conversations, trying to convince me that all was well. In 2023, CNN reported on "Operation Fouled Anchor" and the 2015 Culture of Respect Study, hidden for eight years. Both revealed that the former commandant, Admiral Karl Schultz, and others had hidden these damning reports detailing decades' worth of unpunished sexual assault, harassment, racism, and cover-ups. I understand better why they ignored my request. The navy also ignored my request. I was told unofficially that this decision had been made at the highest levels. Meanwhile, the January 2021 142-page Task Force One Navy Report, containing nearly sixty recommendations (a similar report in 1988 contained seventy-eight recommendations), was submitted to the Culture of Excellence Board and, I assume, added to the existing stack of similar reports, likely soon to be forgotten, just as I had predicted in a CIMSEC article.

Contrast these responses with that from the air force. It gave me 350 pages, equaling ten years' worth of detailed data, as requested. It was broken down by pay grade and included the disposition of each case. I was beyond impressed. When I had the occasion to share that with the chief, General C. Q. Brown, who was then awaiting confirmation as the next Chairman of the Joint Chiefs of Staff, he smiled and said, "We're leading the way." It appears so. The other services were not adequately tracking these complaints or apparently keeping and analyzing these important records and documentation.

I have been interviewed by multiple news organizations and podcast hosts and spoke virtually to a DOD organization during the Secretary of Defense's mandated antiextremism stand-down. I spoke to a group of military and civilian personnel in Suffolk, Virginia, about mentorship and sponsorship with retired navy captain Dr. John Cordle, and we spoke again to a large gathering of naval aviators during their second ever diversity summit in Coronado, San Diego County, California, both in 2022. We have also coauthored articles for the Center for International Maritime Security, including one about DOD's unfinished business regarding diversity, equity, and inclusion. I spoke at the fiftieth National Naval Officers Association symposium in Annapolis and to the US Naval Academy staff and midshipmen as part of their 2023 diversity conference in October 2023. I was warmly received and was extremely impressed with the openness, commitment, candor, and quality of the speakers, distinguished guests, the faculty, and the midshipmen.

Our advocacy appears to be having an effect, despite some in leadership considering us to be nuisances, as were Dennis Denmark Nelson II and William S. Norman, two decades apart. Five decades between nuisances is a pretty good respite, I would say.

In October 2022, the Center for International Maritime Security published an article I coauthored with Doctor Cordle titled "Make Racism a UCMJ Offense." In it, we make eight specific recommendations for change.

In the 2022 Navy Health of the Force Report, issued in February 2023, on pages 11–12, three of our eight recommendations were directly encompassed in the following statement: "An equal opportunity complaint tracking database is in development for Navy and Marine Corps allowing for more accurate reporting of complaints and enhanced ability to analyze and take action on trend data."

Having advocated for that for years, and in light of the responses, or lack thereof, to my FOIA requests for that data, I strongly recommend that the system being used by the US Air Force be adapted and adopted for mandatory use by all the uniformed services subject to the Uniform Code of Military Justice. As General Brown told me, they're "leading the way."

I also hope that the other five recommendations we made are adopted. The rationale for making racism a UCMJ offense is contained in these sea stories and the news stories that have been reported and the input from the troops in various surveys, focus groups, and calls for their written input.

I wrote an article for the Center for International Maritime Security titled "The Navy's Perpetual Racism and How to Fix It," which was translated into French and widely read. I also wrote an article for the United States Naval Institute Proceedings, "The Case for Renaming the USS *John C. Stennis*," which received international attention and was included in a report to Congress by the navy on ship naming conventions shortly thereafter. It was also referenced in the book *Watergate: A New History*, by Garrett M. Graff, and *The Fighting Coast Guard: America's Maritime Guardians at War in the Twentieth Century* edited by Mark A. Snell. In addition, my book was referenced in *In the Shadow of the Golden Thirteen: A Nice Negro Story*, by Gerald A. Collins.

In 2023, in a subsequent report to Congress from the navy, my articles and several others that resulted from it were again included, including one authored by Doctor A. Cordle.

Stennis has had a long reach, but his segregationist efforts and anti–civil rights voting record should disqualify him from the honor of having a diverse capital warship and power projection platform named in his honor. If the navy decides to rename the ship, I'm chalking that up as a win for the advocacy of those who continue to speak out about this ongoing moral injury and injustice.

In May 2023, the DOD inspector general issued Report DODIG-2023-073, which revealed serious, long-standing problems regarding compliance with the DOD Military Equal Opportunity Program. It stated that there was no DOD-approved database for discrimination reporting, ostensibly due to staffing problems and turnover. Each service was using its own method of reporting, including spreadsheets. No method contained all the required data. I find this to be inexcusable.

This database should have been established and maintained when these reports were first required to be reported to Congress decades ago as addenda to the Annual Defense Report, thanks to the efforts of California congressman and former enlisted marine Ronald Dellums, and maintained in a searchable, publicly available, and downloadable format.

The previous reporting requirement ended in 2006–7, under Defense Secretary Donald Rumsfeld's tenure. The DODIG-2023-073 report indicated that 91 percent of complaints were improperly completed or conducted. I have said for years that DOD's equal opportunity complaint programs are failing both leadership and service members. Now I know it's true. Deputy Secretary of Defense Kathleen Hicks, after reviewing this report, issued a memo on June 8, 2023, assigning responsibilities and demanding corrective action and accountability, listing eighteen requirements for corrective action and authorizing supporting funding.

As had President John F. Kennedy, I discovered that things were actually worse than I had been saying they were. The report contained twelve recommendations, all of which I support. One that I have pushed for that is not included is for increased accountability (and tracking, like what is done for drug abusers) for offenders, who should be held accountable for racist behavior under the UCMJ. Likewise, leaders should be held accountable for noncompliance with the equal opportunity complaint program reporting requirements.

I recommend that you read the entire report to understand why I have been advocating that this issue once again receive scrutiny from Congress, equal to the reporting of sexual assaults and harassment. I reiterate that the archived reports that were Addendums to the Department of Defense Annual Defense Reports should be restored to public view for study and context. Historians need this data.

In November 2023, the navy announced that personnel assigned to a vessel that was not in an operational capacity would be able to refuse nonjudicial punishment at captain's mast. This is a positive change and will likely reduce the racial disparity in punishments that has existed for decades across all branches of the uniformed services.

In September 2023, I was invited to speak at the National Museum of the US Navy's Black History Month celebration in Washington, DC, for the upcoming February 2024. The museum staff, especially air force veteran K. Denise Rucker-Krepp, are working to expand their database regarding the history of Black service members in the navy and to better tell their stories. Dennis Denmark Nelson and William S. Norman should be top priorities.

I was contacted by a former naval lieutenant, Gerald Collins, who had an important story to tell, and I convinced him to tell it. Gerald Collins's *In the Shadow of the Golden Thirteen: A Nice Negro Story* revealed his triumph and travails in arranging the famous at-sea reunion of the navy's first Black naval officers and the subsequent destruction of his career. The medals awarded to those who participated peripherally in the at-sea reunion of those pioneers, Collins's brainchild, were in stark contrast to the lack of any medal for the man who conceived, spearheaded, and made it happen. This lack of recognition should be corrected by the navy, including awarding him a well-deserved medal for his singular accomplishment. It has been done before. He will be speaking at the National Navy Museum alongside me. Along with Marv Truhe's book, *Against All Tides: The Untold Story of the USS* Kitty Hawk *Race Riots*, Collins's should be on the chief of naval operations' recommended reading list.

I have paid a psychological price for speaking out, as expected. I filed three separate complaints against a navy doctor providing me care under the TRICARE program and eventually included his chain of command, which apparently was protecting him and themselves. I made the mistake of telling him while under his care that I was writing about my navy experiences and gave him a flyer that made him frown. The next time I saw him, six months later, he angrily called me a liar, twice, as I lay seminaked on an exam table awaiting a prostate biopsy. He accused me of circumventing his department's appointment system and accused me of not working with him as a patient. I forcefully denied his ridiculous allegations and demanded that he get to the bottom of this wrongful accusation as soon as the biopsy was completed. As a show of dominance, he forced me to "ask" him to complete the procedure that had been scheduled by his office. Nine days after the Capitol Insurrection, I once again felt under assault and compromised. He was adding to my anxiety and trauma with moral injury, wrongful accusations, and disrespect, all based on a lie, as were the failures of his command leadership. My counseling with the Veterans Administration (VA) was extended significantly because of this abuse. I don't have to tell you who else he reminded me of. The next time I talked to him, via phone, he told me to find myself another doctor, after he told me that I had prostate cancer. He provided me with no information on why he had accused me and subsequently did not honor his offer to talk to me about it during my next appointment. When he saw me, he ignored me. As had Goodall, they fucked with the wrong guy. Instead of just being pissed about my book, they should have taken time to read it. After 110 days, two separate complaints—including the inspector general complaint that I filed, allegedly "investigated" by a navy captain—and a TRICARE grievance, I received a backdated letter stating that I had not done anything wrong, apparently hand-delivered to my home mailbox. His command had a safety stand-down after my first complaint to correct their admitted administrative deficiencies but shared nothing with me regarding his behavior or the accusations he had made against me. I never let anyone there touch me again, choosing to shift my treatment to the VA system. When pressed for answers in a phone call, his commanding officer informed me that "we may never know why this happened to you," and I told her it was her job to find out. I got crickets. A great deal of effort was spent protecting him and others. No investigator ever interviewed me, or my witness, despite the two investigations into my complaints, which I detailed in more than thirty pages of documentation. You should now understand why I believe the complaint system is broken and that retaliation is complainants' number-one fear in filing a complaint.

My original FOIA request after I was denied closure had been filed in April 2021. After an inquiry from me about it in late 2022, I was informed that it had been assigned a higher priority and "processed" and was awaiting sign-off approval for release by a supervisor on November 8, 2022. As of this writing (in late 2023) it has not been released to me. Documents that are a fifteen-minute drive from my house, which I am legally entitled to receive within twenty days of requesting them, have been illegally withheld from me for more than two years and counting. It makes you wonder what happens to a young sailor or officer who tries to seek justice after being mistreated. My next available steps include requesting assistance from my congressional representative or consulting with an attorney about filing a FOIA lawsuit. It should not be this hard to find out what accusations have been made against you by a uniformed naval officer in the performance of his official duties. This has continued to affect my mental well-being and is another indication that the system needs an overhaul. It is illegal to withhold information simply because it is embarrassing to the holder of that information.

My cancer is now in remission, but the smoldering anger at how I was treated and denied closure, at the hands of yet another naval officer, drives me to continue to seek accountability and transparency for myself and others.

As happened to the young man whom Dennis Denmark Nelson II wrote about in 1951 and my father, I also became wary of white people in positions of authority over me. I have never had another job after I left the navy, at the age of thirty-nine, other than working eighty hours for a friend and navy veteran who owned his own tree service. A guy with my skills and experience was shoving brush into a wood chipper. I've decided that this indicates a significant trauma.

After twenty-two years, at the urging of a fellow officer who had read my story, I finally called the Veterans Crisis Line to talk to a counselor. He informed me that I had multiple issues that would surely result in benefits from the VA. A year later, I submitted the final documents to substantiate my claim and was awarded disability benefits immediately. My claim for racism-induced posttraumatic stress disorder and the increased benefits that claim would provide was denied by the VA. I am not alone. In 2023, the VA was sued for allegedly discriminating against Black veterans for decades and issued a call for such veterans who had previously had claims rejected to resubmit them for reconsideration. Perhaps I'll try. My pride, shame, ignorance, bewilderment, and resentment at how I had been treated cost me an estimated $350,000 in untaxed benefits that I had left on the table. If you know a veteran who you think may need assistance, please advise them to seek help and compensation from the VA. Too many do not. As far as I know, my father never did.

I finally was assigned to an outside counselor under contract with the VA who understood my issues. A Black man, with a daughter serving in the navy, he did not need convincing that discrimination was a life-changing and soul-damaging problem. Unfortunately, the VA, like the military, isn't adequately equipped to deal with the issues of discrimination. It, and the country, does not have the staff or expertise. I hope that changes. The first two white male counselors I was assigned to were visibly uncomfortable while talking with me, which leads me to believe that discrimination is likely here to stay. My military experiences make me wonder what my father must have endured before he behaved in a manner that led him to be charged with inciting a riot on board a naval vessel and punished accordingly without recourse. There was and still is no UCMJ article that specifically addresses racist actions.

If my father were still here, I'd tell him, "I'm sorry, Daddy; I fought as long and as hard as I could, and that was a long, long time. You did warn me. I never went to the brig or captain's mast as you did, but I looked the sharks in the eyes and defended myself when I could. I sometimes spoke truth to powerful lions too. As the Massai warriors once did, I ran toward the lion, sometimes more than once, until my legs gave out, but I never dropped my spear. I wounded a lion or two, and I fought off some sharks. I now understand why you were so volatile, unpredictable, and worried and drank so much. I understand that you were badly damaged too. You walked this earth like a stand-up man, despite losing your own father in a VA hospital when you were twelve years old. We all three served a country that didn't always treat us like men, and we served it well. Thank you for my manhood. I can only imagine what you endured."

There are bound to be more T. D. Goodalls out there. I have no proof, but I think some of the sailors with whom I served might have had a bit of racism or inherent bias or at least showed symptoms. I once thought that they probably would almost never admit it. After my experiences with Goodall and watching what happened at Charlottesville, Virginia, in the summer of 2017 and all that has happened elsewhere afterward, I'm no longer so sure.

Zumwalt's dream of One Navy, like true equality, is still a dream deferred, at least in my time. You now know more than you did. There is still much to learn but not from me. My navy is gone. Someone else has to pick up the spear and run toward the lion.

The officer corps is not as male and white as it used to be, but institutionally, culturally, and traditionally, it is a white male tribe, with adopted members who must adapt or die. Lip service to diversity and equality is not going to fix the problems of bias, harassment, and discrimination. The quote that was on the 2017 CNO's recommended reading list was "Leadership and learning are indispensable to each other." John F. Kennedy said that. I hope everyone from the CNO to Seaman Timmy can learn something from this old sailor's sea stories.

I held no command, I performed no heroics, and I had a mutt's pedigree. I learned to be a good sailor and good officer from good and great ones. I learned things not to do as well. I learned that things like microaggressions, racism, bias, and discrimination can pop up when you least expect them. As my father would say, "You had better be ready, Slick." A son never forgets. Daughters and grandchildren should not as well.